festival voices

festival voices

Plays Written by Students and Teachers for the Sears Ontario Drama Festival

Edited by Wayne Fairhead and Jane Gardner

PLAYWRIGHTS CANADA PRESS
TORONTO • CANADA

Festival Voices: Plays Written by Students and Teachers for the Sears Ontario Drama Festival
© copyright 2010 Wayne Fairhead and Jane Gardner

Playwrights Canada Press
The Canadian Drama Publisher
215 Spadina Ave., Suite 230, Toronto, Ontario, Canada M5T 2C7
phone 416.703.0013 fax 416.408.3402
orders@playwrightscanada.com • www.playwrightscanada.com

The publisher acknowledges the support of the Canadian taxpayers through the Government of
Canada Book Publishing Industry Development Program, the Canada Council for the Arts,
the Ontario Arts Council, and the Ontario Media Development Corporation.

Front cover photograph by Teodoro Dragonieri
Production Editor and Cover Design: Micheline Courtemanche

Library and Archives Canada Cataloguing in Publication

Festival voices : plays written by students & teachers for the Sears
Ontario Drama Festival / edited by Wayne Fairhead and Jane Gardner.

ISBN 978-0-88754-905-2

1. Canadian drama (English)--21st century. 2. Canadian drama
(English)--Ontario. I. Fairhead, Wayne, 1944- II. Gardner, Jane
III. Sears Ontario Drama Festival

PS8315.5.O5F48 2010   C812'.60809713   . C2010-901674-2

First edition: April 2010
Printed and bound in Canada by Gauvin Press, Gatineau

CONTENTS

INTroDucTION

The Sears Ontario Drama Festival involves approximately three hundred and fifty schools annually, between mid-February and mid-May. Ken Watts began the festival in 1946 with three plays. Today's structure has Ontario divided into six regions: Central, North, South, East, West, and Toronto. Each region has between three and six districts. Adjudicators send productions from district festivals to regional showcases based on a set numeric formula. From each regional festival, two productions move on to the Ontario showcase. During the course of the festival, awards and scholarships ranging in value from two hundred and fifty to three thousand dollars are given in all areas of theatrical achievement.

For many years students have been writing original work for the Sears Ontario Drama Festival. The establishment of the Award for Outstanding New Play in 1981 has further encouraged students to submit plays for the festival. As well, teachers—and combinations of students and teachers—have been creating new work as an integral part of their involvement in the festival. In the past, two volumes of outstanding writing from this body of work have been published: *Concrete Daisy and Other Plays*, Volumes One (1991) and Two (1996). Unfortunately these two publications are out of print, but the plays may be accessed by contacting the executive director at Concrete Daisy on the festival website (www.searsdramafestival.com). With *Festival Voices*, we have included plays written during the first decade of this century. Thought had been given to publishing a new anthology to celebrate the sixty-fifth anniversary of the festival, so when Jane suggested doing one co-operatively with Carousel Players and Playwrights Canada Press, we decided that we should move ahead and publish one in the year leading up to the anniversary. It is our hope that this collection will inspire more original work for the coming season and well into the future. All profits from the sale of *Festival Voices* will be donated to the Ken and Ann Watts Memorial Scholarship Foundation.

Three readers—Andrew Lamb, Anusree Roy, and Brian Van Norman—were selected to read all the scripts submitted for inclusion in this anthology, and each chose their ten favourite. We would like to thank these three talented individuals for giving freely of their time and expertise. From these choices, we selected eight for inclusion in this collection. They represent a cross-section of genres and include works written by both students and teachers. Some were written by individuals and some were created collectively. All of these one-act plays are suitable for in-class and after-school exploration and production. As well, many provide material suitable for community- and college-theatre productions. They explore relationships, social issues, humour, ritual, theatre for children, and music as integral to theatre.

We would also like to thank all the students and teachers who submitted the sixty scripts that were considered for inclusion in this anthology. Furthermore, we appreciate the efforts of district representatives who encouraged festival participants to submit work created over the past ten years.

As the selection process was extremely difficult, we decided to give the following seven plays honourable mention, as they came very close to being included:

- *The Cellar* by Richard Bercuson, St. Matthew Catholic High School, Ottawa (2002)

- *Enter Alice* by Aaron Jan, Westdale Secondary School, Hamilton (2009)

- *Saving Chuck* by Nathan Snelgrove, Guelph Collegiate Vocational Institute (2009)

- *Sex and the Saudi* by Christopher Lee Rabba, Cawthra Park Secondary School, Mississauga (2008)

- *Thank You for Everything* by Nyla Benza, Walkerville Centre for the Creative Arts, Windsor (2009)

- *Where There's A Will* by Samantha Marit, Shannon Pucklitz, Elizabeth Martin, and Thomas Preece, T.A. Blakelock High School, Oakville (2005)

- *Zombie: A Teenage Comedy with Brains* by Anthony Reid, Father Henry Carr Catholic Secondary School, Toronto (2008)

This anthology is the result of a unique three-way partnership between Playwrights Canada Press, Carousel Players, and the Sears Ontario Drama Festival. We would especially like to recognize the ongoing commitment and support of Sears Canada, which ensures the life of one of Canada's longest running cultural organizations.

Festival Voices is dedicated to Mira Friedlander, Hélène Gravel, and John Glossop, who all believed in the value and power of the playwright—particularly the voice of students. Before her death in 2000, Mira was considered one of Canada's outstanding arts writers. She was a festival alumni, adjudicator extraordinaire, and staunch advocate of student theatre. After her death and in recognition of her unwavering support of the festival, the MIRAs were established to recognize six students for outstanding achievement in any area of theatre at the provincial showcase. Hélène was a teacher-director who created a powerful francophone youth theatre culture, which continues in the Sudbury area. She wrote specifically about and for her students. Through her work such amazing theatre pieces as *Par Osmose*, which explored francophone identity in Ontario, were created for the festival. John's book, *Directing: The Art and Craft*, includes a chapter titled "The Student Playwright," which all aspiring young writers should read. He, through his reflective adjudications, also influenced many during his long involvement with the festival as a teacher, director, writer, and adjudicator.

We hope that you find these works as exciting as we do and that you decide to recreate them in your school and community. They deserve further exploration. In order to obtain the rights to produce any of these plays, contact the festival's executive director at www.searsdramafestival.com.

Wayne Fairhead and Jane Gardner
May 2010

THE DISPOSABLES

by Jennifer Benson, Emily Tisi,
and Cassandra Van Wyck

The Tree (Brion Neudorf at top), a wise old weeping willow, protects
garbage piles—Socks, Forgottens, and Rottens (Emily Tisi, middle; Sam Cook, left;
Cassandra Van Wyck, right) from Suffix, the terribly toxic waste monster (not shown in photo).

Photo by Jennifer Benson.

In loving memory of Ghislaine Benson,
who stepped gracefully, laughed heartily, and loved profoundly.

The Disposables was first produced by students and teachers from E. L. Crossley Secondary School, Fonthill, at the 2007 Niagara District Festival of the Sears Ontario Drama Festival at Brock University, St. Catharines, and went on to the 2007 Southern Regional Festival at the Sanderson Centre in Brantford.

The play was originally developed by Jennifer Benson and students from the E. L. Crossley Secondary School grade twelve Children's Theatre class, and was workshopped for elementary students, December 2006 to January 2007. The creative team noted below (*) were involved in original ideas, improvisation of dialogue, and script development.

Andrew	Josh Regier*
Dad/the Mayor	Mike Whatling*
Grandma	Genevieve Jones*
Teddy	Tori Godin
Swoopsie/Socks/Litters Two	Emily Tisi*
Tree	Brion Neudorf*
Rottens/Litters One/Bulb One	Cassandra Van Wyck*
Forgottens/Litters Three/Bulb Three	Sam Cook*
Sooki	Sierra Picton*
Suffix	Alan Hoover*
Bulb Two	Jess Peat*
Burbians/Disposables	Kaitlyn Burnham, Sam Cook, Ryan Forneri, Brittany Friesman, Kiersten Hay, Ashlea Kadar, Jess Peat, Meetul Shah, Emily Tisi, Cassandra Van Wyck, Danielle Walker.

Directed by Jennifer Benson
Stage Management by Devaan Ingraham
Set Design by Sherry Wilkinson, Tabitha Stephens
Costume Design by Sherry Wilkinson
Original Music by Rafael Fuentes, Soundtrack Performance Group
Additional Music by Jennifer Benson, Emily Tisi, Kerri Bryant*
Lighting Operation by Shari Edsall*
Sound Operation by Justin Bath
Backstage Crew: Ian Kuckyt,* Tamsynn Secord,* Bailey VanRavenswaay*

NOTES

The Disposables was produced by students and teachers and was the creative by-product of many teenage minds engaged in active learning. Through creative play, music, and improvisation, characters, ideas and dialogue were developed and then scripted into final form. The writers acknowledge their indebtedness to students involved in the Children's Theatre Program for their endless supply of ideas and energy.

Jennifer Benson, Emily Tisi, and Cassandra Van Wyck

Jennifer Benson currently teaches drama and English at E. L. Crossley Secondary School in Fonthill. She attained her honours degree in theatre from Brock University, and her Master's Degree in dramatic literature from the University of Toronto. Both Emily Tisi and Cassandra Van Wyck are currently pursuing degrees at Brock University.

characters

ANDREW	A Burbian boy
GRANDMA	Andrew's grandmother, later Queen of The Land Where all the Garbage Goes
DAD	Mayor of Burbia, Andrew's father
TEDDY	A cuddly teddy bear (played in the tradition of clown)
EIGHT BURBIANS	Militant, yet graceful, with plastic smiles and sunny dispositions—they manipulate flat set pieces
TWO BURBIANS	Carry the Burbian banner
SWOOPSIE	A balletic otherworldly garbage collector
MOUTH	Manipulated by one actor, the mouth represents a garbage chute
TREE	A wise old weeping willow, responsible for sorting Disposables and providing oxygen
SOCKS	The sock pile in The Land Where all the Garbage Goes
ROTTENS	The rotten pile in The Land Where all the Garbage Goes
FORGOTTENS	The Anything that is Forgotten pile in The Land Where all the Garbage Goes
SOOKI	Princess of The Land Where all the Garbage Goes
THREE LITTERS	Forgottens gone rotten
TEN DISPOSABLES	Tossed out from Burbia, they manipulate junk
THREE BULBS	Guards of Trash Tower
SUFFIX	Sludgy by-product of Burbia (the original production made use of a black body bag for this character—played in the tradition of *commedia dell'arte*, he's a blobby version of Il Capitano)

SeTTING

Two distinct locations: Burbia and The Land Where all the Garbage Goes. Chorus actors manipulate objects that add to the appearance of the setting and allow for a variety of fluid arrangements within the location. Within Burbia is Andrew's bedroom. Within The Land Where all the Garbage Goes, the Trash Tower is formed using the junk props, which Disposables manipulate. The only set pieces required are four black two-step risers, three small boxes, a chest, and a bed. Two of the risers are placed upstage centre from the top of the show. The others are floated in as required. A giant mouth appears whenever garbage needs to be disposed of. It disappears when not in use.

Burbia

Uniform. Order. Pastels. Logic. Perfection. Two-dimensional. Burbians manipulate Dr. Seussian placards of homes and businesses. Presentational style of acting. Hats are oversized, characters cartoon-like.

The Land Where all the Garbage Goes

Disorder. Feelings. Imagination. Represents inner journey of characters excluded from Burbia. Steely blue and grey. Toxic. Fog. Disposables manipulate junk to create various locations within the dump.

MUSIC

Music is intricately connected to the physical text of this piece, and in some cases it is intimately tied to characterizations. We are indebted to Gato Fuentes and Soundtrack Performance Group for their performance music library, as it provided great inspiration during the creation of this play. A production CD is available, which includes Soundtrack Performance Group, Junkyard Jam, and sound effects for the play.

Scene One

ANDREW   *(voice-over)* Grandma? Could you tell me a story?

GRANDMA   Sure Andrew… Not so very long ago, there was a little boy named
                Andrew…

ANDREW   Hey… that's me…

                *Parade music. Lights. Jeering. Laughter off. During drum
                roll, ANDREW is thrown in from upstage left, followed by
                his backpack.*

                (picking up his backpack) I am not a four-eyes!

                *Upset, ANDREW grabs a book from his backpack and sits
                on upstage centre risers to read. Grand BURBIAN entrance.
                BURBIANS enter marching, oblivious to the young boy—two
                from upstage left, two from centre stage left; two from upstage
                right, two from centre stage right. The groups of BURBIANS
                move in two tight quadrants, with their positions staggered.
                They meet at the edge of the risers—one quadrant left of centre
                and one right of centre—and acknowledge each other with
                a quick snap of the head on their dialogue. ANDREW watches,
                puzzled, while remaining sitting.*

BURBIANS SL   Good day.

BURBIANS SR   Hello.

                *Burbian quadrants continue marching through to opposite
                side of stage and exit. It is obvious that ANDREW doesn't fit
                in with the pace of this world. He tries to read again but can't
                concentrate, and he stands in front of risers, confused. With
                a quick about-face in the wings, the Burbian quadrants turn
                and march back toward upstage centre. DAD as the mayor and
                the two banner carriers, somewhat hidden behind quadrant
                entering upstage left, enter. Sensing something big is happening,
                ANDREW moves quickly upstage right, so he doesn't get
                trampled, and he gets lost behind the crowd of people. The
                BURBIANS meet upstage centre in front of risers, forming
                a group of eight. This time the BURBIANS, now in a cluster
                of eight, acknowledge the audience with a snap of the head.*

BURBIANS CSL   Fine weather.

BURBIANS CSR   Oh, yes.

DAD as the mayor and two banner carriers step up and on to riser upstage centre. The banner frames the mayor's entrance. The quadrants, having met in front of the riser, turn in sync and part with quadrant upstage right, marching toward downstage right, and quadrant upstage left marching toward downstage left. the mayor and the banner carriers step off the riser and move downstage through the centre of the two quadrants, just as they are parting. BURBIANS march to downstage right and downstage left, forming clusters of four with their placards on either side of the mayor. All of this is done in sync to the music and without missing a beat. Their disposition is hyper-sunny. They are the picture of functionality and organization. ANDREW follows behind the mayor... not quite keeping up with the pace, then is lost behind the BURBIAN grand tableau, framing the mayor downstage centre. The dialogue is timed to the music. The BURBIANS march in place, and the march halts just before the speaking begins. Each cluster manipulates their placards in sync, with simple gestures punctuating the dialogue as they speak. They emulate a moving pop-up book.

DAD	Welcome to our perfect town!
BURBIANS	We have smiles in place of frowns.
DAD	Our town is perfect, just like heaven—on a scale to ten...
BURBIANS	We are eleven!
DAD	The people here are perfect too—
BURBIANS SR	We never get tired or catch the flu. We are happy, all the day— We love to spend and spend away!
BURBIANS SL	We have giant houses that reach the sky. Giant doors and roofs up high! Big huge cars and tiny lawns...
BURBIAN ONE	And where are the trees?
BURBIANS	They're all gone!
DAD	But you see it doesn't matter at all, because instead of trees...
BURBIANS SL	There's a great big mall! Full of stores, with everything...
BURBIANS SR	Oh the beauty! Cha-ching! Cha-ching!

Cluster of BURBIANS intensifying, tightening inward, heightening, obsessive—Broadway musical feel.

ALL	It always has to be top of the line—

It has to sparkle, it has to shine!
We demand more, we need the best—
It must be better, better than the rest!

BURBIAN TWO   But what of the things that grow old and break?
The car without a wheel, the rusty rake?

DAD   Oh don't you worry, don't you fret!
There's no need to be upset.
You see, when something is not wanted anymore—
Plain and simple, toss it on the floor! *(tosses garbage)*

> *Timed with the following dialogue, MOUTH appears downstage left. SWOOPSIE enters through MOUTH, picks up garbage, and disappears through MOUTH. MOUTH exits downstage left.*

BURBIANS   Then come the swoopsies a-creeping and a-crawling!
And pick up all the things on the floor that have fallen.
They *snatch* them up and *clamp* them tight!
Take them away—out of sight!
To a hole in the wall, where every disposable goes...
Down, down, down, and then... and then?
Who knows? Who cares?

> *DAD as the mayor exits downstage left, has obvious business to attend to. ANDREW breaks through crowd of clustered BURBIANS downstage centre. They part centre stage left and centre stage right and are obviously annoyed with him. This happens without breaking the rhythm established.*

ANDREW   I do!
One tiny boy, in one giant room!
Whose grandma told him stories,
of forests in bloom...

> *Lights dissolve as riser is floated in unnoticed. GRANDMA enters centre stage right with her magic staff and meets ANDREW centre stage. BURBIANS are voyeurs, watching from the shadows of the scene. GRANDMA steps on to riser. ANDREW sits down. All of this happens without missing a beat.*

GRANDMA & ANDREW
She told him tales, of times before.
When life wasn't all about what you could buy at the store...

ANDREW   *(wide-eyed)* Really, Grandma?

GRANDMA   And then the weeping willow grew and grew, until he reached all the way up to the brilliant blue sky. All of the other trees looked up to him and he never wept again!

ANDREW	Was the little girl who loved him so much… you, Grandma?
GRANDMA	That's right— I watered him every day, so that he would grow strong and tall.
ANDREW	Taller than Daddy?
GRANDMA	Way taller than Daddy…
ANDREW	*(standing)* I want to be strong and tall one day… like Daddy…
GRANDMA	*(gently patting him on the head as he sits again)* You will Andrew… you will. All things in nature grow… But don't you grow up too soon. *(tickles him)* Do you know that the weeping willow gave me a gift for all of my trouble? He broke off one of his branches, carved it, and I still have it to this day…
ANDREW	Wow…
GRANDMA	*(reveals magic staff)* This has carried me all through life… it is magical for it is made of love…
ANDREW	I wish I had one…
GRANDMA	I can't give you this, for it was entrusted to me… but I can give you this *(sweeping gesture stage right)*, for it too is made of love!
TEDDY	*(entering stage right)* Hello, I'm… I'm… I'm…
ANDREW	Ah! Grandma! He's… I'll name him… Theodore William Bear!
TEDDY	I'm Theodore William Bear!
GRANDMA	Theodore comes with a special map, so you'll never get lost again!
ANDREW	Will this map take me to buried treasures?
GRANDMA	Of course!
DAD	*(off stage right)* Andrew, it's time for hockey practice!
ANDREW	*(whispering)* Grandma, I hate hockey! All of the kids knock me over… and skate circles around me. I'm no good at it!
GRANDMA	Don't worry about that, Andrew… you may not have it *here* yet *(points to arm)* but you have it *here* *(points to heart)*, and *here* *(points to head)*. Some day your dad will come to understand that… Until then, this bear will take care of you, if ever I should have to leave…
ANDREW	But Grandma, I don't ever want you to leave… why would you…
GRANDMA	There are some things you will only understand when you are older… when you're scared, just hug this tight… Teddy is cute and cuddly, just like you *(tickles ANDREW)*, he's smart and well

travelled… he'll get you out of any sticky situation… like… when you meet that blasted pirate who keeps bothering you!

DAD   *(off stage right)* ANDREW!

ANDREW   Coming, Dad!

> *GRANDMA exits stage right. Lights change. BURBIANS move toward ANDREW and TEDDY… taunting.*

BURBIAN THREE

He told me her stories,
Of skies that were blue.
His grandma's a liar!
Plain and true.

BURBIANS   Liar, liar pants on fire!

BURBIAN FOUR

No such thing as trees.
Or squirrels that live there.
No wonder nobody likes him.

> *They jeer and circle ANDREW and TEDDY.*

BURBIAN FIVE   Four-eyes!
You still play with your teddy bear!
You still play with your teddy bear!
You still play with your teddy bear!

> *BURBIANS freeze in taunting tableau clusters that frame ANDREW.*

GRANDMA   *(entering hurriedly stage right)* Andrew, there is something I must tell you… very important… you are old enough now to understand. In the old country, trees were revered and held as sacred. Remember the weeping willow I told you about? He is still alive… way at the bottom of Burbia… He is the only tree left… and he has grown very sick… We must help him or we will never…

ANDREW   *(cuts her off)* I'm a grown-up now!
I'm seven years old.
I don't believe your stories.
Not one that you've told.

BURBIANS   Everyone knows they are lies.

> *BURBIANS exit centre stage left and centre stage right, laughing and taunting. ANDREW exits stage left. GRANDMA exits stage right, defeated. TEDDY is left centre stage, wondering what happened.*

Scene Two

Nightmare. Music. TEDDY is alone centre stage, watching.
The scene change happens around TEDDY. The following bits
of dialogue happen simultaneously as the scene transforms. The
dialogue overlaps, as in a nightmare. Characters cross each other's
paths, but do not connect. The scene has the feel of a pirate ship
on a rocky sea. Seascape images appear and disappear as actors
manipulate set pieces and blankets.

As GRANDMA crosses downstage right and exits downstage
left with her magic staff and a suitcase, ANDREW's bed is floated
in from upstage left by two manipulators and moves to centre
stage. ANDREW enters downstage left, upright with his head on
a pillow and his eyes closed. He turns circles as a chest is floated
in by two manipulators from upstage right and settles downstage
right. A blanket floats in to cover the chest. Another blanket is
floated in by two manipulators from upstage left, which creates
a sail over the risers upstage centre. It floats toward the bed and
settles on ANDREW, who is now in his bed tossing back
and forth.

GRANDMA   *(carrying suitcase, crossing from downstage right to downstage left)*
Andrew... you were my only hope. My only hope.

ANDREW   *(enters from downstage left with pillow, turning circles)* Grandma,
Grandma, where did you go?

TEDDY   *(circling centre stage)* Andrew? Andrew? The pirate is chasing you!
Watch out!

BURBIANS   *(manipulating set pieces)* Four-eyes. You can't skate... *(laughter)*
Mama's boy... Geek... Hockey practice... *(ad lib)*

ANDREW   Teddy? Teddy? The pirate, watch out!

ANDREW gets into bed as the bed settles into position. The
sail, now straightened out, hovers over him. With one blanket
manipulator on either side of the bed, they move the blanket
upward like a parachute, then allow it to settle down upon him.
He continues tossing as all of the manipulators
move around his bed, taunting him.

DAD   Hockey practice! Andrew time to walk the plank!

ANDREW   *(tossing)* I won't go... I won't go... Teddy help me!

ANDREW startles awake. The manipulators gasp, pause for a heightened moment—like a wave about to crash—then dissolve into the background and exit as the music fades. Lights brighten, and ANDREW's consciousness returns.

Just a nightmare.

A game of hide-and-seek commences. TEDDY is always one step ahead of ANDREW, and escapes just before ANDREW goes to where he thinks TEDDY is hiding.

Teddy? Theodore William Bear! Where are you? *(looking downstage)* Are you playing hide-and-seek?

ANDREW checks behind curtain downstage right while TEDDY sneaks behind the curtain upstage left. ANDREW hears him and moves upstage left.

You may be a good hider, but I'm a good seeker! *(He pulls back the curtain, revealing TEDDY, who shrieks.)* There you are! *(They cuddle and giggle, and sit together on the downstage edge of the bed.)* I was having this horrible nightmare... the pirate was chasing us! He was going to make us walk the plank...

DAD's footsteps are heard. ANDREW quickly hides TEDDY behind the chest.

DAD	*(entering downstage right)* Good morning, tiger! Your tenth birthday is coming up... How about we get you some contact lenses?
ANDREW	But I wanted a...
DAD	No son of mine is going to be called four-eyes!
ANDREW	Sure, Dad.
DAD	And last night Mrs. Jones called. Johnny is having a sleepover this weekend. I guess we should fit that into our schedule. My son has got to have good, popular friends!
ANDREW	Of course, Dad. But... um... Johnny always makes fun of me.
DAD	Good man! It'll be good for you to roughhouse like a normal boy!
ANDREW	Dad?
DAD	*(awkward pause)* Yes, junior?
ANDREW	Can Teddy come? *(ANDREW grabs TEDDY from behind chest. TEDDY is unanimated.)* I know you don't let him come to school with me, but I don't think I can sleep without him... and, well...

DAD	You don't need that bear! What are you, afraid of the dark? *(laughs uproariously)*
ANDREW	Well... kind of... I always have nightmares...
DAD	Of course you're not. No son of mine is going to bring a teddy bear to his friend's birthday party! I'm the *mayor*!
ANDREW	Yes, Dad.
DAD	Maybe tomorrow at fifteen hundred hours we can play some ball hockey. You need to learn some stick handling if you're playing for the select team.
ANDREW	But Dad, I didn't make the team...
DAD	I can pencil you in for twenty-eight minutes of play.
ANDREW	But Dad, I got cut...
DAD	What? You cut yourself?
	DAD's cellphone rings.
	Hold on, son. I have to take this.
	DAD exits downstage right. TEDDY becomes animated again.
TEDDY	Shiver me timbers! I thought he'd never leave! *(jumps on bed)* Ahoy there, matey! Here be your blasted treasure map, Captain! All the way from Davy Jones's locker! I can't read it because I only have *(pointing to eye patch)* one eye! And you have...
ANDREW	FOUR! *(takes map)* Well, the map says here that we have to take four backwards bunny hops... one, two, three, four... and three giant steps in this direction... one, two, three... X marks the spot! *(They arrive at the chest.)* Got your shovel?
TEDDY	*(pointing toward the bed)* Andrew look—a pirate!
ANDREW	*(screams and hides behind the chest)* Teddy! Get him!
TEDDY	*(running to meet the pirate, brandishes mimed sword, mimes having it taken)* I can't get him. He stole my sword! *(runs behind ANDREW and urges him forward)*
ANDREW	*(truly scared)* Oh no! *(tentatively gets up to fight pirates)*
TEDDY	Remember what Grandma told you! You may not have it *here*... *(points to his arms)*
ANDREW	But I have it *here (points to brain)*, and *here*! *(ANDREW points to his heart, then thinks, then grabs his glasses as a defence.)* Pirate, I have my ocular spectaculars here and if you take two steps closer

to my shadow you will get a horrible sunburn—and you know there's no more ozone to protect you!

TEDDY   *(imaginary pirate leaves)* Wow, look at him go—he's running faster than the fastest food service...

ANDREW   Faster than my dad's Ferrari...

TEDDY   Faster than the highest speed Internet! Look at him go!

ANDREW   And that's how it's done. Let's get that treasure, matey!

TEDDY   Are you sure it's here?

ANDREW   Course I'm sure. Grandma gave me this map. *(pause)* I miss her. She's been gone a long time. There are some things *only* she can do right... like...

TEDDY   Like sew me when I'm wounded by the sword of Davy Jones!

ANDREW   Like fix my broken glasses when I'm in a fight.

TEDDY   Where'd she go? *(stops to think)*

ANDREW   Daddy said she got lost. It was sometime after we moved into this mega house... with mega disposable options...

TEDDY   Got lost? Grandma?

ANDREW   I know. It doesn't make any sense... *(grows sad)*

TEDDY   *(diverting)* Look out! A whole crew of pirates... we need to get that treasure fast!

ANDREW   Oh yeah! *(whips a blanket off of the treasure chest)* We found it!

TEDDY   Do the honours, Captain! Hurry!

    ANDREW tries to open the chest, but can't.

DAD   *(DAD enters from downstage right, clicking his cellphone off.)* Well, you ready, sport? I can't be late to town hall this morning! I forgot to ask, did you make the hockey team?

ANDREW   Dad, I already...

DAD   You know? The tryouts you went to last night? Did you keep your head up, stick on the ice, did you give 'em what for, did you line the puck the up, did you shoot, did you score?

ANDREW   I got cut.

DAD   You? But you're *the mayor's* son...

ANDREW   I don't like hockey...

DAD	*My* son... I can't believe it... by your age I already had three hat tricks!
ANDREW	What's a hat trick?
DAD	Never mind. You'll get 'em next time. I'll arrange for another tryout... so you can use... this! *(produces amazing hockey stick)* I bought you this special synergistic composite stick... from the Super-Giant, Bigger-Than-Walmart Department Store.
ANDREW	Wow. A magic stick! Just like Grandma's. Thanks, Dad. It's incredible. Will it help me to skate too?
	Without thinking, ANDREW drops TEDDY as he rushes over to DAD to get a hug, but his father puts out his hand and motions for a handshake. They shake hands, then ANDREW excitedly grabs the stick.
DAD	It will help you keep your head up...
ANDREW & DAD	...stick on the ice, give 'em what for, line the puck the up, shoot, and score!
DAD	It works like magic... It'll have you getting hat tricks in no time! You'll make the team for sure!
ANDREW	I'll be a great hockey player just like you!
DAD	With a lot of pract— *(phone rings)* Excuse me, son, I've got to take this call. *(exits downstage right)*
ANDREW	This is the best stick ever! No one can stop me now! I'll have it *here* *(points to his heart)*, here *(points to his head)*, and here! *(points to his arm)* I'm gonna give this a try outside! *(exits downstage right)*
TEDDY	Andrew? You forgot me! Who am I gonna play with now?
	Music. As ANDREW exits downstage right, lining up for a shot with his new stick, MOUTH appears centre stage left, and SWOOPSIE enters through it, dancing a bizarre ballet. The picture of robotic grace, she is intensely passionate about her job, and at times this passion overcomes her robotic nature.
SWOOPSIE	*(enters carrying a giant T, like a magic wand)* I'll play with you! Oopsie doopsie time for Swoopsie. *(robotic voice in italic) Target sighted.* Oooo another one of my trashy little treasures! This one smells warm! *(grabs TEDDY and twirls him inward toward her)* Destination. Bottom of Burbia.

TEDDY   The Land Where all the Garbage Goes? No! NO! NOOOOOOOOO! *(struggling to get free)* I'm still loved! I'm not supposed to go into the trash! Andrew!

        SWOOPSIE dances a vicious ballet/tango with TEDDY, as she moves him toward MOUTH centre stage left.

SWOOPSIE   You are forgotten. He can't hear you now. Oh a feisty one! They all think that they don't belong in the trash. Approaching chute. *Prepare for branding.*

        SWOOPSIE stamps TEDDY with a giant T for trash. TEDDY keeps resisting.

    Stop wiggling! You aren't getting away from me now!

        TEDDY is twirled toward MOUTH and narrowly avoids falling in. SWOOPSIE gracefully gives him one final kick and TEDDY tumbles into MOUTH. SWOOPSIE jumps through excitedly after TEDDY.

TEDDY   *(off, falling)* AHHHHHHHH!

SWOOPSIE   *(off, falling)* WHEEEEEEEE!

ANDREW   *(enters downstage right, upset)* Teddy. I broke the stick. I can't do anything right! *(drops stick)* Dad's gonna hate me now. Teddy? This is no time for playing!

        As ANDREW looks for TEDDY, SWOOPSIE enters through MOUTH to get the broken stick. Music. ANDREW watches with fear and awe as SWOOPSIE tosses his broken stick through the mouth.

    Hey, stop, my dad just gave that to me!

SWOOPSIE   *Broken. No longer usable.*

ANDREW   But I could glue it, I could fix it.

SWOOPSIE   *Go buy another one. There's plenty at the Super-Giant, Bigger-Than-Walmart Department Store. Goodbye.*

ANDREW   Hey, did you take Teddy?

SWOOPSIE   Go buy another one!

ANDREW   *(realizing)* Oh no! Teddy's down there. Mommy said there were monsters down there… but I *have* to go… I promised Grandma I'd always keep Teddy with me… *(He hesitates, then musters all of his courage and jumps through the MOUTH.)*

Scene Three

*Music accompanies ANDREW'S journey down the garbage chute
to the landfill. It also lays the backdrop for the transformation
of the set and characters into the Land Where all the Garbage
Goes. Fog. As ANDREW is tumbling, the set is transforming.
ANDREW's bedroom is playfully floated off the stage, while two
black two-step risers are floated in. One is placed just in from
centre stage left, and one in from centre stage right. MOUTH and
ANDREW, followed by five DISPOSABLES manipulating junk
props, enter upstage left (line one), and five DISPOSABLES with
TEDDY in their midst enter upstage right (line two)—one person
following the other, as if falling down a winding garbage chute.
They turn and circle, sweeping in and out to create chaos and
the appearance of an intricate network of piping. They remain in
lines—much like a game of follow-the-leader. Line one crosses up
and over the risers upstage centre to upstage right, while line two
passes in front of the upstage centre risers to upstage left. TREE
enters upstage right and moves to the riser upstage centre after
line one has crossed over the risers and turned the upstage right
corner. Line one rounds the upstage right corner and proceeds to
downstage left, while line two rounds the upstage left corner and
proceeds to downstage right. There are near collisions between
the two lines of DISPOSABLES as they turn and sweep through
centre stage, creating chaos and pandemonium. TEDDY and
ANDREW hear each other screaming through the echo of the
garbage chute. They reach for each other at various times, but
are unable to connect. MOUTH and ANDREW tumble off
downstage left as line one rounds the downstage left corner.
TEDDY tumbles off downstage right as line two rounds the
downstage right corner. The garbage lines turn and make one
more sweep inward—line one toward the riser centre stage left
and line two toward the riser centre stage right. Still in the same
two lines, still turning circles, the DISPOSABLES climb the riser
one at a time and present themselves at the top by bowing to the
TREE for sorting. In a magical gesture the TREE sweeps each of
the DISPOSABLES to its place upstage left and upstage right of
the tree. Line one members who climb the riser centre stage left,
get swept to upstage right, while line two members who climb
the riser centre stage right, get swept to upstage left. The sorting
happens quickly, alternating from stage left to stage right, each
of the DISPOSABLES jumping off the riser in a final fall before
settling, much like leaves falling, to either side upstage of the
TREE. DISPOSABLES create a collage of garbage that frames
the TREE. As the chaos settles, and as the lighting cross-fades to*

indicate morning, the garbage piles, SOCKS, ROTTENS, and FORGOTTENS, enter asleep and snoring. SOCKS enters centre stage right, and settles riser centre stage right; FORGOTTENS enters upstage left and settles on top step on riser centre stage left; ROTTENS enters centre stage left and settles on bottom step on riser centre stage left. After sorting, TREE falls asleep, snoring and wheezing, obviously unhealthy. Everyone ad libs, muttering their dreams. Just as the set change settles, MOUTH appears upstage right, with ANDREW in tow. MOUTH stops and ANDREW is ejected through it tumbling and screaming. He lands in front of TREE. Music fades.

TREE   *(broken snoring)* More oxygen! *(wakes up and notices ANDREW)* Ahh, a clean boy!

Frightened, ANDREW backs away and runs into SOCKS. SOCKS wakes up.

SOCKS   *(dreaming)* Clean socksies…

Waking up, he notices ANDREW and is upset because he has been woken.

TREE   How peculiar… he must be sorted immediately. Now where to put him? Does he belong in forgottens…

FORGOTTENS   *(waking up)* Forgottens at the ready!

TREE   Rottens…

ROTTENS   *(waking up)* Rottens here!

TREE   Or socks?

SOCKS   *(pulling ANDREW over to her pile)* Oh we wants him we does! We wants his stinky socks for usses!

ROTTENS   *(pulling ANDREW to her pile)* But WE wants him! We wants to soil his clean clothes with the smelly cheeses we hases!

FORGOTTENS   *(pulling ANDREW to her pile)* We wants his memories we does, to take his first steps, his bicycles rides, thoughts of Mom and Dad too…

ROTTENS   *(playing tug-of-war with ANDREW)* Give hims to us 'cause we wants to throw wormies on him…

TREE   Hear me now!

Intake of breath from ROTTENS, FORGOTTENS, and SOCKS.

I decide where things go in this dump, and I say—turn please! He goes… *(ANDREW turns, TREE is shocked.)* Nowhere!

R, F, & S	Nowhere?
TREE	Nowhere! This boy is not branded!
R, F, & S	Not branded? *(running back to risers)* Well wes don't wants him!
TREE	State your business, boy!

SOOKI enters. She sneaks up behind one of the trash piles and listens in on the story.

ANDREW	*(stuttering)* My name is… is… is…
DISPOSABLES	His name is… *is?*
TREE	Is… *(trying to help him)*… Isadora? Isabella?
ANDREW	A… A… A…
FORGOTTENS	A?
ROTTENS	B?
SOCKS	C?
R, F, & S	*(singing)* D, E, F, G…
TREE	Silence!

Intake of breath from ROTTENS, FORGOTTENS, and SOCKS.

ANDREW	Andrew… and I came here to find… to find…
FORGOTTENS	Your hat?
ROTTENS	Your head?
SOCKS	Your socks…
ANDREW	My teddy bear. He was my only friend.
R, F, & S	Your only friend… *(start sniffling)* We has lots of friends…
FORGOTTENS	*(hugging each other)* We loves you, Rottens!
ROTTENS	*(hugging each other)* We loves you, Socks!
SOCKS	*(all hugging centre stage)* We loves you too…
ANDREW	*(breaking through them)* I love my teddy… *(TREE and DISPOSABLES whimper.)* He was a gift… I put him down for just a second, then he was gone…
R, F, & S	*(gasp)* SWOOPSIE!
TREE	I know just how you feel. When I was a young seed, I fell far from the tree. I rolled and rolled until I landed at the bottom of the hill,

	right in this spot. I had a forest of friends, but in the great tree chop of 1999...
R, F, & S	*(gasp)* The great tree chop! *(Looking sad, they grab various bits of garbage to wipe their eyes.)*
TREE	My friends were cut down so that Burbia could be built. My growth was stunted, so they overlooked me. I might have died of sadness anyway, but with the help of a young girl... I grew strong... *(cough)*
R, F, & S	Now he's just hanging on by a limb...
TREE	*(incensed)* Silence!

Intake of breath from ROTTENS, FORGOTTENS, and SOCKS.

	You see, I'm the only one providing oxygen for Burbia. It is a very demanding job, and with all the pollution Burbia is creating, it gets more difficult by the day! I'd take a vacation... but I made a promise to that little girl long ago...
ANDREW	I made a promise too... that I'd never lose my teddy. *(starts to cry)* His name is Theodore William Bear...
R, F, & S	Theodore William Bear!
TREE	Ah, Theodore William... He's brown and cuddly, with stitches on the side...
R, F, S, & ANDREW	Brown and cuddly!
SOOKI	*(aside)* Isn't the Burbian a little old for a teddy bear?
R, F, & S	There. There. No one here gots him...
TREE	I sorted him. He needed repair. His heart was broken!
ANDREW	*(intake of breath, about to cry)* His heart? Oh Teddy...
TREE	I sent him to the queen for mending...
R, F, & S	*(scared)* The queen?
ANDREW	*(frightened)* What's wrong with the queen?
SOOKI	*(aside)* He's a scaredy... I'll fix him...
ROTTENS	She's really rottens, she is...
FORGOTTENS	'Cause she was forgottens...
SOCKS	If you go lookin' for the likes of her, you may never come back...
SOOKI	*(voice, off)* Yes, the deeper you go, the darker it gets, the more you may forget... you might get lost! *(jumps out)*

R, F, & S	It's the queen!
SOOKI	FOREVER!
	All jump in fear.
R, F, & S	*(recognition)* Princess Sooki! Don't scares us like that!
SOOKI	Couldn't help it!
	ROTTENS, FORGOTTENS, and SOCKS crowd around SOOKI centre stage.
SOCKS	Have any nice smelly sockses for us today?
FORGOTTENS	How about a nice photo of a broken-up couple?
ROTTENS	What about some moldy apples for usses?
SOOKI	I'm here on official business. *(turns to ANDREW)* What are you doing here?
ANDREW	I've… I've…
R, F, & S	He's come to get his teddy back!
SOOKI	I've heard his story.
R, F, & S	Ooh!
SOOKI	*(jumps to riser centre stage left)* And I don't believe it.
	ROTTENS, FORGOTTENS, and SOCKS gasp.
	You threw him out! Burbians throw everything out.
TREE	She's got a point. Burbians get rid of everything that doesn't suit them…
ANDREW	But I'm not like that…
SOCKS	*(moving to her place on riser centre stage left)* If it's young, if it's old, if it's meek, if it's bold…
ALL	Throw it out!
	All DISPOSABLES come to life. They take several steps forward on each "Throw it out!" to form a new collage around TREE. Some step up on the riser upstage centre, others step in front of the riser. They shake their junk to punctuate the dialogue, freezing on the word "out."
ANDREW	But…
FORGOTTENS	*(moving to her place on riser centre stage left)* If it's scratched, dented, scarred, or in any way bented…

ALL	*(stepping, menacing)* Throw it out!
ANDREW	But I…
ROTTENS	*(moving to her riser centre stage right)* If it's not the latest, or the greatest, or the biggest, or the fastest, or the loudest or the proudest…
ALL	*(stepping into tableau)* Throw it out!
ANDREW	But… why you?
SOOKI	You have no idea what it is like to be thrown out! *(jumps off riser, at ANDREW)*
ALL	*(moving to ANDREW, trapping him)* Wanna know how it feels?
ANDREW	Ummmm. No? *(He runs downstage right, but is stopped by SOCKS.)*
SOOKI	*(grabbing him)* Where ya goin'… *(She throws ANDREW onto the bottom step of the riser centre stage right.)* We're not finished!

> *SOOKI jumps onto the riser centre stage left and the piles surround ANDREW: ROTTENS kneels on top of the riser centre stage right, FORGOTTENS stands right of the riser centre stage right, and SOCKS stands left of the riser centre stage right. They allow ANDREW no escape. Playful, yet threatening.*

Junkyard Jam

ALL	This is the place of trash!

> *The following is an introduction to "Junkyard Jam," and is sung a cappella.*

SOCKS	*(snuggling into ANDREW)* Nobody loves us.
ROTTENS	*(snuggling into ANDREW)* Nobody cares.
FORGOTTENS	*(snuggling into ANDREW)* Nobody wants us.
DISPOSABLES	And everyone stares!

> *SOCKS, ROTTENS, and FORGOTTENS stare out at the audience while the rest turn to stare at ANDREW. Even the props stare, as the junk is manipulated like puppets. ANDREW runs to centre stage, tries to leave, but is stopped by SOOKI.*

R, F, & S	Sort that trash, baby!

> *"Junkyard Jam" music starts. All begin making rhythmic noises with their junk. In a threatening manner, the DISPOSABLES step toward ANDREW forming two clusters, left and right of*

him. They box him in so there is no escape, though he tries.
DISPOSABLES manipulate their junk props as part of the
choreography. SOCKS, ROTTENS, and FORGOTTENS seize
ANDREW, then dance with him, as in a fifties dance number—
but threatening. ANDREW is twirled from character to character,
and dipped as they tell him their story. ANDREW watches,
fearful, enwrapped in the story, but does not sing. At times he
tries to escape when he sees an opening, but he is stopped and
thrown back into the mire.

ALL	Never thought I'd be thrown out!
	(Oh no)
	By a kid that screams and shouts!
	(Oh yeah)
	I was clearly not needed,
	(Boo hoo)
	She forgot all that we did.
	Don't know what I did wrong.
	But I did it.
	And now I'm down in the dumps.
	Swoopsie caught me, then dropped me,
	and gave me T for trash,
	I was branded underhanded,
	down the tunnel, BOOM, BANG, CRASH!
	'Cause every time we turn around,
	There's always more trash, baby!
ROTTENS	Ain't no debris can smell as bad as me!
SOCKS	Ain't no sock got this many seams…
FORGOTTENS	This the kinda place you don't want to have to see…
DISPOSABLES	We've been hurt, we've been judged,
	we've got slime, toxic sludge!
	Ain't no other place for trash…
	(Watch it!) We're growin' fast!
R, F, & S	Sort that trash, baby!
ALL	Mm, ch, mm, mm, mm, mm.
TREE	I was standing in the woods.
ALL	Mm, ch, mm, mm, mm, mm
TREE	Just chillaxin' in my hood.

ALL	Mm, ch, mm, mm, mm, mm.
TREE	Humans came with their saws-alls.
ALL	Mm, ch, mm, mm, mm, mm.
TREE	Used my friends to build their malls!
ALL	Mm, ch, mm, mm, mm, mm.

Don't know what I did wrong.
But I did it.
And now I'm down in the dumps, dumps, dumps, dumps.

> *All freeze in depressed postures. More ominous music plays.*
> *SUFFIX enters downstage right.*

SUFFIX   Ain't no debris as toxic as me!
Ain't no burn, with this many degrees.
I'm the kinda waste
You don't want to have to see!

I am hurt, I am judged,
I am slime, toxic sludge…

> *All unfreeze.*

ALL   Ain't no other place for trash.
We're growin' fast.
Ain't no other place for trash.
We're growin' fast.
Ain't no other place for trash.
We're growin' fast.
Ain't no other place for trash.
(Watch it!) We're growin' fast!

> *They notice SUFFIX and scream in terror.*

Scene Four

SUFFIX   Feed me! Hungry!

SOOKI   Suffix! Twice in one day! *(jumping to top of riser centre stage left)*
Positions!

> *All get as high as possible on various risers. DISPOSABLES climb*
> *the riser around tree. All are shaking.*

TREE	Andrew, climb! *(ANDREW climbs up the tree.)*
SOOKI	*(SUFFIX oozes toward SOOKI.)* Well somebody… give him something!
SOCKS	Nope.
FORGOTTENS	Nope.
ROTTENS	Nope.
ALL	We're running out!
SUFFIX	*(to SOOKI)* Mmmmm. Orphans are delectable. Ahhhh! You're really full of toxicity! MMMM! All that anger! I could live on your fumes for quite a while!
SOOKI	Someone throw carcinogens! He's really hungry!
R, F, & S	Carcinowhats?
ANDREW	Carcinogens… *(to ROTTENS)* You have some asbestos… I've seen it… give it to him!
SUFFIX	Mmmm. Asbestos…
ROTTENS	Here Suffix, here boy, here
	SUFFIX turns from vicious monster to panting puppy as he ogles the special treat. ROTTENS throws the asbestos off stage left, and SUFFIX pursues it offstage.
ANDREW	*(afraid)* What was it?
SOOKI	Just Suffix.
R, F, & S	Suffix!
ANDREW	Suffix… the end of a word.
R, F, & S	*(whimpering)* The end…
SOOKI	He slowly creeps up on his prey and eats them! *(SOOKI jumps off of the riser and scares ANDREW.)* What are you so afraid of? I'm not afraid of Suffix.
ANDREW	Well… you sure looked pretty scared when he had you by the legs!
FORGOTTENS	We thoughts…
SOCKS	He was going to eats you, Sooki!
ROTTENS	Like a giant cookie!
SOOKI	Well, I wasn't scared!

ANDREW	He said you were… an orphan… is that why you're here? You have no…
R, F, & S	Ssssshhhh, Andrew…
SOOKI	*(ignoring ANDREW's comment)* Go back to your mega house… I can handle him…
TREE	But Sooki, he has come twice today…
R, F, & S	That's never happened before…
ROTTENS	He used to come once a week.
FORGOTTENS	Before that once a month.
SOCKS	Before that once a year.
TREE	Suffix is eating everything…
FORGOTTENS	Next he'll eat us!
R, F, & S	Sooki, what do we do?
SOOKI	Ummm…
TREE	Andrew, you're quite an intelligent Burbian…
R, F, & S	Do you have an idea?
ANDREW	Well…
SOOKI	The B-b-b-burbian? Yeah right. I know what to do! We still have a ton of teddy bears left, and he loves forgotten teddy bears!
R, F, & S	Yes, teddy bears…
ANDREW	Oh no! Do you think Theodore has been… eaten? *(starts crying)*
SOOKI	So what if he has? It's just a dumb teddy!
R, F, & S	*(intake of breath)* Sooki!
SOOKI	*(starts to pace)* What? I have to worry about myself… Did you see how he attacked me?
ANDREW	It might have something to do with your rudeness and anger!
R, F, & S	She can be pretty toxic…
SOOKI	You haven't seen the half of my anger… Neither has Suffix! Oh, what I plan to do to him!
R, F, & S	Tell it, sister!
SOOKI	I'll… I'll… *(at a loss)*
ANDREW	You've got nothin' to tell… do you…

TREE	Sooki?
SOOKI	I… don't know what to do about Suffix.
R, F, & S	You're out of ideas? But we named you our princess because you had all the ideas…
TREE	There's only one thing you can do… You must visit the queen!
R, F, & S	(shivering) The queen!
SOCKS	I wouldsn't wanna be in your socks!
ANDREW	How mean can a queen be?
ROTTENS	Likes a queen bee… bzzzzzzzzzzzzz bite!
ANDREW	How could you send my Theodore to her!
TREE	Don't worry, Andrew… She'd never harm him… She has a special spot for animals… Just not… people. When she first came here… she mended everything that was broken…
SOCKS	Even Burbians…
ROTTENS	She wrote books.
FORGOTTENS	And told us stories.
R & F	Of the way things used to be…
TREE	She grew sadder and sadder when nobody came for her…
SOCKS	And angrier and angrier…
ROTTENS	She whipped up storms that blews us all over the place…
R, F, & S	Then she wents (pause) in there… (all pointing stage left)
SOOKI	The deeper in you go, the more treacherous the landfill gets…
TREE	You'd better know what you're getting into, Andrew… Your parents might miss you
ANDREW	(more to himself) Dad probably hasn't even noticed I'm gone…
R, F, & S	We are just the outskirts…
ROTTENS	The really rottens, the angry forgottens, and the litters are in there…
FORGOTTENS	No one here has ever been…
R, F, & S	In there…
TREE	Except the queen.
R, F, & S	Except the queen.
ROTTENS	And she hasn't returned for years.

TREE	She's working on a plan…
R, F, & S	A dangerous one… to stop Suffix.
ROTTENS	She even builts herself a magical tower!
ANDREW	How do you know?
TREE	Her plans, carried on the winds of her rage, are sometimes blown to us.
	I fear for my old friend… So much anger…
SOCKS	Somes say she is so angry you burn up in her gaze if you look at her!

ROTTENS, FORGOTTENS, and SOCKS all shudder— even SOOKI.

ANDREW	That's okay. Princess Sooki isn't afraid of anything… We'll go together…
TREE	Sooki… are you sure you're…
SOOKI	I'm a princess, aren't I? What are we waiting for?

General cries of hurrah.

ANDREW	So which way is Trash Tower?
R, F, & S	Nobody knows…
TREE	The tower is constantly moving…
ANDREW	Well, if it's always moving, then can't we just wait here until it comes to us?
R, F, & S	The queen won't find what doesn't seek…
ANDREW	Well… I'm a good seeker… Let's go!
SOOKI	Onward!

SOOKI heads downstage left, then stops and considers. She then heads downstage right. The trash piles follow her movements.

ANDREW	Why don't we follow a map?
SOOKI	(frustrated now) Okay, wiz kid. Do you have a map?
ANDREW	(checks his pockets) I have this one my grandma gave me…
SOOKI	(rips map out of ANDREW's hands) Let me see this. (inspects closely) It says: You *are* here. Well look at that, pretty accurate. You are here. There's the tower! Let's go!

DISPOSABLES clap and cheer them on. All exit downstage left.

Scene Five

---

*Ominous music. Fog. The scene shifts as SOOKI and ANDREW
enter upstage left, climbing onto upstage risers and peering out
through the darkness. Rottens, Forgottens, and Socks transform
into LITTERS ONE, TWO, and THREE by removing their outer
costume and putting on enlarged noses. The LITTERS transform
slowly before the audience into ominous and threatening
creatures. TEDDY enters downstage right, calling out toward the
audience for ANDREW. TEDDY is scared and alone. LITTERS
scuttle about the stage in shifty and unpredictable movement
patterns—like crabs. Other times they are stone still, so as not to
be seen. When engaged with ANDREW, they are hypnotic, casting
spells with their voices and movements.*

TEDDY   *(enters downstage right)* Andrew, where are you?

LITTERS   *(repeats in a whispering voice, mocking)* Andrew, where are you?

ANDREW   Teddy, Teddy?

LITTERS   *(whispers, taunting)* Teddy, Teddy, where are you?

SUFFIX   *(enters from downstage right, drinking from a pesticide can)*
Pesticides. Hmmm... Empty! *(angry)* I need more food!
(throws can off right)

TEDDY   *(stops downstage centre, calling out to audience)* Andrew!

SUFFIX   *(notices TEDDY, aside to audience)* A teddy bear, a sweet delectable
teddy bear...

     TEDDY notices SUFFIX.

(He attempts to be pleasant.) I don't want to hurt you...

     TEDDY screams and exits downstage left.

(passionately) I just want some of your nice, gooey stuffing...
(chasing after)

ANDREW   *(crossing from upstage right toward centre stage)* Oh no, Suffix is
after Teddy! *(calling)* Teddy?

SOOKI   What makes you say that?

ANDREW   I heard him...

SOOKI   It's just the wind...

LITTERS   *(repeat in a whisper)* Just the wind...

SOOKI   Andrew, stay here in case the tower comes this way… I'm going to search over there…

SOOKI walks off upstage right, searching.

ANDREW   Sooki? It's better if we stick together… Sooki?

All LITTERS corner ANDREW downstage centre. They circle him.

LITTERS ONE   You're in litters territory now…

ANDREW   Don't hurt me!

LITTERS TWO   *(mocking)* Don't hurt me!

They all throw large pieces of what appears to be TEDDY'S stuffing at ANDREW.

LITTERS ONE   We throw things at Burbians, because you threw us out!

LITTERS   It's only fair…

LITTERS TWO   You left us for dead on the streets…

LITTERS THREE   With nothing to eats!

LITTERS ONE   When you had plenty…

ANDREW   *(shocked)* Teddy? *(tries to put the pieces of the teddy bear back together… then hoping)* You're not Teddy…

LITTERS THREE   You did this to him…

LITTERS   Not only his heart needs mending… *(laugh)*

ANDREW   Sooki…

LITTERS   *(mocking)* Sooki!

LITTERS TWO   SUCKIE!

LITTERS THREE   FOUR-EYES!

LITTERS ONE   You'll never get to Trash Tower.

LITTERS   Never! *(cackling)*

ANDREW   *(falls to his knees)* My teddy…

LITTERS all freeze as SOOKI enters.

SOOKI   *(re-entering from downstage right)* Well, it's not here… did you find it?… Andrew, what's wrong?

ANDREW   *(really upset)* It's… Teddy…

SOOKI   *(grabbing stuffing, moves downstage right)* This is not a teddy…

ANDREW   It's not?

>*LITTERS begin circling ANDREW, trying to get at him.*

LITTERS ONE   Four-eyes!

LITTERS TWO   Trouble seeing?

LITTERS THREE   Why don't you get six eyes?

SOOKI   Andrew! Don't listen. They can't hurt you if you don't listen to them!

>*ANDREW puts his hand over his ears. The insults get exceedingly lame, and have no further effect on ANDREW. The insults begin to literally bounce off of ANDREW and hit the unsuspecting LITTER. They become easily confused, and they start hurling insults at each other. This comical effect can be produced by hand gestures and eyes that follow the insult as they hit and bounce off of their target. The LITTERS lose their ominous trance and hypnotic rhythm as they grow more and more confused.*

LITTERS TWO   Bat face!

LITTERS THREE   Mosquito!

LITTERS ONE   Litter... bug!

>*They turn insults on each other.*

LITTERS TWO   Stinky!

LITTERS ONE   Smelly!

LITTERS THREE   Lizard breath!

LITTERS TWO   Putrid!

LITTERS ONE   Messy!

>*They exit upstage left, ad libbing more insults.*

SOOKI   You okay?

ANDREW   Yeah... if I don't listen... they can't hurt me...

SOOKI   It's an old trick I learned when I lived in Burbia... Otherwise I never would have survived. *(looking at map)* The map's cleared! We've got to hurry, it's getting darker... *(They exit downstage left.)*

Scene Six

> *More fog. Music. DISPOSABLES enter from various places, manipulating junk. All are isolated, never looking at each other, never connecting. They are lost, floating, weaving, vacant, empty. Their presence on stage provides a moving maze through which the main characters must find their way. Deep depression. TEDDY enters pursued by SUFFIX.*

TEDDY *(entering upstage right, moving to centre)* Andrew?

SUFFIX *(entering upstage right, sneaking, following TEDDY)* Mmm... teddy bear!

> *SUFFIX thinks, then grabs a garbage can lid from one of the DISPOSABLES. He uses it to hide behind and sneaks up on TEDDY, who is by this time standing downstage centre.*

> *Hearing SUFFIX and thinking it could be ANDREW, TEDDY looks over his right shoulder and SUFFIX is nearly caught. SUFFIX hides behind the trash lid.*

TEDDY Andrew?

SUFFIX *(can hardly contain himself, peeks out from behind trash lid)* Mmm... teddy bear!

> *Again, TEDDY hears SUFFIX and looks over his left shoulder. SUFFIX quickly hides behind the trash lid.*

TEDDY Andrew?

> *SUFFIX lurks over TEDDY. Sensing his presence, TEDDY looks up over his head, sees him, and screams. He runs off downstage left, as SUFFIX just misses capturing him.*

SUFFIX Curse my gelatinous body! *(follows TEDDY off)*

ANDREW *(on riser upstage centre)* This place is weird... but I don't feel scared anymore.

> *DISPOSABLES begin to shake props, threatening, like distant thunder—the promise of something spectacular about to happen. SOOKI and ANDREW try to remain calm.*

SOOKI *(travelling downstage right, peeking off right)* Neither do I...

> *Music. Lighting shift. DISPOSABLES shake harder and form Trash Tower on and around the riser centre stage left. GRANDMA enters centre stage left behind DISPOSABLES,*

unseen, and takes her place on the top step, inside the newly formed tower. Three BULBS enter unnoticed, carrying boxes downstage left. They take their places seated on boxes that form three levels in front of Trash Tower. BULB ONE is seated lowest, stage right of BULB TWO, who is seated at medium height, stage right of BULB THREE, who sits highest. The BULBS are immobile, except for their heads. The BULBS appear as though they are on a string, wrapped around the tower. They are asleep.

According to the map it should be here… *(pointing off downstage right)* but I don't see it!

Waking up, the BULBS notice SOOKI and ANDREW, and though they are guards, they aren't very good at what they do.

BULB ONE	*(whispering, snapping head right)* Someone's coming!
BULB TWO	*(whispering, snapping head right)* Someone's coming!
BULB THREE	*(whispering, snapping head right)* Someone's coming!
BULBS	*(gasp)* HIDE!

There is nowhere for the BULBS to go, so in unison they tuck their shoulders around their ears and squeeze their eyes shut.

SOOKI	Look, it's Trash Tower!
ANDREW	Right in front of us… How could I miss that?
SOOKI	Wahoooo! We made it! We made it!

SOOKIE grabs ANDREW's hands and starts to dance. Both SOOKI and ANDREW enjoy the dancing, realize what they are doing… then stop.

ANDREW	This is a fortified tower! No stairs…
SOOKI	No door!
ANDREW & SOOKI	
	(pointing at each other) Your turn…
SOOKI	Fine, I'll do it!
BULBS	*(jerking heads to the right)* STOP!
ANDREW	Excuse me, umm, we have to get to the top…
BULB ONE	*(jerking head back centre)* They have to get to the…
BULB TWO	*(jerking head back centre)* have to get to the…
BULB THREE	*(jerking head back centre)* have to get to the top?!
BULBS	*(turning heads to right in unison)* WHY?

ANDREW & SOOKI	We have to see the queen.
BULBS	*(gasp, heads centre)* The queen! *(They shake in fear.)*
ANDREW	*(scared)* I need to get my bear back...
SOOKI	And I need to stop Suffix *(hard for her)* Please...
BULBS	Please? *(laugh)*
SOOKI	Let us up or I'll step on each and every one of you!

> *In sequence from BULB ONE to BULB THREE, the BULBS imagine that they are being stepped on, and they physicalize the possibility.*

BULBS	*(awareness in unison)* Not good.
ANDREW	Sooki, don't be mean. They're obviously broken!

> *Intake of air from BULB ONE.*
>
> *Intake of air from BULB TWO.*
>
> *Intake of air from BULB THREE.*

BULBS	Broken? We're broken! *(They all sob uncontrollably... then sing to the tune of "Jingle Bells.")* We don't work, we don't work, that's why we are here... We burned out, we're thrown out, no more Christmas cheer. Hey!
SOOKI	*(to BULBS)* I'll make you a deal. If Andrew fixes you, will you let us up?
BULBS	What's in it for us?
SOOKI	*(making it clear)* Fix...

> *SOOKI and ANDREW look at each other exasperated.*

BULBS	Ahh... *(clueing in)* right! Fix...
ANDREW	Christmas lights are powered by electricity, and electricity comes from a power source. So, if we follow the cord, we should find the problem!

> *As ANDREW runs his hand along the cord, following it from BULB THREE to BULB TWO then to BULB ONE, each bulb responds as though being tickled.*

> *(following the cord around and behind the tower and exiting centre stage left)* ...And the cord seems to go over here to...

> *BULBS light up.*

BULBS	We're all toasty… Thanks!
ANDREW	You're welcome. Now, it's time to let us up!
BULBS	No! Good night.

BULBS go back to sleep.

SOOKI	Hold on just one minute!

BULBS wake up.

BULBS	Yes?
ANDREW	You said you would let us up!

BULBS look at each other, then shrug and go back to sleep.

SOOKI	*(frustrated)* That's it!

SOOKI tries to climb but burns her hands on the bulbs.

Owwwww! *(scared)* The queen's anger burned me!

ANDREW	Ummm Sooki? You clearly touched the Christmas lights, which can get very hot. They're powered by electricity, which then creates heat, which then…
SOOKI	Okay whatever, Andrew.
ANDREW	We could try knocking politely…
SOOKI	You knock… I'm not touching the tower…
ANDREW	*(knocking)* Umm… Queen? Your Majesty? Hello? I need to talk to you!
QUEEN	*(growls)* Go away!

The tower shakes when the QUEEN speaks, punctuating her words.

ANDREW	But I…
BULB ONE	She isn't…
BULB TWO	Seeing anyone…
BULB THREE	Today!
BULBS	Or ever!

BULBS all laugh, then stop at the same time.

ANDREW	I came all this way to see you.
QUEEN	No time, no time at all! Get lost!

ANDREW	*(to himself)* Come on, Andrew. Think. I may not have it here *(points to his arms)*, but I have it here *(points to his head)* and here *(points to his heart)*...
QUEEN	*(intrigued, peaking out from behind the junk)* I've heard that somewhere before...
ANDREW	My grandma always told me that.
QUEEN	Okay boy, your grandmother thinks you are so smart, then prove it! I will see you today *if* you can answer this riddle.
BULB ONE	Oh, the riddle. You'll never get it.
QUEEN	If you get it wrong...
BULBS	You'll burn up in her gaze.
SOOKI	Careful, Andrew!
QUEEN	Okay, here is the riddle. What is cherished by some, forgotten by others, but is always somewhere in your head?
ANDREW	My grandmother used to ask me that... I wish I could remember... it's memories!
QUEEN	No!... Ha, ha, ha!

The BULBS giggle.

Wait... YES... That's correct. Ahhhh!

Music. Thunder. Lightning. Fog. The DISPOSABLES making up Trash Tower explode up and out, creating chaos. GRANDMA slips out centre stage left and reappears on upstage centre riser unseen, shielded by the chaos. DISPOSABLES exits, as though blown off by a raging storm, and the QUEEN suddenly appears, backlit, raising her magic stick in the air... in a tremendous rage. The BULBS remain seated, circling upright in their seats to add to the chaos, ad libbing: woah... what's happening... I'm scared... etc.

(in a rage) Now, boy, what do you want? *(slams cane, music stops, lights flash on, silence and stillness)* I am busy saving the world!

ANDREW	*(shaking)* I ah... ah... *(moving toward her)* Your friend the tree... sent... *(recognition)* Grandma?
QUEEN	What, boy? *(to SOOKI)* What are you doing here?... I expressly forbid...
ANDREW	Grandma! I can't believe it's you!

SOOKI	Grandma?
BULBS	Grandma?
QUEEN	Grandma? Ha ha ha.

The BULBS giggle.

I am no Grandma. I am the Queen of Trash Tower!

BULBS	She hasn't the heart to be a grandma...
QUEEN	I hate kids! *(goes to the BULBS)*
ANDREW	Don't you remember me? It's Andrew! You told me stories, and I've found out since... they are true... And you gave me Theodore William Bear... Here... here's the map, the map you gave me to look for treasure with. Please remember... *(hands map to QUEEN)*
SOOKI	His map helped us to find you...
QUEEN	It is a good map. I think I... Oh my my my my! You are my Andrew.

Intake of air from the BULBS.

ANDREW	Your Andrew! *(goes to hug QUEEN)*
QUEEN	*(stops ANDREW)* My Andrew that stopped believing me! My Andrew that called me a liar! You were my last hope in Burbia. My last hope, Andrew! I'm glad your family has forgotten you! Now you know what this feels like!
ANDREW	But Grandma...
SOOKI	*(shocked)* Did you really do those things, Andrew?
ANDREW	Well, I did but—
SOOKI	I thought you were different! I guess all of you Burbians are the same!
ANDREW	But I've changed... *(The BULBS sob and weep.)*
SOOKI	Pff. You'll never change!
QUEEN	*(to SOOKI)* Now, why did you come?
SOOKI	I came with Andrew... Suffix is getting bigger and stronger... He even attacked me... We can't control him anymore... If it weren't for Andrew... I might have been...
QUEEN	Ahhh. No need to worry now... Suffix is, as we speak... meeting his end...
DAD	*(offstage)* Andrew! ...Andrew!

	DAD enters from upstage right covered in muck and a black sheet. He looks like SUFFIX.
QUEEN	What is that?
ANDREW	Why is it calling my name?
DAD	*(entering upstage right, seeing ANDREW)* ANDREW!
ALL	Ahhhhh! *(pointing at father)* Suffix!
DAD	Where? Ahh!
	DAD screams because the others are screaming. He turns and looks for SUFFIX from where he came, then backs away toward the BULBS downstage left.
ALL	Ahhh! *(scream because DAD is screaming)*
DAD	*(backs into the BULBS)* AHHH! *(The BULBS start to bite at DAD, causing the sheet to come off.)*
ALL	*(recognition)* AHHHH!
DAD	I just got bit by a light bulb! What's wrong with this place?
BULBS	Self-defence!
DAD	Andrew, I finally found you! Let's get out of this disgusting place! There's this thing that's been following me, it's been trying to eat me. I had to disguise myself to look like him... that's how I escaped! Let's get out of here!
ANDREW	You didn't forget about me! *(to GRANDMA)* Daddy didn't forget about me!
DAD	What makes you think I'd forget about you? I love you! *(They hug each other.)*
QUEEN	*(pokes her way through them with her magic stick)* Hey! Don't you go believing that nonsense! He just wants you back and perfect so he can win the next election! He may have it here and here *(points to DAD's head and arm)* but he's never had it here! *(points to heart)*
DAD	That's not true! Don't say that! Wait—Mother? How did you get here? *(DAD's phone rings as QUEEN takes a deep breath to tell her story.)* Hold that thought—I must take this! *(He answers the phone call, moving centre stage left.)*
BULBS	Tsk tsk. *(rolling eyes)*
QUEEN	See that, Andrew? You'll never be more important than his cellphone!

ANDREW   I'm sure it's an important call...

DAD   *(concern)* Could you guys keep it down a bit?

        The BULBS huff.

QUEEN   Do you really want to go back to that? Honestly?

DAD   *(comes back to group)* That was my assistant. There's something attacking Burbia!

BULB ONE   Is it big?

DAD   Very big.

BULB TWO   Is it black?

DAD   Very black.

BULB THREE   Is it swallowing everything up?

DAD   Yes! And it's getting bigger and bigger!

BULBS   It's SUFFIX! *(all gasp)*

ANDREW   What is Suffix doing in Burbia?... Grandma, I thought you...

QUEEN   I put it there!

DAD   Then move it back here!

SOOKI   *(to DAD)* What about us?

QUEEN   Burbia created it, therefore if Suffix destroys Burbia, he will ultimately destroy himself!

ANDREW   Don't you see? When it's finished with Burbia, it will just return here! Moving it changes nothing.

QUEEN   *(cowering)* Oops...

ANDREW   We've got to think of something!

BULBS   We've tried everything!

QUEEN   I'm out of ideas...

DAD   Have you tried to swoopsie it?

        They ALL roll their eyes.

ANDREW   I've got it! No time to explain! We've got to go now! To Burbia!

        ANDREW charges in one direction, and all follow, but they don't know which way to go.

QUEEN	Andrew, the only way to get to Burbia fast enough is my way. Everyone, grab.

All except the BULBS grab a part of the magic stick. It is held horizontally in front of them.

Think really hard about something you love!

ANDREW	Teddy!
SOOKI	Disposables!
DAD	My son! *(nudge from QUEEN)* And my mother…
BULBS	Electricity!
QUEEN	The birds, the bees, the flowers, oooh, and the trees…
DAD	Mom…
ANDREW	Grandma…
SOOKI	Your Majesty…
ALL	*(no BULBS, no QUEEN)* We have to go! To Burbia!
QUEEN & BULBS	
	To Burbia!

Music as in opening. The drum roll ushers characters offstage and march music ushers the new scene on stage. BULBS exit downstage left ad libbing goodbye, good luck, etc. The others, as if carried on the winds of the magical staff, are pulled centre stage right, then up and toward audience with the staff high over their heads, then back with the cane down low, then out centre stage right. All ad lib sounds as if on a roller coaster to punctuate their movements.

TEDDY enters upstage left. He sees everyone just as they are exiting, and gets left behind.

TEDDY	Wait for me… oh no, how do I get there?

MOUTH appears downstage right.

Oh!

TEDDY enters MOUTH. MOUTH and TEDDY exit together, twirling.

Scene Seven

*Parade music continues as in opening. The grand Burbian
entrance echoes the opening. The BURBIANS enter marching
and carrying placards tucked under their arms, two from upstage
left, two from centre stage left, two from upstage right, and two
from centre stage right. SUFFIX enters unnoticed and takes
his position on the riser upstage centre, surveying Burbia. The
BURBIANS move in two quadrants toward upstage centre, with
their positions staggered. The banner carriers step up over the
back riser, framing SUFFIX. They don't notice that it is SUFFIX
who is with them, or that the mayor is missing. SUFFIX enjoys
all of the attention. The dialogue is timed to the music.*

BURBIANS SL *(at corner of upstage left riser, looking up, continuing to march on
the spot)* A cloud?

BURBIANS SR *(at corner of upstage right riser, looking up, continuing to march on
the spot)* In Burbia?

BURBIANS *(looking toward the audience)* Impossible!

*SUFFIX stretches high in the air and is just about to suffocate
the BURBIANS when the quadrants turn in sync and march
forward, quadrant stage right marching toward stage right,
and quadrant stage left marching toward stage left. SUFFIX
and the banner carriers step off the riser, and move downstage
through the centre of the two quadrants, just as they are parting.
The BURBIANS march to downstage right and downstage
left, forming clusters of four with their placards on either side
of SUFFIX. The march halts. The dialogue is still timed to the
music. All of this happens without missing a beat.*

Welcome to our perfect town!
We have smiles in place of— *(turn to look at SUFFIX)* AHHHH!

SUFFIX Your town is delectable... *(looks stage left and the BURBIANS shake)*
Just like heaven! *(looks stage right and the BURBIANS shake)*
On a scale to ten—

BURBIANS *(not certain)* We are eleven?

*SUFFIX relishes in his power, and notices the townspeople
are shaking.*

SUFFIX *(playfully)* Boo!

The BURBIANS scream. They are frantic and run everywhere. Fog. SUFFIX consumes them metaphorically with sweeping gestures and laughter. As he approaches DISPOSABLES, they crumble to the ground. Burbia is destroyed. DISPOSABLES hang over their placards, lie on floor, over risers, barely alive, forming a tableau of destruction.

(surveying, noticing nothing left to eat) More food! *(exits downstage right)*

Enter ANDREW, GRANDMA, DAD, and SOOKI centre stage left. They are all holding the magic stick, spinning and screaming. They come to a crashing halt at centre stage.

ANDREW   I'm so glad we made it!

SOOKI   That was one crazy ride!

DAD   *(seeing the devastation)* What has happened to my town? My beautiful, perfect town!

GRANDMA   Well it's Suffix of course, and he's doing exactly as I told him.

DAD   Mom, how could you?

GRANDMA   Son, how could you?

ANDREW   What's done is done! We have to stop Suffix now! What is he made of?

GRANDMA   Greed.

SOOKI   Things that are discarded.

DAD   He *is* a by-product of my town.

ANDREW   So what is the opposite of all that...

GRANDMA   Not greedy.

SOOKI   Things that aren't discarded.

DAD   Something that *isn't* a by-product of my town?

ANDREW   Something that is loved!

Enter MOUTH downstage left. TEDDY enters through MOUTH.

TEDDY   Andrew, Grandma!

ANDREW & GRANDMA
Theodore William Bear! *(They all hug.)*

SUFFIX enters centre stage left and oozes over. He gets on top of the riser centre stage left, increasing his height.

DAD   Watch out, son! *(He steps in front of ANDREW.)* You will not hurt my son or my town!

TEDDY   I'll save you!

> *TEDDY runs in front of SUFFIX, and SUFFIX attempts to eat TEDDY. The crowd gasps. TEDDY cowers at the oncoming onslaught. SUFFIX is stopped by something invisible. SUFFIX pauses. There's a protective shield around TEDDY that SUFFIX can't penetrate. SUFFIX tries again from a different angle. The crowd gasps. Pause.*

SUFFIX   Why can't I eat you?

> *Another of SUFFIX's gargantuan attacks fails. The crowd gasps. Pause. TEDDY realizes he can't be harmed and musters all the courage he has. He gently pokes at SUFFIX. SUFFIX hisses and screeches in horrible pain, then shrinks slightly. All pause.*

TEDDY   *(looking around for encouragement)* I'm scared!

> *The crowd nods encouragement. TEDDY pokes SUFFIX again, and SUFFIX shrinks further, writhing in pain. All pause. TEDDY pokes at him again, gaining more courage and watching the others for their reaction. With one grand writhing, screeching movement, SUFFIX attaches to TEDDY's back, becoming a part of the bear.*

What happened? Andrew, I feel different...

ANDREW   Teddy! *(walks around him, carefully)* I think you are... containing Suffix.

GRANDMA   *(investigating)* How peculiar!

DAD   *(backing away)* Teddy, you need to go... you'll make us all sick...

ANDREW   You're just saying that because you don't like him...

GRANDMA   No Andrew, your dad is right. Teddy must go...

DAD   The love you gave Teddy has saved us all...

ANDREW   Teddy, don't go... I need you...

TEDDY   I can't stay here... I'll make you sick... don't worry, I'll be okay...

ANDREW   Well, where will you go?

TEDDY   I don't know, far away. I'll miss you... but it's okay... I'll find my way... You will too, Andrew. I believe in you.

ANDREW   Here, take the map, Teddy... so you'll always know your way home.

GRANDMA	And here, take this. It was a gift from an old friend... It will protect you as long as you have love...
SOOKI	You are so brave... take this. *(offers TEDDY her crown)*
TEDDY	Oh it fits!
DAD	*(searches and finds cellphone)* Teddy... I have nothing worth giving you...

ALL are astonished.

...But my word. I'll do everything in my power to make things right again. I promise I won't forget you, Teddy, or the sacrifice you're making...

Murmurs of agreement from all.

TEDDY	Thank you. I have to go...
ANDREW	Goodbye, Theodore William Bear, I love you. *(They hug.)*
TEDDY	I love you too, Andrew.

SUFFIX growls.

All watch TEDDY leave downstage right with SUFFIX attached. Silence. All look around then down, recognizing their own responsibility in the loss of TEDDY. They freeze. ANDREW steps out.

ANDREW	It was a long time before anybody spoke. We didn't have any answers. Only questions. We knew one thing was for sure. We had to change. It took us a *long* time to put the pieces back together. Then *(pause)* Grandma wrote this story... so that no one would ever forget.

Blackout.

Alternate Ending

ALL watch TEDDY leave downstage right. Silence.

GRANDMA   Well I guess if we're going to make changes, we should start now.

SOOKI   I'm going to build homes for people who don't have them.

DAD   I'll give you money for your projects. City council will plant trees, allow bees, and start charging garbage fees...

ANDREW   I'm going to be a scientist that helps the environment.

GRANDMA   I'm going to write this story... so no one ever forgets...

ALL   *(turning out to the audience)* What can you do?

Blackout.

Swoopsie (Emily Tisi) sneaks into Andrew's bedroom
and swipes his teddy (Tori Godin) as her trashy treasure.
Photo by Jennifer Benson.

enter my goddess

by Carmela Arangio, Marguerite Jack-Vermey,
and the ensemble of soothemysisters productions

The poster designed by Stephanie Sanchez was created for
the 2005 SummerWorks presentation of *Enter My Goddess* in Toronto.

Enter My Goddess was first produced by the students of Notre Dame High School, Toronto, in February 2004 as part of the Toronto East District of the Sears Ontario Drama Festival. It was initially mounted at Sir Wilfrid Laurier Collegiate Institute, Scarborough, with subsequent performances at the Toronto Regional Festival, Hart House Theatre, in April 2005, and in the Provincial Showcase at Brock University, St. Catharines, in May 2005. *Enter My Goddess* was also presented at the SummerWorks Theatre Festival, Factory Theatre, Toronto, in August 2005.

Ancient Women

Abuya	Christie Tang
Badru	Trisha Villanueva
Buquisi	Angela Rosales
Yetunde	Kanika Ambrose
Mayasa	Beverly Hestick
Jalili	Bea Palanca
Shakila	Tanya D'Costa
Etana	Monique Wery
Matuko	Ali Bertrumen

Contemporary Women

Faaizah Ahmed, Chelsea Dowling, Julie Fernandes, Erika Gonzales, Chevone Griffith, Tavia Heaven, Amanda Kevins, Na Kyung Kim, Christina Mohlala, Erica Russo, and Rowan Williams.

Directed by Carmela Arangio and Marguerite Jack-Vermey
Stage Management by Maria Lyon
Costumes by Terry Weatherhead
Head Wraps by Mrs. Mohlala and Gemma Hyppolite
Lighting Operation by Megan Robinson
Projection by Pablo Padilla
Percussion by Marsha Courneya
Backstage Crew: Johannah Smith and Erica Van Velson

We thank Valerie Root Wolpe for her poem "As My Daughter Bleeds So Do I," which is incorporated into Buquisi's words to her daughter in the opening scene.

A DVD recording of the 2005 SummerWorks production is available upon request from Marguerite Jack-Vermey at marguerite.jack-vermey@tcdsb.org.

NOTES

soothemysisters productions and *Enter My Goddess* were birthed in the same year. The all-female ensemble imagined a time when we were rooted in our own power—manifest in the ancient women we created. We talked, laughed, cried, and soothed each other with coming-of-age and first-blood tales current and remembered. What began as a grade ten ritual unit, quickly galvanized the cast of twenty and lent structure to the ancient's path. Thank you to Creator and to the Women Who Always Walk With Us.

carmela arangio and marguerite jack-vermey

In 2005, Carmela Arangio and Marguerite Jack-Vermey met as staff members new to Notre Dame; together they renewed the school's drama program. Realizing that they had an extraordinary opportunity in an all female cast, they sought to give voice to the soul-experiences of their students. Six years later, soothemysisters has birthed five student/teacher collaborations, four of which were Sears Ontario Drama Festival provincial festival winners, two SummerWorks selections, an appearance at Luminato, and a performance at the IDEA Conference. Carmela and Marguerite feel blessed to have worked with these courageous young women, who were willing to entrust their hearts and stories to them and the theatre community.

characters

Ancient Women

ABUYA (AH-boo-yah) Born when the garden was overgrown.
BADRU (BAH-droo) Born at the full moon.
BUQUISI (BOOH-kee-see) Queen of Sabaa.
ETANA (eh-TAH-nah) Strong one.
JALILI (JAH-lee-lee) Exalted, dignified.
MATUKO (MAH-too-koh) Elegance.
MAYASA (MAH-yah-sah) Walks proudly.
SHAKILA (shah-KEE-lah) Shapely.
YETUNDE (yeh-TOON-deh) Mother returns.

Contemporaries

AMANDA
CHELSEA
CHEVONE
CHRISTINA
ERICA
ERIKA G
FAAIZAH
JULIE
NA KYUNG
TAVIA

Ancients: Opening

*Lights come up slowly on the shaman centre stage. A djembe
always underscores the ancients' movement and dialogue. Their
music must have a primeval and tribal quality. In the opening,
we hear them offstage singing a celebratory song, slow in tempo.
BADRU and BUQUISI sleep downstage centre—they are lit
only by spill. The contemporary women stand with their backs
to the central scene, encircling them. Behind them, throughout
the course of the show, an oversized full moon rises.*

ABUYA

My sisters. My brothers. My people. We are all bound by this truth:
that the water, the earth, and the stones are the three great mothers,
and that our kindred wait for us within them. It is in the stones,
waters, and the many fish, which inhabit the sacred ponds, that
the spirits of the dead wait to be born again. They wait for us.
It is through our strength, our knowing, that they will be reborn.

Should we forget this truth, we will not recognize our own, and
they will wait as fish, their mouths opening and closing, asking,
"Do you not know us anymore?"

And if we forget, then your daughters and their daughters and their
daughters will feel as though they swim alone. We must lend our
ears to the call of their voices; the ancient ones who speak from
the depths of each still pool. Should we forget, we will be unhewn
stones buried so deeply in the silt that we shall not know Isong, our
Mother, or Eka Abassi herself in the moon.

We will not hear the voices of our elders calling to our girls,
reassuring them. They will not be able to hear them say: "In your
first blood, you are as sacred and holy as Her." Our power will be
disregarded, even controlled. And she will struggle, not knowing
her own strength is rooted in The Mother of All.

Ancients: Separation

*The djembe plays through the transition. The light fades on
ABUYA and the scene opens with BADRU lying on her side
downstage centre, with BUQUISI curled around her. They
awaken slowly. BADRU is sleepy and child-like in her waking.
The djembe continues through the scene as though in the*

> *distance. There is a quiet moment before BUQUISI speaks.*
> *She gently holds her, hums, and rocks her; reminiscent of*
> *another time.*

BUQUISI It is your time, my daughter. Listen! Do you hear the drums? They are calling to you already. Tonight you will lead the people, and carry A Kwa Ba forward. You will even walk ahead of the chief!

BADRU Yes, Mama.

BUQUISI You are not afraid.

BADRU No… *(hesitating)* Will you walk with me, Mama?

BUQUISI *(firmly, gently)* Badru. I have walked behind you throughout your childhood. I held you in my arms when you were too tiny to know that you were born at the full moon. You learned to walk at my fingers, tipping and balancing on them. I have tilled with your hands secured between my knees. I have steadied the water as you swayed ahead of me, and I have woven the cloth around your waist to guide your fingers. My time to walk behind you is finished. It is time for you to move without me, and to know your own power.

BADRU I will walk alone?

BUQUISI You know you are never alone. The ancient ones always walk alongside. And today, Yetunde will guide you. Tonight, my daughter, I will walk beside you. As a woman. Come.

> *BUQUISI invites BADRU into her arms, and they hold one*
> *another. BADRU draws back from her mother.*

BADRU You are sad.

BUQUISI I am proud.

BADRU But you are crying.

BUQUISI I am holding my little girl one last time.

> *They hold each other one more time until BUQUISI firmly moves*
> *BADRU away from her.*

(tying on BADRU's head wrap) Eka Abassi, you know my daughter, Badru. You gave her to me at the height of the moon, and I thank you for the gift of her life. As she bleeds now, so do I. Yet her womb is learning its own rhythm, while mine is missing beats. This is right and sacred. How quickly her body finds its own balance, just as quickly as she learned to walk. Now she moves away from me: in her body's rhythm, out of girlhood. Her womb is on its own, in free-flowing richness. This your gift. This is her power. One day, only my daughter will bleed and my womb will rest in full stop.

(with humour and hope) Perhaps she too will sleep with babies in her bed, and then only my heart will move blood, in love for my grandchildren. *(finished with the formalities)* There. You are ready.

YETUNDE   *(entering)* Badru. I am here to walk with you. I am here to teach you, and to guide you to the woman's house.

BADRU   I am ready.

The ancient women exit. The djembe *supports them.*

Contemporaries: Separation

The contemporary women continue to hold their circle. They face away from centre stage. They exchange positions so that each new monologue is rotated to the downstage centre position.

NA KYUNG   *(alternating between Korean and English—translating for the audience as she goes)* Mama. Wait. Don't go home without me. Don't leave me here. I don't think I am strong enough. I don't want you to be ashamed of me. I want the family to be proud. I've tried to be brave about coming to Canada, but I think it's a mistake. I need you.

———————

ERIKA G   You have to understand—there are only three important events in a Latina's life: her birth, her wedding, and her sweet fifteen, her *Quinceañera*. A girl becoming a woman is taken very seriously in my culture. I always imagined mine in Mexico. It would be the real thing, not like the ones they have here. It would be in a huge banquet hall with the mariachi's playing. I'd be wearing a pink spaghetti-strap dress, fitted at the top, but A-line down the bottom. It would be trimmed with sequins. I'd sparkle like a princess. There would have to be at least seven *damas* and *caballeros* processing in pairs as everyone stands applauding. And as the last pair makes their grand entrance, there I'd be, accompanied my father: "*Mi Princessa es una mujer.* My princess is now a woman." The guests whispering among themselves about my beauty. And that day would be all about me. Me and that big pink dress. Sadly, it never happened.

———————

CHEVONE   Mommy! I'm over here in the men's department. I found the most wickedest shirt, and it's just my size: 5X! I know you don't like it when they're too baggy on me but just think, Matthew can wear it too. Mommy! Okay, I'll put it back. *(addressing the audience)*

I like the way I dress. I love my mother, and I do listen to her, but I'm trying to find me. On a typical day you can find me in running shoes, big jeans or track pants, a jersey or a white tee, one earring, a hat, and my bag. My wardrobe consists of extra-large shirts, jerseys galore, track suits, and ONE pair of shoes. When I dress "like a boy," I feel powerful, strong, and appreciated. I can present myself as intimidating. Dressing this way makes me feel wanted in society; that I am seen as equal to everyone else. So if you could get all of that by dressing like a boy, why wouldn't you?

CHRISTINA (*in a cramp*) Why does it have to hurt so much? Oh, it's so beautiful how God created the female anatomy! It kind of makes you wonder was She... oh boogers... was HE still mad at the female population for the fact that Eve made Adam eat the fruit? Yes, the fruit! That same fruit that makes North American men drool over the covers of degrading *Maxim* or *FHM*. He suddenly realized after he had taken a bite that it was "wrong." So he blamed the whole affair on Eve. Ever since then, we've been doomed. We're viewed as seducers, things that can be owned and pre-owned. We're just an accessory with seed-sized brains that surely can't hold any information except how to clean, cook, and reproduce. (*another cramp*) So that's what I'm supposed to believe when I'm cursing and complaining that this is all because of Eve's little stint!

CHELSEA (*to the audience*) So, it goes like this. When I ask my mother about it, ninety-two per cent of the time we end up fighting. I will say: "Mom, what's my background?" She will say, "Canadian." I will say, "NO, Mom really, what's my background?!" She will say, "I was born in Canada. So were you. You are Canadian." Then I will say, "Mom, what is my father's background?" She will say, "Canadian." I will say, "NO, Mom, what is *his* background?" Then she will say, "He was born in Canada, his mother and your grandmother talk white— whiter than me. They sound like: 'Yallow. Hi. How ya doin'?'" Then I get mad and tell her to stop and tell me. She always says, "African. All black people come from Africa before slavery."

FAAIZAH Why am I doing this? I don't even know who I'm doing this for. Well, I know, but is Allah really there? What if there really isn't a "supreme being"? Would our prayers be lost, unheard by anyone? And even if something was there, wouldn't I be able to feel Him, or know that He was there? Of course, just thinking this is a sin. You don't question God, you just do.

Ancients: The Teaching

> *The ancients begin a melody, which is heard slowly at first from the wings. The contemporary women use the music to contract/collapse to the ground holding their circle. The tempo increases and becomes celebratory from the wings and the ancients enter and set up the women's house/red tent for the teaching scene. BADRU's moon time/sleeping mat is brought in with her, as well as a mortar and pestle with ochre in it. ABUYA brings in a medicine bowl with sage and a goddess-shaped vessel with wine in it. The djembe supports their song and then plays quietly underneath after they finish.*

MAYASA   Come Badru, rest with us for a while, you'll need your strength soon enough. My, how quickly the Great Mother moves the seasons. Your first blood already! Do you remember, Buquisi, was it not just yesterday that we sang to announce Badru's birth?

ETANA   I remember your mother's joy, Badru, when the full moon came and there was no blood between her thighs. She came to me and put my hand on her belly. I smiled and told her it would be a girl, a daughter to keep her memories alive.

SHAKILA   A daughter to cost her a dowry!

ETANA   Oh, hush up, Shakila, and sew, no one wants to hear your grumbling here. Badru, how does this night find you? Are you sure in your footing?

BADRU   Yes Etana, it is a privilege I have long awaited.

SHAKILA   So long so that *some* girls cannot wait.

> *Everyone laughs knowingly, looking at JALILI.*

JALILI   *(embarrassed)* Fine then, bring that old story up again! Can we not get through a first-blood gathering without bringing up that silly story?

MAYASA   You didn't think we'd let you get away without telling that one, did you?

BADRU   What story, Jalili? Please, for me.

JALILI   As long as you remember that what is said in this house remains in this house.

> *BADRU nods in agreement.*

Well, Eka Abassi wanted it so that I waited many, many moons to come to my power. I watched longingly as my friends and sisters became women. With each new moon, new girls were showered with honours; with each new moon, I grew more impatient.

SHAKILA Even my youngest, little Adusa, became a woman while Jalili still waited.

JALILI Impatience gave way to fear when I began to see, at each new announcement of a girl's ripening, the worry in my mother's eyes, the doubt. I knew what she was thinking, what everyone was thinking. Was I being punished? Was my mother? Would I never bleed? What was to become of me? I prayed many prayers and made many offerings, and the moon continued to wax and wane, and still a child I remained. Something had to be done! So one evening, I began complaining about stomach pains. Before going to bed, I mixed some ochre with water and smeared it on my thighs and my sleeping mat. The next morning when my mama found me, she was overjoyed! Immediately, she scooped me up in her arms and held me, caressing my hair and rocking me back and forth with relief. Once she had caught her breath, she told me to clean up and we would head down to see Abuya so that I could be inspected and announced. Blissfully, I made my way to the well to wash, but once there, it did not take me long to realize that my ruse was over. For as the water ran over my skin, it left behind unnatural red stains. My thighs, my hands, my fingers, exposed my shame.

Women all burst out in laughter.

SHAKILA You lied to bring about your womanhood, while Mayasa lied to try to hide it!

BADRU What!

MAYASA Well what would you do if you had that hyena-faced Liyongo (*LEE-yohn-go*) making eyes at you! I was *not* going to marry that man!

JALILI Speaking of making eyes, Badru, I've noticed Akram watching you lately. What do you think, does it look promising?

SHAKILA I think Badru's hips look promising!

MAYASA (*with humour*) Badru! You make sure Akram has your bride price set aside before he touches your skirt!

ETANA I remember the first time I laid eyes on Bomani (*BOH-MAH-nee*). He was working in the cassava fields. I watched him from behind. I worked and watched. He was beautiful…

SHAKILA	*(intending innuendo)* Is he as gentle a warrior as his name claims? Did he conquer you?!
ETANA	He captured my heart, and together we have gathered back some of our people.
SHAKILA	A whole tribe between you!
ETANA	Yes, we have been greatly blessed. But with Aina *(ah-ee-NAH)* I thought I would die.
YETUNDE	Badru, this gift we possess is a great power. It has the power to open and close the mouthpiece of Eka Abassi. We labour under its force, we surrender to it. At times it swallows us whole.
MATUKO	*(quietly)* And at times we must give Her gifts back. How often my hearth has been left desolate. Three times I have clipped curls from the heads of my lost and placed them in a hole in the rocks dedicated to Her. I pray that she will speedily set the feet of my little ones back upon the road to life.
YETUNDE	This is what lies before you, Badru. This is what it means to be a woman. It is the bitterness of kola nuts, and the sweetness of yams.
BADRU	To be a woman, must I give up everything I have been before?
YETUNDE	Yes. And no. Not long ago, I too crossed this threshold with Etana.

The women begin to collect around BADRU and start to massage her. They all work together—it is ceremonial.

Like you, I was just a child, playful and carefree. But like Etana and my mother, and all the women before me, I was born a second time, I was born into womanhood. Now with your first blood, you stand between the power of two worlds. It is time to leave behind your childhood ways; you will be as the Earth Mother, and will be able to bear children. You are in your moment of truth. There is nothing in your body that lies. *(They mark BADRU's body with the ochre.)* All that is new is telling the truth. You are holy. Walk with honour and dignity. Be strong for the mother of all people, the mother of all things, has given her power to you.

ABUYA smudges the women for the ceremony, echoing the blessing with the medicine bowl.

(with formality now) Eka Abassi who alone is great, upon whom men lean and do not fall, receive this wine and drink. *(She acknowledges the sky.)* Isong, Earth Mother, whose arms hold and support us, from whom women are fruitful, receive this wine and drink. *(She pours the wine onto the earth.)* Our ancestors, when I mention one, I mention all, receive this wine and drink. My sisters

and mothers, who gather today to guide their daughter, receive this wine and drink.

Each woman passes the wine and drinks

Badru, upon whom the blessings of The Mother will be given, receive this wine and drink.

They hold the vessel for her and she drinks.

The ancient women exit upstage centre with the djembe *and now widely encircle the contemporary women. They watch them from their outer circle through the transformation.*

Contemporaries: Transformation

The contemporary women now use the "step" to break out of the circle and set up each location. For each monologue a single line is made choral as they "step" the transition. This single line is indicated in brackets with quotation marks before each character speaks.

NA KYUNG   *("Don't Go".) (to audience)* My mom warned me that it would be different, but I had no idea how different it would be. Even lunchtime is a challenge.

The ensemble brings the lunch scene to life.

ERICA   *(as LUNCH LADY)* I sweat over a hot stove all day, I get paid minimum wage, and then I have to deal with these punks!

ERIKA G   *(as LUNCH LADY TWO, in Spanish, crossing herself)* Jesus, Mary, and Joseph, give me strength!

ERICA   Say one for me!

CHEVONE & CHELSEA
    Hey girl!

NA KYUNG is pushed to the back of the lunch line. As she approaches the lunch ladies, they begin speaking in gibberish.

ERICA   *(gibberish into)* Pizza?

ERIKA G   *(gibberish into)* Fries? *(She waits—NA KYUNG clearly doesn't understand—and then decides for her.)* Fries.

NA KYUNG   *(to the audience)* I didn't want to have lunch by myself but I didn't know how to approach other students to join them. I flip-flopped back and forth. Should I ask? Yes, no, yes, no. I had to put aside my pride.

She approaches the first group of girls.

CHELSEA Girl, you'll never believe who I saw at the mall yesterday—Clint! And he looked so fine!

CHEVONE He's the finest thing in MNE!

BOTH Damn!

NA KYUNG tries to join them. They talk in gibberish about her and finally finish with—

Wack!! *(They freeze.)*

FAAIZAH Oh my God, guys, look at my hair! Ever since I've started using Pantene it's been so soft and silky!

NA KYUNG approaches the group. They speak in gibberish and finish with—

FAAIZAH & CHRISTINA
(indicating NA KYUNG) Cute!

TAVIA *(gibberish as she introduces herself)* Tavia. *(more gibberish as she points at NA KYUNG, asking for her name)*

NA KYUNG doesn't understand and just laughs.

FAAIZAH Cute? *(They freeze.)*

NA KYUNG *(to the audience)* I think those girls ignore me because I'm Korean.

JULIE Oh yeah! We have a math test today!

AMANDA Math test? What math test? I never heard about any math test.

JULIE Calm down. Don't worry about it. Cheat off the new girl, she's Asian!

Both go into gibberish as NA KYUNG approaches.

BOTH Functions. *(gibberish)* Number five? *(They freeze.)*

NA KYUNG *(to the audience)* Even now, though I do have some friends, I still feel alone.

————————

ERIKA G *("Like a Princess")* Yeah, my *Quinceañera* was going to be the real thing. Not at all like that *creida* Maria's… really stuck up, you know?

CHELSEA *(as Maria)* Hi Erika! I know we have our differences, but I want you to come to my *Quinceañera*. My dad says that we are going to have the mariachi's there. *(sarcastically)* Oooooh. I forgot. You didn't have yours. *(smugly)* But it's okay. You can come to mine!

ERIKA G   *(to the audience)* I have to admit, the card was nice, with the fancy trimmings and flowers printed on it, but then again, it IS professional. But I have to say it would look better with MY name on it—Erika Citcallli Gonzalez... *(turns to CHELSEA)* See you there! *(CHELSEA walks away. ERICA reads the invitation to the audience.)* "Mr. and Mrs. Lopez request the honour of your presence at their daughter Maria Lopez's *Quinceañera.*" Honour her? Yeah, I'll honour her with a present from the dollar store!

CHEVONE   *("Dressed like a Boy")* On a typical weekend, on the quiet street of Mason Road, I can usually be found outside with the boys playing basketball or just chillin'. *(basketball scene comes to life)*

ERIKA G   *(as ADAM)* Here, Chevone... you want the ball...

CHEVONE   I got you!

      ADAM passes ball to ERICA.

ERICA   *(as ERIC)* You want this, you want this? *(ERICA knocks CHEVONE over as she dribbles past her.)*

ALL THE GUYS   Ohhhhhhh!

CHEVONE   It wasn't that bad, it wasn't that bad. *(to the audience)* I have to admit that I enjoy hanging out with the boys more than the girls sometimes.

      The girls enter scene, and the boys all holler and catcall.

Yo, that's my foul, I want my foul!

      TAVIA as DAVID prowls after the girls, and the boys continue to holler.

ERIKA G   *(to DAVID)* You're not going to get anything that way. Trust me, I know! *(to CHEVONE)* Hey Chevone, when are you going to start dressing like that?

ERICA   *(as ERIC)* Yeah, Chevone, when are you going to start dressing in some tight clothes? *(The boys all laugh.)*

CHEVONE   Are you mad?! Don't you have any sense? *(flicks him)*

ERICA & ERIKA G
      Hey, lighten up, Chevone! *(boys freeze)*

CHEVONE   *(to the audience)* They laugh but that's not the only stress I get about my appearance. My friends at school don't make my life any less stressful...

The girls reset and come downstage, walking to a mirror in a school bathroom.

CHELSEA   Oh my gosh! My mom bought me the worst bra ever! It makes my boobs look so saggy.

CHRISTINA   Stuff!

CHELSEA   Stuff?

BOTH   Stuff!

AMANDA   Ewwwww Erika, I think I'm growing a moustache. Nair! Quick!

JULIE   Damn! Look at my butt in these jeans, need I say more?

ERICA   You have a nice butt... Speaking of butts, how does my butt look in this skirt?

ERIKA G   It just needs to be a bit shorter. *(She pulls at the skirt.)* Trust me, I know.

ERICA   You think? *(to all girls)* Hey, you know what would be funny? To see Chevone in a skirt!

             They all laugh. CHEVONE enters the bathroom.

ALL   Hi Chevone!

FAAIZAH   Hey Amanda, I have an idea.

CHEVONE   I wanna know the idea...

FAAIZAH   Let's take this damn scrunchie off her hair. Hold her down! *(They wrestle it off her.)*

ERIKA G   Chevone, you have really nice eyes...

NA KYUNG   I know.

ERIKA G   I think you just need a little mascara... *(They wrestle it on her.)*

CHELSEA   Chevone, your boobs, umm, they look sort of saggy. Let's stuff!

ERICA   Perky, perky, perky! *(struggle continues)*

CHRISTINA   Chevone, you know you have really great legs...

JULIE   I think you should try on this skirt!

CHEVONE   *(as they struggle to put it on her)* I don't need no skirt! I like my big jeans.

TAVIA   Stop! Leave her alone! *(They all freeze.)*

———————————

CHRISTINA *("Eve's Little Stint")* It all started with the process of growing *(indicates breasts) these.*

NA KYUNG, FAAIZAH, & CHRISTINA
(CHRISTINA is the only one of these little girls with developed breasts. She holds them as she jumps.) Itsy bitsy lollipop, itsy bitsy boo, itsy bitsy lollipop, boys love you! *(indicating CHRISTINA)* Ewwww! Boys love you!

Enter C.C. Club girls.

ERIKA G Oh Christina, you are so pretty!

AMANDA Yeah, why are you hanging out with them?

ERICA Yeah, you should be hanging out with us. Do you want to be in our C.C. Club?

CHRISTINA What's the C.C. Club?

ERIKA G It's the cute...

AMANDA ...and...

CHELSEA ...cool...

JULIE ...club!

ERICA So, what do you say, Christina?

CHRISTINA Well. *(looking at her younger friends)* I... ah... I don't know.

ERIKA G C'mon, you belong with us.

CHRISTINA *(hesitates... then)* Okay!

Together the girls ad lib approval.

CHELSEA So, I was at the mall last night...

The boys enter, and the girls notice—flirting and coupling off ensues. In particular, CHEVONE as DEVANTE pairs up with ERIKA G, but then notices CHRISTINA.

CHEVONE *(to CHRISTINA)* Yo, yo, yo, who's this? You is fine! What's yo name, shorty?

CHRISTINA *(shyly)* Christina.

ERIKA G *(to CHRISTINA)* Who do you think you are?! What do you think you are doing? You're supposed to be my friend! You aren't in the C.C. Club anymore! Girls, lets get out of here...! Devante, NOW!

Each couple freezes as they turn and exit, leaving CHRISTINA alone on stage.

CHRISTINA   The funny thing is, all I was thinking about was what new Barbie to add to my tea set.

CHELSEA   (*"What's My Background?"*) When I go to school, I just feel like I'm not good enough. The white people say I am a "nigger" or I act "too black." Then the black people call me an Oreo, or say that I'm whitewashed. The Hispanic people come up to me and ask if I'm Dominican or Cuban; I say, no, I'm white and black. The only family I know is the woman who raised me and she's white. Because of that, I get the name half-breed. Dogs breed. I'm not a dog. (*pause*) Last year, we did this pavilion thing at my school. Well, I went into the West Indian one... because I am black.

> *The pavilion comes to life.*

CHEVONE   J-A-M Jamaica! A-I-C Jamaica! A-Jamaica! A-Jamaica...

ERICA   I always miss that last cue, that's all right eh?

CHEVONE   (*ignoring ERICA*) Hey Chelsea! Who you representin'?

CHELSEA   I'm representing... I'm representing...

TAVIA   (*with the Trinidad group*) Yo man! What are you doing over there for? (*kissing her teeth*) Yo man, flag them off!

FAAIZAH & NA KYUNG
Bap bap Trinidad!

CHEVONE   Bap bap Jamaica!

CHELSEA   Bap bap... black?

FAAIZAH   (*"Why Am I Doing This?"*)

ERICA   (*singing*) Amen, amen, amen.

ALL WOMEN   (*joining*) Amen, amen, amen. (*in chorus*) In the name of the Father, and of the Son, and of the Holy Spirit. Amen. (*FAAIZAH struggles to fake the sign of the cross.*)

> *All the contemporary women have arrived on the edge of the stage.*

FAAIZAH   People in my school seem to have this unshakable faith. It seems to me that they don't need any reassurance that God exists. They just trust in Him without question. They don't need proof of him, because they already believe. And... if God is a he and I'm a she, then where does that leave me?

Ancients: Transformation

The djembe *provides a segue for the crossover between the ancients and contemporaries, and also provides a "collapse" for the contemporary women at the edge of the stage. The* djembe *continues and evolves through the scene. Through movement, the ancients recreate the swim to the bottom and the rise back up to the top.*

YETUNDE   Grandmother moon. You know all women from birth to death. We seek your knowledge, we seek your strength. Grandmother, lighten Badru's path in the dark. Keep her safe from harm and guide her hands until she finds her own strength rooted in the gift of an oval stone.

The ancient women form a circle, creating the pond around BADRU and the shaman. They use aspects of Sowu in slow motion to create the boundaries of the pond. The women witness the vision quest, as well as BADRU's journey.

BADRU   *(anxious and peering into the water)* What is my task?

YETUNDE   You must swim to the centre of the pond, the centre of the mother, and retrieve a single white stone. It is in this stone that the spirits of our ancestors wait. They wait for you. Badru, as you descend, be sure of yourself, a white stone, a good stone.

BADRU begins to swim to the bottom of the pond. The ancient women create the boundaries of the pond, and the action of the quest itself. The moon behind the women is now fully risen and has turned red. ABUYA tells this story as BADRU swims down.

ABUYA   At the beginning of time, Eka Abassi's power was so great that she did not need a husband for the birth of her babes. By *her* might alone, did the first of her children spring forth; but to none of her descendants was this power transmitted. When she saw that all the first earth-women were barren, long she pondered; then sent down to them a great white bird that, upon reaching the earth, laid a gleaming egg—the symbol of fertility. Eka Abassi declared that all eggs and oval stones must be honoured as earthly representations of her. By making sacrifice to the Great Mother, the gift of fruitfulness might be won. She flew back to her home in the sky; whence, with folded wings, soft brooding, she still watches over her children. Mortals call her moon and sometimes, when all people are sleeping, the moon-bird floats down from her place in the sky and looks around to see that all is well with the earth folk.

> *As BADRU swims downward, she spirals, losing control and her sense of direction. The pond turns red, and the drum beat turns into a heartbeat.*

BADRU *(very afraid for the first time)* Abuya! I am lost.

ABUYA No, Badru. You know yourself. You know your power. You know the way.

BADRU *(seeing contemporary women downstage)* I do not know these women.

ABUYA They are of a time to come.

BADRU Look at their bodies. Look at their faces. Why do they grieve?

ABUYA *They* do not know themselves, their power, the way.

BADRU How did they get so lost?

ABUYA Some have forgotten, some have not been told. Others are surrounded by a force so strong that it conspires to keep them in the darkness, out of the light of the moon. They do not know they are walking into changing woman. They do not know that they are sacred.

BADRU Why am I here?

ABUYA You are within the within. You are between the worlds. Between the spirit world and the earth, between time and time. Your power is greatest now. What do you wish?

BADRU To comfort them.

ABUYA Speak. Use your woman's voice and call to them from your depths.

BADRU They will hear me!

ABUYA Not with their ears. Not within time, but in their bodies and hearts.

BADRU What do I tell them?

ABUYA Tell them what you know.

> *BADRU picks up the stone at the centre of the pond, and as she picks it up, a similar stone appears in the hands of the contemporaries.*

BADRU My sisters. You are in your moment of truth. There is nothing in your body that lies. All that is new is telling the truth. You are holy. Walk with honour and dignity. Be strong for the mother of all people, the mother of all things, has given her power to you. Stand still at your door, sure of yourself, a white stone, a good stone. Do not forget.

BADRU rises to the top of the pond with her stone. She is embraced first by her mother. BADRU offers her stone first to BUQUISI, who folds it back into BADRU's hand. A celebration among the ancients ensues and they sing. As they celebrate, BADRU is re-dressed on stage into white with red trim. The full moon is restored to white. The ancients continue singing quietly as the contemporaries stand up to speak.

Contemporaries: Rejoining

NA KYUNG	All I can do is my best.
ERIKA G	I would have been beautiful.
CHEVONE	At times I can hear people whisper, right in front of me, "Is that a boy or a girl?" They can just figure it out for themselves.
CHRISTINA	Sometimes it's hard being a woman, but it sure as hell beats being a man!
CHELSEA	Yesterday, my mom gave me my uncle's phone number. It may not seem like a big deal, but it is to me. This is my uncle, from my black side.
FAAIZAH	I don't have to see God the way others do. I can just let Him… or… Her come to me.

The celebration becomes very lively with the ancients dancing Sowu. Their celebratory singing is accompanied by the djembe. A coming together occurs with the dance; the ancients surround and support the contemporaries. The contemporaries' steps blend with the ancient dance. The contemporaries finish in a circle turned toward the audience, which is surrounded and supported by the ancients. They all take a breath in and out together.

Lights out.

Abuya (Christie Tang) and the voices of other ancestors weave
into the modern stories of young women struggling with life's obstacles.
Photo by Mary Douglas-Kadey.

HOW NOUS avons MET

A One-Act Bilingual Comedy
in Five Scenes About Love, Language, and Canada

By John Anthony Nabben

Let us be French, let us be English, but most importantly, let us be Canadian.

—Sir John Alexander Macdonald

How Nous Avons Met was written and created by John Anthony Nabben. It was produced by Joseph Picard and the students from École secondaire l'Essor, for the 2004 Windsor-Essex District Festival of the Sears Ontario Drama Festival at the Capital Theatre, Windsor, in March 2004, with further performances at the Southern Regional Festival at Brock University in St. Catharines in April 2004 and the Provincial Showcase at Centrepointe Theatre in Ottawa in May 2004.

Maître d'	Sophie LeBlanc
Voice	Melanie Raymond
Mel	Jesse Gras-Gagné
Nada	Renée Guilbeault
Théa	Caroline Leal
Bono	Kingston Ihuwan
Can	Steven Gouin
Arty	Brendan Drouillard

Directed by John Anthony Nabben
Stage Management by Nancy Lefebvre
Assistant Stage Management by Sophie LeBlanc
Choreography by Mélanie Sylvestre and Natalie Joy Quesnel
Lighting Design/Operation by J. P. Neilson
Sound Operation by Jean-François Papineau

NOTes

This is a bilingual play that does not necessarily require bilingual actors. The cast is made up of three English males, three French females, and a baby's voice. A waiter(s), a maître d', a live band, and restaurant patrons are all options for scene four. In order for this play to be most effective, the accents should be authentic and genuine. Therefore try to cast, if available, the female roles with francophone actresses and male roles with anglophone actors. You can also cast all males or mix it up as you wish.

For the set, we used a sofa and a flat for scenes one, two, three, and five. We used a table and two chairs for scene four.

Scene four is yours to have fun with. There is very little dialogue because the emphasis should be on non-verbal physical theatre. In this scene the characters speak through body language, emotion, and facial expressions. Some stage directions have been included in order to help you understand what the scene requires. The length of this scene can also be adjusted depending on your time frame. In the original production, there was enough time to add a musical number with waiters and a singing maître d'.

A dash at the end of a line indicates that the dialogue has been cut off by another character. When necessary, the thought was completed so the actor knows what the character was going to say before being interrupted.

Feel free to substitute location names with local references to the place where the play is being performed. As well, the musical references in the play can be substituted with others if necessary. The expletives used in the play can also be adjusted to words that are more suitable for your audience.

JOHN anthony naBBen

John Anthony Nabben currently runs the dramatic arts program at Walkerville Centre for the Creative Arts (WCCA) in Windsor, Ontario, a specialized enriched arts secondary school program. *How Nous Avons Met* was inspired by his experience studying theatre at the University of Ottawa. John Anthony was a student-teacher when he approached École secondaire l'Essor and asked to work with the students.

Since starting his position at WCCA in 2005, John Anthony has worked with two Regional Finals in the Sears Ontario Drama Festival (*Match With the Devil,* 2006) and (*Tuesdays and Sundays,* 2008) and one Provincial Showcase (*Insanity of Mary Girard,* 2009).

characters

Les filles (high-school grads)

THÉA, short for Théa-Marie
MEL, short for Mélanie
NADA, pronounced NAH-DAH, Nadine's nickname

The boys (high-school grads)

ARTY, Arthur's nickname
BONO, Adreano's nickname
CAN, short for Canton

Scene One: As-tu Ever?

Present day. Anywhere. A sofa is placed centre stage. Behind the sofa is a wall used throughout the play to hang various posters, flags, and pictures to represent the different settings. THÉA and ARTY are standing downstage, ARTY stage right and THÉA stage left. They do not notice each other. The other boys and girls are seated frozen on either side of the sofa as though they are in the middle of a conversation.

ARTY   Hey. Have you ever been forced on a blind date, or known someone who has? Have you ever been made to do something you absolutely hate or didn't want to do? Have you?

THÉA   Connaissez-vous quelqu'un dans votre vie qui n'est pas compatible avec vous? Ton opposé totale? Ton extrême polaire? Si tu étais une machine DVD et il étais une casette VCR... ça ne marcherais pas ensemble? As-tu déjà vécu une situation pareille?

ARTY   Now, by all logical means and according to all spiritual, ethical, moral, divine, and zodiac laws, it's easy for anyone to see: if you don't want it, it won't work, right?

THÉA   Ça va jamais fonctionner!

ARTY   My friends are blind!

THÉA   Mais les gens continue a insister a soumettre d'autres dans des situations pareilles. Je me retrouve souvent dans des situations impossibles, et ces, grâce à mes amies.

ARTY   But whether you've experienced this or not, it doesn't really matter. I'm telling you these things happen to people all the time, no matter how hard you try to fight it.

THÉA   Voici Nadine et Mélanie. Tous les deux ont des gros, mais parfois elles essaient trop fort. On se connait depuis notre première année a l'école. On est toutes allé voir *Les Belles-Soeurs* ensemble et on a découvert qu'on adore le théâtre. Nous vivons ensemble dans un appartement depuis qu'on est venu ici à l'Université d'Ottawa. Elles sont mes amies les plus proches au monde. Elles adorent se mêler dans ma vie personnelle. Je sais qu'elles ont de bonnes intentions, mais des fois ça va un peu loin.

THÉA and girls exit. ARTY moves toward CAN and BONO, who are sitting frozen on the sofa.

ARTY	These are the boys! This is Bono. His real name's Adreano, but we call him Bono 'cause he's the world's biggest U2 fan. It's a great nickname. This guy's Canton. He wanted a wicked nickname too so... we call him... Can. We were tired. He likes it. Done. We met in grade ten when we were all cast in the school play. We got along ever since. Bono and I were the leads. Can had a silent role. When it came time to pick a university, we all chose to go to the University of Ottawa 'cause of the theatre program there! Rez was full so we rented out a house. We love it. But these guys have become more than roommates; they're my friends, my brothers, the *boys*! And now that we're here at the U, they're family! But like all family, they think they know what's best for me!

Scene Two: The Boys

	The boys unfreeze and we flash back to sometime earlier. The wall changes to reveal the boys in the living room of their apartment. They are mid-conversation.
ARTY	Then what?
BONO	So when we get to the university pub, I spot these two hotties on the dance floor. They were playing "Mysterious Ways" of all songs.
ARTY	Nice.
BONO	They were dancing like pros. And they're both wearing those black boots; you know the ones, right up to the knees, highlighting the curves of the legs, sexy... but classy. So I point them out to Can. He wants to rush over right away but I tell him, "Whoa tiger, remember the three rules: One: *Scan for boyfriends.* I give it a look. Nothing! Two: *Freshen breath.* I finish my beer and wait for Can to finish his Kool-Aid cooler. We pop in a Juicy Fruit; he starts singing the song, I slap him. And three... *(looks to ARTY)*
ARTY	Never make it obvious.
BONO	Exactly! *(to CAN)* See!
CAN	Damn.
BONO	*Never make it obvious.*
ARTY	Go on.
BONO	So we start movin' in slowly, real slowly. Keeping it cool, real cool. A bit of head bouncing, *(CAN and BONO bounce heads.)* nothing

dramatic. A little shoulder, some hand slices, till we get within range. Now you know how girls can appear good from far but once you get closer they're far from good? Well, these girls appeared hot from far, so I was naturally apprehensive. But when we got closer they were drop-dead gorgeous! And I've only had one beer, so I know what I'm seeing is real. I mean, these girls were on fire! I notice one of them mouthing the song as she's dancing. You know the scene. Check it. *(starts mouthing the song)* So I ask her: "Do you like U2?" She smiles and says, "Oui! Toi aussi?" Well no wonder she's hot; she's French! So I say, "Oui, moi aussi!" Thank God for grade nine French class. Then she introduces her friend Nada to us, who was definitely checking out Can the whole time. *(high fives CAN)* So now the four of us start tearing up the dance floor. Can does his worm thing. They're impressed. He does it again. They laugh. He does it again, I tell him to stop. So as we're shooting the shit, I find out they're from Quebec, studying here at the U, and living off campus, with a third girl who couldn't make it that night—which worked out for us right. Now get this! They're taking theatre, just like us! Only their courses are in French, so we never had the same classes.

CAN	I didn't even know you could do theatre in French.
BONO	What are the odds, right? Here we are, dancing, with two of the hottest French theatre chicks in the world. I quote some Billy Shakes, make 'em laugh, showed 'em some moves, and we tore up the floor some more.
ARTY	That's great, man. *(goes to leave)*
CAN	Wait, there's more.
BONO	Now you won't believe this, but you know how I keep auditioning for professional plays? Well, while Can is busy putting the moves on Nada, Mel tells me that her uncle's directing a show for the Great Canadian Theatre Company this season.
ARTY	The GCTC?
BONO	Swear to God. So right away I'm like telling her how sick and tired I am of community theatre and feel ready for the big leagues and blah blah blah. Make a long story short, she promises to get me an audition!
ARTY	Yeah right.
CAN	It's true!
ARTY	What's the catch?
BONO	"What's the catch"?!

CAN	There's no catch!
ARTY	There's always a catch.
BONO	Why does there have to be a catch? We met, she likes me, she wants to hook me up. It's that simple. Wha? That doesn't happen in real life? It's not about who you know or being in the right place at the right time?
CAN	Jeez guy!
BONO	Now as we're slow dancing—and man she's fine—I'm holdin' her close. Real close. Looking at her perfect neck, the little hairs that you can't see unless you're right up holdin' her close, looking at her perfect neck. I whiff her perfume. You know what I'm talking about. So I tell her, *(deep voice)* "Merci beaucoup, mon amour, this has truly been le bestest soirée of mon life." To which she replies, *(cute French accent)* "Moi aussi, bébé!" So I look right into her big beautiful French eyes and ask, "Est-ce que you have any plans for tomorrow soirée?" "Oui" she says... "Wit you!" God! That! Accent! I just wept. Then after the last slow song, we all leave and go for a walk by the canal. So I take us to the spot. You know the one... And there... under the stars... by the light of moon, I lean in... close my eyes... and experience the greatest kiss of my life...
CAN	That's when I interrupted 'cause Nada kissed me too and I had to tell him.
BONO	Last night was perfect, Arty, and tonight promises to be even better!
ARTY	That's awesome boys!
BONO	Now here's the catch! As we're all enjoying the night, Nada mentions how it's too bad that while they're here with us having so much fun, their roommate's home alone again. They went Eeyore just thinking about it. Then—get this—in true girl logic, they feel so guilty about *leaving her* alone *again*, that they cancel *our* plans for tonight!
ARTY	That's shitty.
CAN	I'm devastated and Bono's about to cry.
BONO	I said nothing. You ran away.
ARTY	That really sucks, boys.
CAN	Girls are funny that way, Arty. Always thinking of each other. They're just like us, only different.
BONO	They can leave one of their own alone once, never twice. Naturally, I had to think fast, right. So I'm like: "I've got it... We'll find a date

for your roommate! This way, the four of us can still go out, and your roommate won't be left alone." Well... it was brilliant. They went nuts! And by nuts I mean she kissed me again. The mother ship of all kisses...

CAN   Nada's sooo excited, she's on her cell calling her roommate before we could say... roommate.

BONO   So we discussed a few things, made a few *a-rain-ge-men-tays*, and voilà! Problem solved!

ARTY   Well, that's not so bad. It all worked all out in the end, eh? Well done, boys. Excellent. *(short pause)* What...? Okay, stop looking at me like that! *(realizing what they want)* Oh my God! No no no no no no. No way!

BONO & CAN   *(overlapping)* What/Come on. Why not/Buddy!

ARTY   Tonight!?

BONO   Yeah.

ARTY   No!

CAN   Arty, c'mon man, she's French!

ARTY   I don't care!

BONO   You haven't been on a date since Joan.

ARTY   So!

BONO   Soooo it's time!

ARTY   No, it's not time!

BONO   Yes, it is! Can, is it time?

CAN   It's definitely time!

ARTY   No, it's not time. It's not time at all—

BONO   Hell yeah! Can!

ARTY   No, Can—

CAN   It's *go* time, baby!

ARTY   Please not the hockey analogy.

BONO   Listen! *(BONO hums hockey music.)*

CAN   Arthur my friend, you're ready to coach again—

ARTY   Can—

CAN   Time to strap on the ol' skates and go hit the ice!

ARTY   Please—

CAN   There's so much talent out there—

ARTY   Okay—

CAN   Just dying to play—

ARTY   Listen to me—

CAN   Tired of being in the minors! Ready for a major contract—

ARTY   Please don't—

CAN   Ready to go into overtime and score that big goal—

ARTY   I'M NOT READY TO GO ON ANOTHER BLIND DATE!

BONO   Why not?

ARTY   Where have you been? What happened the last time?

BONO   You weren't compatible.

ARTY   She didn't show up! I was stood up.

BONO   She was running late—

ARTY   I waited three hours. I sat there at that stupid restaurant, all alone, with this sick sinking feeling of utter rejection.

CAN   It happens to all of us once or twice—

ARTY   Not eleven times in a row it doesn't. And the one time when the girl actually did show up was even worse. I suck at relationships. You know that. I never know what to say. I see their big eyes. Their big what-the-hell-are-you-talking-about eyes. I never know what to say. So I get rejected. Well I'm sick and tired of being rejected, okay. You have no idea what it's like. *(looks at BONO who shakes his head "no")* Remember how excited you were when you landed your upper-bowl seats for the U2 Air Canada Centre concert in Toronto… Well, imagine landing tickets to your dream concert: U2, unplugged, live in Dublin! Backstage passes. All expenses paid.

CAN   Holy shit.

ARTY   You walk in. The place is packed. Every seat taken except one. Yours. See it… Front row, dead centre, seat number… eight… You go over and sit down. Everyone else is staring at you with envy. You're so close you can reach out and touch the mics… As a matter of fact, you're so close that the real Bono will be within make-out range. You need a moment just to let it all in… And as you sit there, getting comfortable in your seat, thanking God for this moment… a man comes on stage and announces: "U2 will not perform this evening unless the loser in seat number eight leaves." Suddenly you feel all those people staring at you again, only this time it's not out of envy. Everyone in the room wants you gone…! And at that moment, the best place you could be… is dead! That's how it feels to be rejected: total, utter, heart-ripping disappointment…! So, like I said, I hate blind dates!

CAN   *(short pause)* Well that's good news!

ARTY   How's that *good* news?

CAN   'Cause this ain't a blind date.

ARTY   It *ain't a blind date?*

CAN   Nope!

> *BONO looks at CAN as if to say "Where are you going with this?"*

ARTY   What is it then?

CAN   A *rendez-vous*!

ARTY   A rendez-vous?

BONO   Yeah! *A rendez-vous*!

CAN   A *French* blind date.

ARTY   It's still a *blind date!*

CAN   Nope. *Rendez-vous* are different!

ARTY   How are they any different, Can?

BONO   Can.

CAN   Because… *(making it up as he goes along)* historically… when the pioneers settled here from France—due to the excessive time spent working on the lumber fields… and sap plantations—many lost their sight from the great plague of 1605… Withermore and thus, as a result, these "habitants" had to have arranged courtships, hockey-style, and whatnot, within their log cabins called Marie Chadelaine or what have you quid pro quo on account of the blindness—

> *BONO looks at him.*

I googled it.

BONO   Thank you, Heritage Canada, for that infomercial. *(to ARTY)* Arty, what you went through was bad. I know. And I don't blame you one bit for feeling the way you do. But the fact of the matter is that's the past. This is now. And that shitty experience won't happen this time.

ARTY	Thanks guys, really, but no thanks! I'd rather wait for the right girl to come along instead of sitting at some random restaurant across the table from a girl I don't know. Stop forcing this on me. I mean, c'mon. What will we talk about? I don't just make stuff up like you two. I hate improv—you know that. I'm the method actor here, remember! God! That awful uncomfortable silence... sitting there... wondering who is gonna speak first. Miming everything. I'm getting nauseous just thinking about it. I get nervous with silences. My palms sweat. I slur my words. I start getting clumsy. I forget things. My nose starts to run. You all know this!
CAN	But Arty, that's what's so great about this!
ARTY	What?
CAN	You won't have to do the talking man! Nada said this girl's a talking machine! Isn't that right, Bono?
BONO	Yeah... right... She's a virtual conversation factory was what I was told...
CAN	Arty, girls love to talk, man. Especially French chicks.
ARTY	Right.
CAN	Tourtière, réveillon, cabanes à sucre, messe de Minuit, the Rocket, how many times the Canadiens won the Stanley Cup—
BONO	See!
CAN	And they remember everything, too. Je me souviens, it even says so on their licence plates.
BONO	You can't go wrong.
CAN	Just don't mention Trudeau, or the rebellion of 1838, or the Bloc Québécois, or règlement 17, the separation—
BONO	Can—
CAN	...or the deportation of Acadiens, or the referendum, or the Nordiques. And don't mention the Leafs; they hate that team!
BONO	And... scene!
CAN	Besides, you're both in theatre. So it's not like you'll have anything in common not to talk about that you won't have to say and/or that of which you can mention to her as resulting of not having a thing in common with her to talk about when...
BONO	CAN! The important thing is you both have a lot in common.
ARTY	Like what?

BONO	She's just studying theatre.
CAN	Just like you.
BONO	You both have high standards.
CAN	Just like you.
BONO	She only likes a certain type of guy.
CAN	Just like you—
BONO	*(to CAN)* Shut. Up. *(to ARTY)* It's all good. It's all been taken care of anyway.
ARTY	What?!
BONO	What? We planned out a few details is all. And we did it because I know how you don't like surprises, man. I care about you.
ARTY	What?!
CAN	It's how blind dates are done now, Arty! See it. Plan it. Do it.
BONO	You're meeting at Donovan's!
ARTY	Donovan's?
BONO	Great food.
CAN	Intimate atmosphere.
BONO	And there's a dance floor.
ARTY	What about a dance floor?
CAN	You need one for dancing.
ARTY	Since when do they have a dance floor?
BONO	On Saturdays they move the tables and...?
ARTY	I never go on Saturdays precise— Why dancing?!
BONO	It was part of the deal.
ARTY	But I can't dance. That's why I didn't go out with you last night. *(realizing what was said)* "Part of the deal"? What the hell does that mean?
BONO	I made one—or two—promises... They were really impressed with his worm, so I said, "If you think he's got moves, you should see Arty tear it up." They made me promise you would ask her to dance. Apparently she loves it. I was—we were—trying to impress the girls with the quality of date you were—
ARTY	That was stupid!

BONO	Yes, but it worked.
ARTY	BUT I CAN'T DANCE!
CAN	No one'll notice.
ARTY	CAN! I CAN'T DANCE: L-I-T-E-R-A-L-L-Y! My knee! Your slap shot! Remember? I'm still in physio! The therapist wants me resting my knee.
CAN	Meaning don't tango or do your Michael Jackson impression.
BONO	Which is probably a good idea anyway.
CAN	But this is slow dancing. And it's easy, Arty! You just move in a circle.
ARTY	No dancing! I can't and I won't.
BONO	You did it at prom.
ARTY	She was in a wheelchair and her dad moved her around me!
CAN	Dude! It's just a circle!
ARTY	I can't dance, dipshit! My knee! And even if I could, which I can't, so I won't, she might still say no.
BONO	Okay! We have a minor problem with the dancing!
ARTY	Dancing... Jesus... Sometimes I really don't understand you two!
CAN	Arty, it's circles! Just circles. Watch my circle.
BONO	*(thinking)* "You two..." 2... U... That's it!
ARTY	What?
BONO	U2! It's perfect! Mel and Nada love them. Their roommate must too!
ARTY	How do you know that?
CAN	Because chicks like doing things in clusters. Like going to the bathroom. They like to bond. They become one. They even say that girls who live together eventually synchronize their periods due to the psychological—
BONO	Enough, Can! The point is... you know how to dance to U2 songs. You've watched their videos many times with me. Especially the slow ones! They're easy to dance to. You stay in one spot and move. Can. Here. Now. Look. Like this! *(demonstrates)* See, it's easy! No pressure on your knee. Now you can dance and look good doing it—
CAN	*(to BONO)* How is this any different from any other slow song?

BONO	Shut it.
ARTY	NO! I CAN'T!
CAN	Yes, you can!
ARTY	Even if I could—which again, I can't—so I won't— Donovan's doesn't play U2. They play that other kind of music, the "Wind Beneath My Wings" kind. The classical-impossible-to-dance-to-waltzy-slash-tangoish kind. I can't risk it. You know I hate surprises!
BONO & CAN	My nose runs, I sweat, my asthma kicks in, I slur my words, I can't breathe.
ARTY	I can't risk it. I know what they play there, and it's not music I am familiar with.
CAN	It really doesn't matter what they play because in the end it's all the same: circles! Small circles!
BONO	Solved! I'll call and tell the manager to *make sure* they play a U2 song! It's that simple. I'll ask for… "With or Without You"! Girls love that song.
CAN	Especially the French chicks. It reminds them of Quebec's attitude to the rest of Canada. They cry every time they hear it. Emo all the way, dude.
BONO	How's that? Now you won't have any surprises. You'll know the song so you can comfortably manage to move to that beat in a… circle… Arty, picture this… You arrive. You walk in. You see a hot Frenchy wearing a red shirt—that's what we arranged she'd be wearing so you know it's her. You sit down. You listen to her yap yap yap your ear off. You just listen 'cause, like Can said, she's a talker. Right?
CAN	Fa shizzle.
BONO	Suddenly the song comes on, a song you know, a song she loves, a song that makes people fall in love… you ask her to dance. She gladly accepts. No rejection, Arty… and you know the song so well, a song that all slow dancers move to in the same circle. You can dance to it without legs… You can even sing along…
CAN	Sing in her ear, dude. French girls love that shit!
BONO	One slow song, Arty, and it's all over. Then… take her back to her seat.
CAN	Then order some food.
ARTY	It costs a fortune there—

CAN	She'll pay. That's the way it's done now.
BONO	Consider it pro *bono*... *(short pause—his joke bombs)* Order some fries.
CAN	Make it a poutine!
BONO	Yeah, a small poutine.
CAN	Make it large. French girls love that shit!
BONO	A garden salad.
CAN	With *French* dressing.
BONO	Some wine.
CAN	*French* wine!
BONO	Okay! We get it, Can. French. Yes. Good. Now sleep! *(to ARTY)* Order dessert too. Girls love ice cream.
CAN	French vanilla, motherfu—
BONO	Can! See, Arty. It's easy. Just don't order dumb things like milk and sardines like you often do. Be cool.
CAN	Check it. Read the English side of the menu, then find the matching item on the French side, then order it in French. Totally cool. Example: Find soup. Flip le menu over and...
BONO	It's still *soup*, asswipe. Listen, Arty. What's critical is the wine.
ARTY	Why?
BONO	It's like water for the French. Not to mention, it's an aphrodisiac. It epitomizes a romantic night.
ARTY	You know what happens when I have a glass of wine—
BONO	Yes, I do. So as you eat dinner, listen to her talk, allow the wine to settle in so you're nice and relaxed. Give her the occasional "yes," "uh huh," so she thinks you're listening. Then—after the dance—just let me finish. All you have to do is take her home. Easy peasy Japanesey. But I'm so convinced that you'll enjoy her company so much, you'll wanna take her to the *spot*.
ARTY	The spot?
CAN	Le spot...
BONO	And once you're there, enjoying the moonlight, you'll reach down, take hold of her soft little hand... Feel that perfect little cold, trembling hand in yours, and—
CAN	Say, "Merci pour la belle soirée!"

BONO	Or say nothing at all… Just lean in… and… kiss her…
ARTY	Kiss?!
BONO	Kiss.
CAN	French kiss.

> *BONO does not even look at CAN. He simply takes his hand and gives him a face wash.*

BONO	When you go out with a lady, the polite thing to do is to kiss her good night.
ARTY	It is, eh?! C'mon, Bono! What? Is this another part of your *deal*?
BONO	Yes. But it's still the right thing to do. When was the last time you kissed a girl?
ARTY	This whole thing is sooo whacked! Dinner, dance, kiss a complete stranger. Who makes these kinds of arrangements for their friends anyway? You're suppose to have my back, boys! A blind date is bad enough, but to make me have to meet certain objectives—
CAN	Just like theatre, man! Objectives, goals, tactics, and high stakes!
ARTY	You're douchebags, you know that? Forget it. Bye!
BONO	Why? 'Cause you've been burdened with the horrible misfortune of having to eat and dance with a beautiful girl?
ARTY	You've never seen her!
BONO	I have in my mind's eye! And in my heart.
CAN	And he saw a picture!
ARTY	Forget it!
BONO	Arty! Listen! You sit here night after night doing nothing. Now you have a chance to get out and what? Am I suppose to feel sorry for you? Woe is you. What a poor guy. What a cross you bear. You poor Sisyphus! No way, man. My job, as your friend, is to kick your ass and get you back in the game. Stop being a suck! What's your problem, Arty? 'Cause Can would do this for you in a heartbeat. Is it the kiss? The dance? Or is this really all because of *Joan*? 'Cause if it is, you've got to get over her, man!
ARTY	I loved her.
BONO	Joan dumped you. That whole thing went up in flames!
CAN	You were burned—
ARTY	I miss her.

CAN	She threw a candle at you.
ARTY	She was mad.
BONO	She was sick of you doing too many weird things. Like your stupid Michael Jackson impression shit. You freak people out with that.
ARTY	He was a legend!
BONO	Okay, but you don't honour his memory by grabbing your crotch every time his song comes on at a bar then ask yourself why everyone circles around you—and you especially don't go on eBay and spend your tuition on a replica glove.
ARTY	Limited edition!
CAN	That's why you're single, Arty, you do weird shit like that.
ARTY	She was my first love, man.
BONO	We didn't like her.
CAN	Arty, it's her loss.
BONO	She's gone. So accept it! Get over it. Let it go! And move on.
CAN	There are more fish in the sea.
ARTY	She said I was a bad kisser.
BONO	You are.
CAN	It's your technique man.
ARTY	I can't do it, guys. I'm sorry.
BONO	Arty! Stop with this depression bullshit.
ARTY	Why kissing?
CAN	It's a French tradition to kiss people. It's like a handshake to them. They do it every time they greet each other. It's easy, watch. *(goes to BONO, BONO looks at him, he backs down)* They call it giving a "bees," man. Like the birds and the bees. Don't deny her her rights, man! They get screwed out of so much already.
ARTY	Why did you make all those promises, Bono?
BONO	Because. Duh. I wanted to make it special for you. And her. It was in the heat of the moment. I was still buzzing, And Arty, you're the only guy I know who's a real gentleman, single and available. Come on! You've got everything going for you—
CAN	You're talented.
BONO	You're intelligent.

CAN	You're smart.
BONO	You've got a great sense of humour.
CAN	You're funny. And you're good looking *(catching himself as the other two look at him)* for things… we lose in the couch, you find 'em quickly—
BONO	*(ARTY isn't convinced.)* You know you haven't been yourself since Joan dumped you. This will really do you some good.
ARTY	Tell me the truth, Bono. Why do I have to do this?
BONO	Because I'm thinking of her. This girl is hurting and just wants a date with a great guy like you. *(ARTY still isn't convinced.)* Dammit! Okay, I want this audition!
ARTY	Always about you.
BONO	And I really like Mel! And Can likes Nada. And you need to get out. But I really need this audition man. This is the closest I've ever come to professional theatre. Please, Arty… One tiny little dinner, one tiny little dance, one tiny little peck, and you're golden!
CAN	I'll clean the apartment for the rest of the month.
BONO	And Can will do your laundry… *(ARTY is not impressed and starts to walk out.)* I'll stop ripping on you for keeping your glove under your *Aladdin* pillow, and for owning an *Aladdin* pillow. Or winning the Belle River moonwalk contest… *(ARTY stops. BONO to himself.)* Forgive me, boys. *(Looks at his U2 T-shirt. Pause. Takes a deep breath.)* Instead of going to see U2 at the Air Canada Centre… I'll sell the tickets… and we'll go to that Michael Jackson tribute concert in Montreal.

There is a moment of silence. ARTY stares at BONO in disbelief.

ARTY	MJ tickets…? You don't have that kind of money!
CAN	OSAP. *(short pause)*
ARTY	You'd give up U2 for MJ?

BONO hangs his head in shame and nods yes.

All this for a girl?

BONO	She's French…
ARTY	This really means that much to you…
BOTH	Bro…
ARTY	Really…

BONO	It's the chance to be in a professional play, man... Please Arthur... do it for us... please...
	ARTY hesitates. BONO and CAN start chanting "MJ! MJ!" They begin dancing like Michael Jackson. CAN sings a Michael Jackson tune.
ARTY	Swear to me you'll get those tickets.
CAN & BONO	Done!
	Pause.
ARTY	What's her name?
	BONO and CAN scream with happiness, then jump on ARTY and hug him.
BONO	Théa! Her name is Théa!
CAN	It's French for tea and then enjoying the taste: "Thé... ahhh..."
	Oh my God...
ARTY & BONO	What?
CAN	You guys are so meant to be!
ARTY	What are you talking about?
CAN	Take her name, add your name, put them together, say it fast, what do you get?
BONO	Théa-and-Arty?
CAN	No man. You get TAY-ART. It's French for theatre. Which is what we're all studying... You see! It's a sign! Like in a play. We're all connected in the cosmic circle of life. And French girls love that shit!
ARTY	You promise she'll do the talking?
BONO	Until the cows come home! No worries.
CAN	But you should talk a little too. Use this. *(tosses him a French-English dictionary)*
ARTY	Why? You said she'll do all the talking.
BONO	Yes, she will but just in case—
CAN	To have a little something something to throw in. So you don't look like a prop, you can point to something on the table, say the word in French. Look it up, say the word. For example: You see some butter. Look it up. It's called beurre. You say, hey, babe, beurre.

Guess what? She starts to melt like butter 'cause you're so hot with your words.

BONO   She's talking, you feel good, you wanna say something intelligent, you've got this puppy for backup. Only for backup, but there won't be a need 'cause there's so much to talk about with a French chick that there will never be silence.

CAN   Yes, I googled this too—French chicks are Catholic and they pray a lot. So you can always bring up the saints... Like Sain Jean Baptiste and Sain Sacrement! French chicks love their *sains*!

ARTY   Boys, listen to me very carefully. This is my last blind date. Okay?

BOTH   Okay!

ARTY   You're lucky I'm a good friend.

BONO   No, you're a best friend! I promise you, you won't regret this!

CAN   You better go get ready so you're not late! French girls hate th—
(Both boys take a pillow and beat CAN.)

ARTY   I'm gonna get ready. I will hold you to those tickets.

BONO   Yeah. For sure. Wear your black blazer so she can recognize you. Don't wear a plain T-shirt underneath. Wear something that says, "Hey, I am aware of you and respect your culture, and this is who I am." She'll be wearing a red shirt.

CAN   Colour of love.

BONO   And please do something with your hair—you don't want to scare her. Use my gel. Just a little—you always put too much. And only one squirt of cologne, Arty, no more!

    ARTY exits.

    (big sigh and a pause) Well, that was easy...

CAN   Not really, dude... Actually, you know what, Bono? Even though I'm getting a date with Nada out of this, I really feel I'm helping Arty. It's gonna be fun for him. I mean, if Théa looks anything like Nada... he'll be a happy man.

BONO   Right...

CAN   What's wrong?

BONO   Nothing...

CAN   What is it?

BONO   It's about Théa...

CAN	What?
BONO	Something Mel mentioned to me when you were showing Nada your worm.
CAN	What...? Oh my God! She's a charity friend... I should have known. With two hot girls there's always an ugly one. Stupid, stupid, stupid.
BONO	No! That's not the rule. When there's three hot girls, there's a charity friend. When there's two, the third's just as hot. It has nothing to do with her looks. She's cute. Mel showed me her picture on her phone.
CAN	Well, what then?
BONO	It's how she talks...
CAN	She stutters...? She has a lisp...? Then what then? Nada said she never shuts up.
BONO	She doesn't speak a word of English.
CAN	Holy fu—
BONO	I know.
CAN	He's done... *(There is a sudden realization and they both start laughing.)* Dude! I should of known this was too good to be true.
BONO	Mel probably assumed Arty spoke French 'cause we both do.
CAN	We don't.
BONO	I could kill Arty for dropping French—
CAN	What a douche.
BONO	I told him French would open doors one day—you can't drop it.
CAN	Things would be so much easier if we were all born bilingual.
BONO	I know, dude. I know... I almost feel bad. I couldn't say anything. It happened so fast. It was this close from being perfect...
CAN	It's like being up two-nothing the whole game, and with only three seconds left in the third period, they score a goal. All that work and just like that, the shutout is ruined. Oh well. I'll go tell him.
BONO	Yeah... Yeah. Wait...! The shutout is ruined, but, in the end, we still win the game, right!
CAN	C'mon, Bono, they won't be able to talk. He'll panic! He'll—
BONO	A minor detail for his own good! For the good of the team. Sometimes you gotta take one for the team, right? Besides, what's

the worst that could happen? A dinner, a dance, and a small kiss good night—

CAN   She doesn't speak a word of English! *He's fu—*

BONO   Love is its own language. It's something we feel. Something we all get. He'll get a beautiful date, we both get our ladies… And I get an audition.

Scene Three: Les filles

At the same time, in the girls apartment.

NADA   *(NADA pretends to be THÉA.)* Oui! Oui! Oui! Quelle excellente idée! Je vais l' faire! Mais dis-moi tout, parce que, moi, j'aime ça les détails!

MEL   *(MEL is practising her speech to THÉA.)* On est là en train de danser. Pis ces deux gars n'arrête pas de nous regarder. Ils essaient d'être suave et cool, mais ça ressemble plus le cours de clown du départe de théâtre. Ils étaient tellement "cute." En tous cas, ils s'approchent de nous comme deux autruches gelées… Leurs corps touts par touts.

NADA   Fait-le!

MEL imitates their dance and they both laugh.

MEL   L'autre n'arrête pas de se jeter par terre et nous montrer son "worm." Il était mignon comme tout… Pour un vers de terre. Check ben ça; ils étudient le théâtre aussi!

NADA   *(as THÉA)* Excellent!

MEL   Nada!

NADA   Okay! *(as THÉA)* À non! Pas d'autres gars qui étudient théâtre! S'ils sont pas gays, ils sont arrogants… ou ambiguës.

MEL   Pas eux! Et en passant c'est pas tous les gars en théâtre qui sont comme ça. *(to NADA)* Il faut démystifié les stéréotypes. *(She resumes her speech to THÉA.)* En tous cas, ils nous ont amené au SPOT, c'était tellement romantique!

NADA   Quel spot?

MEL   Nada.

NADA   *(as THÉA)* Oh le spot! Alors il faut que je sorte avec leur copain?

MEL   Mais attend au moins que je te le demande!

NADA   *(as THÉA)* J'accepte! Vous êtes les meilleures amies du monde. Merci de m'avoir trouvé une date! Maintenant, viens m'aider à trouver ma chemise rouge. *(as herself)* Très bien, Mel! Tu m'as complètement convaincu mais soit juste un peu moins raide au début—okay? Comment était mon imitation du Théa?

MEL   Un peut trop gentille, je trouve! Écoute, ce qui est nécessaire est que tu suis mon lead. Théa aime les détails… Il ne faut pas mentir, simplement lui mettre l'eau à la bouche. *(hears THÉA coming)* Okay! Fait comme d'habitude. Laisse-moi installer la situation comme on à pratiquée. Si les choses vont mal tu peu improvisé *un peu.* Un peu! Et Nada, soit plus discrète?

NADA   Okay!

      THÉA enters.

      (shouting) Bonjour Théa! Comment vas-tu aujourd'hui?

THÉA   Ça va…

NADA   *(shouting)* Géniale! Ça va, moi aussi! Merci! Mel, as-tu de quoi à dire?

MEL   Ça va, Nada. Merci.

NADA   *(shouting)* Oui! Et en parlant de—

MEL   Merci, Nada! Théa, pourrais-tu t'asseoir?

      THÉA looks at both of them. Silence.

THÉA   Qu'est-ce qui se passe?

      Neither knows where to begin. They shuffle around as THÉA stares at them.

      Vous voulez me demander quelque chose…? *(They nod their heads yes.)*

      Qu'est ce que vous voulez…? *(They look at each other.)* On va fonctionner comme ça? Okay… Vous me parler en même temps… alors vous voulez une faveur. Mmm… Mel, t'a lavée tes cheveux… alors tu sors ce soir… Nada, tu portes tes bottes et ta jupes… alors vous sortez ensemble avec des gars… Mel, tu m'as demandé de m'assoire… alors ce que vous voulez c'est un service que je ne voudrais pas vous rendre… Nada a ses mains serrées, alors ça concerne un gars que je connais pas. Okay, je sais! Vous voulez que je sorte ce soir avec un gars que je ne connais pas!

NADA & MEL   *(shouting)* Wow! Oui!

THÉA	NON! Espèce de rendez-vous. Oublie ça! J'ai tout entendu dans l'autre salle. Tu parles trop fort, Nada. Puis en passant, c'était la pire imitation que j'ai jamais entendue.
MEL	S'il te plaît, Théa, écoute nous deux secondes.
THÉA	Vous ne le connaissez même pas.
MEL	Bien sûr on connaît des choses.
NADA	Yé tellement charmant!
MEL	Un véritable prince!
NADA	Un Prince Charmant!
THÉA	L'as-tu déjà vu?
NADA	En personne?
THÉA	Oui, en personne!
NADA	Oui! Absolument! Plusieurs fois! Pas vraiment. C'est-à-dire; non! Je veux dire oui, je l'ai vu, mais pas en personne. J'ai vu une photo!
THÉA	Montre moi la photo.
NADA	Ce n'est pas vraiment une photo. C'était une description qui m'a fait pensée à une photo.
MEL	*(changing the subject)* Son nom c'est Arty!
THÉA	Hardie?
MEL	Ca veut dire "comme l'art" ou "*presque* de l'art" en anglais.
THÉA	Arty… c'est-un anglo?
NADA	Oui, mais ça paraît pas!
THÉA	Qu'est ce que tu veux dire "Ça paraît pas"?
MEL	Il n'est pas un vrai anglo!
THÉA	"Vrai anglo"?
NADA	Un anglo-Anglais!
THÉA	Un quoi?
MEL	Un anglo qui parle que l'Anglais.
THÉA	Alors il parle Français?
MEL	Français-français?
NADA	Oui!
MEL	Non!

THÉA	Quoi?
MEL	Parfois.
THÉA	Parfois?
NADA	Comme un francophone—
MEL	Un francophone Anglais—
NADA	Il parle franglais.
MEL	Comme un anglophone—
NADA	Parle l'Anglais!
MEL	Comme nous.
NADA	Vive le Québec!
MEL	Penses-tu qu'on t'arrangerait un *rendez-vous* avec quelqu'un qui ne parle pas Français? Et toi qui parle pas un mot d'Anglais. Hahaha! *(regarde a NADA)*
NADA	…Hahaha… Ben non! *(making it up)* Quelqu'un dans le département qui connaît quelqu'un d'autre, qui a dit à l'amie de Sandrine…
MEL	Ah! Oui… SANDRINE!
THÉA	C'est qui, Sandrine?
NADA	Tu te souviens pas de Sandrine? Mel va tout t'expliquer.
MEL	Elle était dans notre cours de mouvement. Celle qui s'est cassée le nez. En tout cas, elle était la très bonne amie de la fille qui était bien chum avec le colocataire de l'autre. Apparemment, Arty dansait pour gagner de l'argent pour aider sa mère qui est handicapée, à cause de l'accident…
THÉA	Quelle accident?
NADA	Bye Bye… quat—
MEL	—tre—
NADA	Vingt!
MEL & NADA	Dix?
NADA	Huit.
MEL	Oui!
MEL & NADA	Quatre-vingt-dix!
NADA	Elle chantait et elle a pêté ses cordes vocales. Juste comme ça.

THÉA	Vraiment!
MEL	Malheureusement, oui!
NADA	Mais, son malheur fini pas là.
THÉA	Non?
MEL	Non…
NADA	Non! Il s'est cassé la jambe durant le Bye Bye '95.
MEL	Nada, comment ça se fait que j'avais oubliée tout ça?!
THÉA	Il est anglophone, non? Comment ça se fait qu'il dansait au Bye Bye?
NADA	Son grand-père… un Irlandais! *(MEL and THÉA are confused.)* Voyons, Théa, réfléchit un peut!
MEL	Hahaha… *(changing the subject)* J'ai entendu dire qu'il a les mêmes intérêts que toi! C'est juste qu'il na pas réussit à trouver la bonne personne.
THÉA	Mêmes intérêts?
MEL	Tu veux une famille, et il veut une famille.
NADA	Une grande famille.
THÉA	Grande?
NADA	Un vrai famille Québécoise avec quinze enfants.
THÉA	Quoi?
MEL	Cinq!
THÉA	Cinq? Moi, j'veux seulement deux!
MEL	Quelle coïncidence! Il cherche une intellectuelle, pour une relation a long terme, qui adore danser, la poésie, et qui veut deux enfants!
NADA	Et un chalet à Saint-Sauveur.
THÉA	Vous me prenez vraiment pour une conne! Vous êtes les pires menteuses au monde. Je ne pense pas que notre prof de jeux vous trouverait très convaincantes.
MEL	Oh! Okay. Madame qui regarde *CSI* chaque soir. Félicitation! T'a tous découvert. C'est vrai! On veut que tu sortes ce soir. C'est un rendez-vous avec un gars qu'on connaît pas. On a déjà fait les arrangements avec ses amis. Es-tu contente maintenant?
NADA	On voulais juste t'encourager a sortir…
THÉA	Où?

MEL	Chez Donovan's.
THÉA	Ce soir?
MEL	Salsa night! *(short pause)*
THÉA	C'est bien trop cher!
MEL	T'inquiète pas, c'est un gars, il va payer!
NADA	C'est fun ça. T'adores la salsa et apparemment il est un bon danseur! Et il adore le vin.
THÉA	Ça pourrait être le fun! Mais…
MEL & NADA	Jean-Sébastien. On le sait. T'en parles chaque seconde.
THÉA	C'était pendant notre chanson préférée…
MEL & NADA	"With Or Without You."
THÉA	On dansait. Ma tête était accoté sur son épaule, mes yeux fermés, c'était parfait! Mais comme toutes bonnes choses ça n'a pas duré longtemps. J'ai senti qu'il regardait quelque chose. J'me suis ouvert les yeux, et là, je l'ai vue assise toute seule, entrain de fumer, en nous regardant. Joan Smith. Son "tuteur" d'Anglais. J'ai compris toute suite! Il a senti que je l'savais. Il s'est arrâté, en plein milieu de la chanson, a reculé d'un pas, puis a OSÉ me dire qu'il ne voulait plus sortir avec moi! Il a "découvert" une fille de l'Ontario. Il "voulait un changement." Alors je lui ai dis: "Merci pour la danse!" Et je suis partie seule en pleurant. Si c'était à refaire j'aurais du lui dire: "She's *Yours To Discover*, asshole!" Je pouvais pas le croire! Une Anglaise avait volé mon chum! Espèce de… de… AHHH! Le problème c'est qu'elles prennent toutes! Le bas Canada! Notre bois! Elles ont même l'audace d'utiliser les couleurs de notre drapeau, blue et blanc, pour les Leafs de Toronto! La pire équipe au Canada. Pauvre Potvin. Puis une autre chose qui m'énerve! Elles ajoutent French devant toute! French fries! French onion! French-ip! *(friendship)* Et y a pas une seule qui parlent FRENCH! Osti! Elles sont trop occupée entrain de voler nos chums (parce que leurs chums sont nulles) pour apprendre l'autre langue nationale de notre pays! Ça lit du Tremblay pis ça pensent que ça nous comprend. Ha! Moi! J'hais ça le bingo! Puis le pire, c'est qu'elles sont toujours en train de parler de nos accents—c'est eux avec l'accent, sacrement!
MEL	Whoa là!
NADA	Okay… tu penses pas que t'exagères un petit peu?
MEL	Toi qui as un petit accent du sud de l'Ontario?

NADA   Puis en plus, tu ne parles pas les deux langues nationales de notre pays.

THÉA   C'est différent!

MEL   C'est toujours différent quand ça nous convient. De toute façon, il y a deux raisons qui garantie de jamais revivre cette mauvaise expérience. Et de un; il ne joue jamais des chansons comme ça dans un club salsa. Et de deux, je lui ai dit que tu n'aimais pas U2. Il m'a même répondue: you too… toi aussi… okay!

THÉA   S'il faut que je sorte, j'aimerais au moins sortir avec un gars qui est intéressé à moi et qui me comprend. Pas qui veux être compris.

MEL   On comprend!

THÉA   Un gars honnête, j'hais les surprises!

NADA   Compris! Et qui n'est pas comme les autres gars du département.

THÉA   VOILÀ!

MEL   C'est pour ça qu'Arty est parfait.

NADA   T'en fais pas, je leur ai déjà tout expliqué!

THÉA   Uh?

MEL   Aux gars, comment tu es…

THÉA   Pardon?…

NADA   On leurs a expliqué, tes attentes, tes inquiétudes, que tu veux être aimée—

THÉA   Quoi!

NADA   On voulait te faire une surprise!

THÉA   Marie Nadine Mireille St-Denis! Dis-moi que t'as pas dis ça!

NADA   Surprise!

MEL   On leur a simplement dit qu'une date serait le remède parfait pour quelqu'un seul et triste comme toi!

THÉA   Jésus-Sainte-Marie…

MEL   Calme-toi, Théa. C'était juste— (pour ton propre bien-être)

THÉA   Maintenant, ils vont penser que je suis désespérée!

NADA   Tu l'es!

THÉA   QUOI?!

MEL	Ce n'est pas bien de rester ici, seule dans l'appart. Si on te poussais pas, j'imagine que tu resterais ici... *(calmly)* Théa, on sait bien que c'était difficile pour toi et Jean-Sébastien. Il a vraiment brisé ton cœur. Mais ça fait déjà deux ans!
THÉA	Et sept mois!
MEL	D'accord, "et sept mois!"
THÉA	Et trois semaines!
MEL	*(getting impatient)* Et "trois semaines" et deux jours, et une heure, et six minutes... blah blah... Bien, maintenant! Aujourd'hui! A cette heure-ci! C'est le temps de sortir et de rencontrer du nouveau monde!
THÉA	Et votre solution est de me sacrifier! De me jeter dans la rue avec un gars que tu ne connais même pas! NON! Je vais pas aller!
MEL	Ça y est! Je suis tanné de te voir ici chaque nuit en train de rien faire! Chaque fois que je reçois un appel de quelqu'un pour sortir, je vois que T'ES JALOUSE! Tu ne peux pas le cacher! Tu n'es pas une assez bonne actrice pour me faire croire le contraire! On a fait des demandes spécifiques pour s'assurer que tu vas t'amuser!
THÉA	Je n'ai pas demandé pour cela!
MEL	Tu l'as besoin!
THÉA	NON! NON! NON! Je refuse!
NADA	*(calm)* Permet-moi, Mel. *(really upset and frustrated)* Écoute, Théa! Ça-suffit là! Grouille tes fesses, et arrête de faire ton bébé, ta baboune, et ta premadona. Tu es toujours en train de te plaindre en disant que tu trouveras jamais ton Roméo. Voilà ta chance!
MEL	Ça va être une nouvelle expérience pour toi... Ou tu pourrais être moins égoïste; ça serait une très, très bonne expérience pour lui...
NADA	Pour au moins une soirée, tu ne penseras plus à JS!
	Pause.
THÉA	'Kay.
	NADA and MEL scream with excitement. They hug THÉA and thank her.
	Si, et seulement si, je peux emprunter vos vêtements quand je veux.
MEL & NADA	Okay...
THÉA	Et j'ai la salle de bain a chaque matin aussi longtemps que je veux.
MEL	Ben okay, Théa, mais ça va faire—

THÉA	Et je ne veux plus entendre ton CD de Céline Dion, Nada.
NADA	Aye!
MEL	Elle a raison, Nada.
THÉA	Ou Mario Pelchat, Mel.
MEL	Ben là!
THÉA	Vous devez laver la salle de bain à chaque semaine! ET toi, je ne veux plus jamais entendre parler du nombre de fois que tu as été choisis pour les premiers rôles, ni comment les critiques raffolent de tes présentations.
MEL	Ok! Ça suffit!
THÉA	Bon. *(short pause)* Qu'est-ce que je vais porter?
MEL	Ta chemise rouge! C'est avec cela qu'il va t'identifier. Il port une manteau noir.
THÉA	Rouge?
NADA	Couleur de la passion…
THÉA	Que devrais-je commander?
MEL	Une salade, un verre d'eau, et c'est tout! Il paye alors c'est pas poli de prendre avantage d'un repas freebee.
NADA	Alors vas-y prépares-toi! Tu n'as pas de temps à perdre.

THÉA leaves to change.

Ça va lui faire du bien de sortir. Y a rien d'mieux qu'un bon compagnon et de la bonne conversation… *(MEL looks worried.)* T'en fait pas… je sais.

MEL	Quoi?
NADA	Bono t'a dit.
MEL	Oui… Mais comment est ce— *(que tu le sais)*
NADA	Intuition.
MEL	Ah… C'est dommage, eh?
NADA	C'est normale.
MEL	Je suppose…

Pause.

Juste par hasard… qu'est ce que tu penses que je pense?

NADA	Arty… il est beau… gentil… et en théâtre…

MEL	Oui…
NADA	Il est gay!
MEL	Non! C'est pas ça, pas du tout!
NADA	Alors c'est quoi?
MEL	Il ne parle pas un mot de Français!
NADA	Oui, mais Théa ne parle pas un mot d'An— Oh holy shit!
MEL	Merde! Je me sens tellement mal—je voulais lui dire mais-t'es tellement convainquante quand tu parlent. Pis j'ai pas voulus—
NADA	On annule la soirée.
MEL	Si j'annule, on sort plus avec Bono et Can… et je vais avoir une réputation à l'université—tu sais bien comment les rumeurs circulent vite. De plus si on arrangent ça, Bono ma promise de me trouver un audition avec un théâtre Anglais. J'aimerai me diversifier un peu. C'est bon pour mon CV. De toute façon c'est bon pour Théa et aparament, le gars a vraiment besoin de quelqu'un.
NADA	Mais on ne peut pas laisser Théa sortir avec Arty. Tu sais bien ce qui est arrivé la dernière fois qu'elle a sortie avec un gars qui ne communiquait pas. C'était un désastre total, et le restaurant va jamais être le même.
MEL	On fait rien! Le gars va se débrouiller. Okay, ils vont pas parler mais ils vont danser et rire. Non, le tout va s'arranger! Ca sert à rien de s'inquiéter.
NADA	T'as raison.
MEL	Mais juste en cas, on fait une autre chose.
NADA	Quoi?
MEL	On prie! *(They both get down on their knees.)*

Scene Four: Le rendez-vous

ARTY walks in and sees THÉA. He takes off his glasses. She falls in love at first sight. The music starts. They dance out the perfect date. He is a total Casanova and they hit it off perfectly. When the music ends, they go back to their original places and the real date begins.

Please note, these are just guidelines. This is the scene for non-verbal communication! A constant play on facial expressions and body language. Physical acting is necessary in order to achieve the comedy and the communication. The bigger the better. Throughout this scene, it is important to maintain awkward silences followed by fidgeting and moving. If desired, you can add a waiter, play with menus, add other customers, have ARTY take off and put on his jacket, have the characters eat food, etc. The waiter can get the bill and no one pays. Wine can also be a gag. Allergies, asthma, a live band. Play it out, have fun—everything that could possibly go wrong, slapstick, or not. But have fun!

Donovan's restaurant. One table. Two glasses of water. A bottle of wine and two wine glasses with a basket of bread. THÉA is sitting at the table looking at her watch. She taps her fingers on the table impatiently. Clearly he is late. ARTY enters with too much gel in his hair. He looks around and then sees her. He points to his shirt as if to say, "You have the red shirt on, I have the jacket." We see his shirt underneath is Cailloux or Céline Dion or Michael Jackson, or something ridiculous that only ARTY would wear to try and impress her. He motions a hello with his hand. She stands up and waves him over. He points to his watch as if to say, "Sorry I'm late." He sits down. She stands up to greet him. He gets back up. She leans in to give him a "bise." At the same time, ARTY thrusts his hand out for a handshake. He inadvertently touches her chest while she misses her target and gives him a peck on the lips. They freeze in that position. They are both horrified. They slowly disengage. Both sit down looking away from each other to try and recuperate from the bizarre introduction. He wants to start over and offers his hand. She takes it. She clearly feels his sweaty palm and tries to discreetly wipe in on the table. He tries to dry his palm by trying to discreetly blow on it to dry it out. Uncomfortable silence. They both go for their water. ARTY drinks the whole glass, save two drops, as though dehydrated. He makes a motion as if to say, "How rude of me," and offers her the remaining water. She motions that she has her own. He then wipes his head and gets a hand full of gel. He puts his hand on the tablecloth and it gets stuck to it. More silence, more shifting and motions that make it clear things are uncomfortable. They both look around the room. ARTY checks his watch discreetly so only audience sees. He notices the nice art piece on the wall and points to it. They both nod their heads in appreciation and smile. And start to laugh and laugh without really knowing why. At the same time, ARTY points to the art, THÉA points to him, and ARTY points to her.

ARTY   Art.

THÉA   Arty.

ARTY   Théa.

> *Brief pause. Laughter. He slaps his leg while laughing and hurts it. The laughter slowly fades to complete silence. He looks at the dance floor and his watch. He goes for more water. Without looking, he accidentally touches her hand. They both realize it. Neither knows what to do. He's impatiently waiting for a U2 song to start when THÉA, taken by the urge to fill the silence with something, anything, motions to dance. ARTY refuses; it's not time yet and they are playing salsa music. She grabs him. They go. Disaster unfolds. Because of his knee, he can't dance. She tries to show him but it doesn't work. He wants to cry. The song dies down and THÉA is about to go back to her seat when U2 comes on. This is ARTY's cue. He takes her and brings her back onto the dance floor as the song cuts out. More silence and shifting. ARTY anticipates the song starting again. He is anxious and quickly motions for her to dance. He stares at her. She has no idea why and goes back to her seat. He is waiting for the music. He starts to sob because it is not coming on. He looks at his watch. Why hasn't it started yet? Suddenly the music comes on. He looks up to the heavens thankfully. He gets up to help her out of the chair. The chair does not move right away. He tries harder and pushes the chair, pinning her to the table. He gets her out by pulling the chair back very hard and she is whirled around. He helps her up and takes her to the middle of the dance floor. He leaves her there and goes back to the table to get a napkin to hold so she won't feel his sweaty palms. They both just stand ready to dance. Finally the music begins. He smiles with relief, and he gets in place. They dance like high-school students: distance between them, very stiff, looking different ways. As they turn around slowly (when the audience can see her face), THÉA is crying. ARTY starts yelling "Vive le Quebec, vive le Quebec," thinking this will help calm her down. She kicks him in the crotch. He takes her back to the table. She won't stop crying, which makes him nervous. He drinks his water and realizes her glass is empty, so he pours his water into her glass. She is grossed out. He does not know what to do. He goes over and tries to burp her. She is still crying. He takes the glass and pours the water on her face out of desperation. She is completely shocked. She takes the water and splashes him. They reach a point and then burst out at the same time—not listening to each other, just blurting it all out at the same time so the last word is in sync.*

ARTY | I'm so sorry, this was not my idea! I am so embarrassed. I hate blind dates. I knew this was a bad idea from the start. But my friends are such jerks. You're too good for me, you probably think I'm a complete idiot. I'm sorry. You're so beautiful—

THÉA | Je m'excuse pour cela! Je n'aime pas les blind dates comme ça! Tu penses que je suis une idiote, une folle! Je suis trop stressée. Mes amies sont naiseuses. Tu penses je suis folle, je suis tellement nerveuse, j'ai pas sortie depuis longtemps, tu es tellement beau—

ARTY | You look amazing!

THÉA | T'es tellement beau!

Silence. ARTY and THÉA speak at the same time again.

ARTY | Sorry.

THÉA | Je m'excuse.

Pause.

ARTY | Sorry, go ahead.

THÉA | Vas-y je t'écoute.

Finally ARTY puts his hand up a little to let her know he's going to talk, and they stop talking at the same time.

ARTY | I'm sorry for tonight—

THÉA | Je te comprends pas…

ARTY | *(louder)* I'm very sorry for tonight.

THÉA | Parle Français s'il vous plaît… *(un peut genée)* Je ne comprend pas l'Anglais.

Pause.

ARTY | I AM VERY SOR—how come you're looking at m— *(realizing she doesn't speak English)*

Holy shit. You don't speak English.

THÉA | *(looks at him with blank stare)* Tu ne parles pas Français?

ARTY | You don't speak English? *(THÉA gives him a blank look.)* What the fu—of course you can't answer me because you have no idea what I am saying—

THÉA | Il ne parle pas Français! Merde. Je parle pas l'Anglais—

ARTY | Shit. Shit. Shit. Shit… *(looks at her)* uh… merde.

THÉA | No! Shit.

ARTY Ah… Tut no parla Englishé—

THÉA I… spoke… non… Anglais—

ARTY Ge non speaky no Frenchy! Noooooo…

Understanding everything all at once and realizing the doom he is about to face, ARTY reaches into his pocket to get his cellphone and tries to call the guys without being noticed by her.

Help…

THÉA Qu'est-ce que je fais maintenant, sacrements!

ARTY "Sacrements" the sacrements. Church… the saints… Saints. Ah, ah! Yes! I know this one… Me also aimer beaucoup your sains. *(THÉA throws water at him.)* What did I say? I have no idea what I'm saying! I'm sorry! X-CUZY me! *(She slaps him.)* OW! Pain. Beacoup pain. *(points to his face)* Except that I also love the sains. *(slapped again)* You donner me PAIN!

THÉA Ah oui, tu veux du pain, voici ton pain, espèce de pervert—

THÉA throws a piece of bread at him, followed by the whole basket.

ARTY This is awesome. BONO! Can! I am going to kill you guys! *(cries)*

THÉA Excuse! Je sais tu fais un effort! Mais, MEL! Nada! Merde!

ARTY God, what do I do. The dictionary. I don't want wine. I want milk. I need milk. Milk… Order some milk. *(the waiter comes by)* Wait, be a gentleman… Keep it together, man… Ask her if she wants some… milk… *(finds the word)* Good…! Ah… Tut es lait?

THÉA looks to throw the entire wine decanter over him. She moves very slowly. He no longer cares or protests.

Bring it…

THÉA pours the entire wine decanter on him. ARTY starts to cry a little. She feels bad. Realizing he probably has no idea what he said, realizing they are both in an awkward situation, they look at each other, realizing they were both bamboozled. They laugh a little.

You can't understand me but… I hate my friends!

THÉA J'ai aucune idée se que tu dis. Mais tes amis son nuls.

ARTY Since you don't understand a word I am saying, I am just going to tell you everything without worrying about formalities. Okay? I am going to speak my mind. I've done that before. But tonight… You… You know what? You're trés beautiful… *(thinks about a word)* belle. You're... extremely belle. Can we try this again? *(tries to break down his speech for her using big gestures)* I—Yo-meo-moy. Really... um... really, want... ahh voulez... this night... seven... sept! Noché...! Two... marché. *(slow song comes on)* Oh thank God, the music...

THÉA   J'aimerais essayer de nouveau aussi.

> *ARTY motions her to dance again. They use their body language to communicate and get things in order and they dance. She relaxes and he holds her a bit closer. They are both obviously very relaxed, happy, and really enjoying the slow dance. ARTY is suddenly very suave and THÉA moves with ease. Allow the dance to go a while so the audience can enjoy the new energy. They stare at each other as they dance, saying nothing, letting their eyes talk. They fall in love. A final gentle kiss.*

Scene Five: Some temps After

> *Standing as they did in scene one. To audience.*

ARTY   So that's how—

THÉA   Nous avons— *(they look at each other)*

ARTY   Met! Okay, so we left out a lot of details and the whole second and third act, but you get the idea. It's funny how relationships are born out of the strangest circumstances; I went to an English high school, she went to a French high school but somehow... we gave it a chance... I mean... two different people, two different cultures, completely different languages...

THÉA   On a trouvé des choses en commun. Avec le temps, tout est possible et tout peut fonctionner. Quand on aime quelqu'un, on est près à travailler ensemble.

ARTY   Moi, j'ai apprend un petit Français.

THÉA   Slowly h'I learn to speaks h'English. *(They get closer at centre stage.)*

ARTY   And you know how to really get a relationship going? You listen to them. Pay attention to their smile, their laugh, the look in their eyes—that's what really speaks. Languages are the least of our worries as long as we accept, encourage, try, and LISTEN... There are, of course, other, more exciting ways of communicating... *(He holds her and kisses her lovingly.)*

THÉA	Bono et Mel, ET Can et Nada sont toujours ensemble. À nos noces Can l'a demandé en mariage.
ARTY	Did you tell them about Can's proposal at our wedding reception?
THÉA	Yes, h'I did!
ARTY	*(whispers to the audience)* I don't know if Bono will marry Mel too, but "petit a petit l'oiseau fait son nid"!
THÉA	C'est bon, mon amour!
ARTY	So in the end, the six of us worked out! We spent a lot of time together, met the families. I experienced le réveillon and she's taking ESL. We don't always agree—but we still listen. And yeah, blind dates suck. Doing something you hate sucks. But in the end everything always works out. Especially when you take the situation and go with it.
THÉA	Espécialement when da Habs smash da leaf.
CAN	Oh my God!
EVERYONE	What?
CAN	If you take my name and mix it up with my fiancée's name, you know what you get?
BONO	No Can, no one understands…
NADA	I do! I thought of it too, Can. You get CAN-NADA, like CANADA… It's a sign!
CAN	And the cosmic play of life continues… *(They kiss.)*
BONO	Why…
MEL	CAN! Can it! Get it? Good…
BONO	God, I love you! *(They kiss while CAN and NADA are looking at each other lovingly.)*
CAN	And the cosmic play of life—
EVERYONE	CAN!
THÉA	Une relation développe avec du temps et de la patience.
ARTY	Et ensemble tout est possible. *(He comes out with their baby.)*
THÉA	La vie est vraiment pleine de surprise. J'adore les surprise!
ARTY	Surprises. You have to roll with them. Take 'em as they come. Even if it's not what you planned… you never know what great things will come.

> *Together they make a great family-picture scene with both couples in the back.*

THÉA   We decided dat bébé would learn boats language. Dat bébé now will 'ave—as mon amour says—"De best of boat world."

ARTY   Écoute tout-le-monde! The baby is about to say his first word!

EVERYONE   SHHH!

> *Silence, as they listen intently. There are big smiles on everyone's faces.*

BABY VOICE   Ola!

> *ARTY and THÉA look at each other, then at the audience, in disbelief.*

THE IMPRESSIONIST WING

by Mia Rose Yugo

William Shakespeare (Stephen Djan) drops in on Jake's (Roberto Esteves) conversation with the two explorers, Dr. Sanjay (Tiago Abreu) and Dr. Misha (Tiago Ortega), who are attempting to explain the physics of the Wing.

Photo by Marianne Yugo.

The Impressionist Wing was first produced by students from Dante Alighieri Academy, Toronto, at the Toronto Central District Festival of the Sears Ontario Drama Festival in February 2009, with subsequent performances at the Toronto Regional Festival at Hart House Theatre in April 2009 and the Provincial Showcase at the Grand Theatre in Kingston in May 2009. Student playwright Mia Rose Yugo received the 2009 Outstanding New Play Award at the Provincial Showcase for *The Impressionist Wing*.

Misha	Tiago Ortega
Sanjay/Don Juan	Tiago Abreu
Jake	Roberto Esteves
Alexander the Great	Michael Anthony Dos Santos
Shakespeare	Stephen Djan
Joe Shmoe	Ian Gonzalez
Dark Side of Joe Shmoe	Philip Carvalho
Gabriel/Wizard/Tradesman	Josie Franchi
Giuseppe Verdi/Nurse	Gaspare Bellissimo
Hospital Nurse	Cynthia Casasanta
Queens and Student Nurses	Melanie Costa, Jessica Cuello-Gatica, Alessia Lalomia, Stefania Macchiocchi-Lancia, Erica Parisi, Monica Serodio

Directed by Mia Rose Yugo
Stage Management by Ashley Nicholson
Set & Costume Design by Mia Rose Yugo
Lighting & Sound by Ashley Nicholson and Mia Rose Yugo
Musicians: Kevin Dutra and Anthony Pannozzo
Music Advisor: M. Pilaf
Artistic Advisors: L. Reedy, L. Dragonieri
Backstage Crew: Derek Bujeya, Cesar Calero, Karen Calero, Keisha Lewis, Chad Targatt
Staff Advisor: Mr. Teodoro Dragonieri

NOTes

All music is to be performed live. No recordings should be used for any of the songs. Below is a list of songs appearing in the play and instructions on how to acquire the sheet music. The portion of each song to be sung is indicated in the script alongside its duration.

1. "Libiamo ne'lieti calici" from Giuseppe Verdi's opera *La traviata*.
2. "La Donna è mobile" from Giuseppe Verdi's opera *Rigoletto*.
3. The Triumphal March from Verdi's *Aida*.
4. The theme from Beethoven's Symphony No. 5.
5. "Hallelujah" from Handel's *Messiah*.
6. Short excerpts from the song "Put A Little Love in Your Heart," music and lyrics by Jackie DeShannon, Randy Myers, and Jimmy Holiday.

Sheet music for Giuseppe Verdi's operas, Beethoven's Symphony No. 5, and Handel's *Messiah* can be found for free in many public reference libraries or online. This music is in the public domain and permission for its use is not needed. Sheet music for "Put A Little Love in Your Heart" can also be found in many public reference libraries, but please note that permission from the rights holders is needed to perform this piece. Alternatively, a different song with a similar theme may be substituted.

Mia rose yugo

Mia Rose Yugo wrote *The Impressionist Wing* in 2008 at the age of seventeen. It was picked up for a professional reading at the SummerWorks Theatre Festival in 2009. Her interest in the dramatic arts was sparked by the influence of her teacher, mentor, and friend, Mr. Teodoro Dragonieri. In 2008, she was the winner of the Human Rights and Race Relations Centre Essay Contest. Other works include *Blind Spot* (co-written for the 2008 Paprika Festival) and *Lifeline* (an anti-bullying play). She now attends University of Toronto.

characters

Dr. MISHA
Dr. SANJAY
DON JUAN
JAKE
ALEXANDER the Great
SHAKESPEARE
JOE Shmoe
DARK SIDE of Joe Shmoe
GABRIEL
WIZARD
TRADESMAN
VERDI
NURSES
QUEENS
JANITOR

Scene One

Two men are lying on a raised platform. Giant picture frames for the actors to walk through, prints of Impressionist paintings, a big triangle, busts on pedestals, etc. are scattered across the stage. A music box is on one man's chest. This man is MISHA. The lights come on as he opens the box and music begins to play. The drums cue the second man, SANJAY, to get up first. He stretches his arms, walks over to the music box and closes it. Music stops. Both men are now up. They are dressed in doctors' attire, wearing white lab coats and the same thick, black-framed, round glasses. They greet each other with a funny handshake.

MISHA   *(in heavy Russian accent)* Zdrastvuitye! Hyello, my friend.

SANJAY   *(in heavy Indian accent)* Hello, Misha. *(looks at his music box)* Working, I see.

MISHA   Da, working.

SANJAY   And how are things?

MISHA   Is very busy lately. The alien visitations have become more frequent. Is increasingly difficult to hide and invyestigate them. Even the American, Larry King, he speaks of them.

SANJAY   Allow me to translate: You have more crazy Russian cases to solve, which you call aliens.

MISHA   Vell is fancy vay to say so. Ha ha ha.

Suddenly, a disoriented, twenty-year-old off-balance man— dressed casually in jeans—stumbles in. He has a cut on his forehead.

SANJAY   *(raises his hand in alien greeting)* Greetings!

JAKE   *(hands on head)* Whoa, what's that ringing?

MISHA   Is no ringing. Is delayed shock.

JAKE   *(hysterical)* Huhhh? Then I'm dead? I am. I knew it. That girl was the end of me. I said it, I said she'd kill me some day. Oh, I'm too young to die.

Sad music plays as JAKE weeps loudly and kneels down to wipe his face against SANJAY's attire.

And look where they sent me. *(bewildered and almost disgusted)* This is heaven? You don't look like St. Peter.

SANJAY	Looks can be deceiving, but in this case, they are not. Ha ha ha ha. St. Peter I am not.
JAKE	*(asks MISHA)* And you're definitely not Gabriel?
MISHA	No, but speaking of Gabriel, she vill drop by later.
JAKE	Drop by? So I am dead? This *is* heaven? Ohhhh *man. (in Russian accent imitates MISHA)* Is no ringing. Is delayed shock. *(mutters)* Crazy Russian dude. Delayed shock?! I'm DEAD, man!
MISHA	Nyet, not dyead. Temporarily indisposed. *(MISHA and SANJAY look at each other in agreement and nod.)* Yes, indisposed.
JAKE	So what is this place?
SANJAY	Misha, tell the boy.
MISHA	Is called Impressionist Wing.
JAKE	What?
MISHA	Is enough information.
JAKE	But how did I get here?
SANJAY	You were hit by automobile.
JAKE	So I am dead, what's the matter with you?
MISHA	No, my friend, you are in coma.
JAKE	So are you in a coma too?
SANJAY	No, I'm afraid not.
JAKE	So who are you?
MISHA	Allow me to introduce myself. I am Dr. Misha Zlatanov Pametovich, colonel of the Russian army, psychiatrist and head of the Bureau of Paranormal Research, PhD in Parapsychology. Hyeadquarters, Moscow.
JAKE	*(nods)* Uh huh, and you are? *(pointing in the direction of SANJAY)*
MISHA	This is my good friend Dr. Sanjay Bengali, general supervisor of the Calcutta Institute of Advanced Science and Nuclear Engineering.
JAKE	*(a little impatient)* Nice, you lost me at the Moscow Bureau of something something, mister doctors.

Scene Two

The warrior ALEXANDER runs in. He is in full armour, wears sandals with thin leather straps, and his toenails are painted red. He falls, and his helmet falls off his head and rolls down the stage. He picks up his helmet.

ALEXANDER   Bucephalus!? Bucephalus, where are you?! *(He turns to the two explorers.)*

MISHA   Hyello Alexei. Nyet, I have not seen your horse today.

ALEXANDER   Sir, you will address me as Alexander the Great, conqueror of… *(He's cut off.)*

SANJAY   Calm down, Alexander.

> *ALEXANDER remains still, making only steaming noises and building up anger. SANJAY runs over to ALEXANDER.*

Shhh… Quiet. Listen… *(silence and then a loud noise)* That's the sound of the fourth wall breaking. Go… go… go on! *(He nudges him forward.)*

ALEXANDER   *(runs out into the audience in search of his horse)* Bucephalus?! Have you seen my horse Bucephalus? I can't seem to find him. *(ALEXANDER runs back onto the stage and exits.)*

MISHA   Have a nice day, Alexei.

JAKE   Jeez, what a nutcase. *(laughs at ALEXANDER's expense)* Wait a second, did you say Alexander *the* Great? As in *the* Alexander the Great?

MISHA   Vat do *you* think?

SANJAY   Congratulations. You have just met the greatest conqueror of the world.

MISHA   Apart from Genghis Khan. *(The explorers laugh hard.)*

SANJAY   Oh, you're bad. You're very bad. *(Again they laugh.)*

JAKE   I don't get it.

SANJAY   What's to get?

JAKE   You're telling me that's Alexander?

MISHA   Da.

> *JAKE shakes his head at SANJAY as if to ask: "What does that mean?"*

SANJAY	It means "yes" in Russian.

SHAKESPEARE enters, carrying a skull from Hamlet, *which he pets non-stop and is never comfortable with throughout the whole play; he is always changing its position, never quite knowing how to hold it.*

JAKE	Oh. And I guess this is Shakespeare, right?
SANJAY	Yes! How did you know?
JAKE	What?
SHAKESPEARE	*(theatrically)* To be or not to be, that is the question. *(smiles crazily and reveals to the audience)*
JAKE	You know, you're *pretty convincing (laughs)* but that Alexander actor was better *(mocking).*
SHAKESPEARE	*(Completely ignoring JAKE, again he poses the question theatrically.)* To be or not to be, that is the question.
MISHA	Villiam, that's been the question for over four hundred years.
SHAKESPEARE	Pish-posh. I just came up with this brilliant question this morning. Who are you, anyhow?
SANJAY	We are explorers, William.
SHAKESPEARE	And what, may I ask, are you exploring?
MISHA	Amongst other things, *you* my friyend.
SHAKESPEARE	Pish-posh. *(Theatrically. Each time he says "pish-posh," his spit reaches MISHA, SANJAY, and JAKE. They react to it, and it becomes a running gag.)* To be or not to be, that is the question.
JAKE	Hey buddy, can't you come up with something else? If you're gonna play Shakespeare, you might as well get into character. Come on, try something from ah… *Othello*, or one of the other plays.
SHAKESPEARE	*(confused)* What *place* is this Othello you speak of?
JAKE	No, it's not a *place*. It's a character, from one of your *plays*… if you *are* Shakespeare, that is.
SHAKESPEARE	Plays? What plays? Who are you? *(theatrically)* To be or not to be, that is the question. *(He leaves.)*

Scene Three

JAKE	Wow, this is some cuckoo house you got going here.
MISHA	Is no cuckoo house.

VERDI enters humming "Libiamo ne'lieti calici." He is followed by the six QUEENS, who are tied together with a rope and wearing white tutus. Each queen has her own quirk. Two of them have nail files, two have fans. One has a mirror and is always checking her makeup, and one is always playing with her hair. QUEEN ONE stops abruptly, causing them to start falling over each other as they begin to sing

(QUEENS sing. VERDI is their conductor. Song: "Libiamo ne'lieti calici." Duration: approximately forty seconds.)

Libiamo, libiamo ne'lieti calici
che la belleza infiora.
E la fuggevol, fuggevol ora s'inebrii
a voluttà.
Libiam ne'dolci fremiti
che suscita l'amore,
poiché quell'ochio al core onnipotente va.
Libiamo, amore, amor fra i calici
più caldi baci avrà.

JAKE	*(hysterical: laughing, crying)* Ha ha ha. Why hello...

VERDI has a long black coat, a white scarf, and a wooden stick he carries around, which he does not use as a cane. It has more of a slapstick function—to make sounds, to use for conducting, and to cue the QUEENS.

VERDI	*(in heavy Italian accent)* Hello there, young man.
QUEENS	Oh, *helloooo.*

They giggle. All of them keep laughing too long and VERDI signals them to stop with his stick. All of them except one stop laughing right away and change their expression to guilty/serious. QUEEN TWO continues laughing very loudly and snorts until VERDI stops her for a second time.

VERDI	Giuseppe Verdi at your service, but for you, Joe Green. *(He bows.)* Signor Misha, Signor Sanjay. Glad to see you. *(hums the tune of "Libiamo ne'lieti calici" in "la la la" form)*

JAKE	So now how come *this* guy knows who you are and Shakespeare doesn't?
MISHA	Signor Giuseppe is here by his own vill.
SANJAY	He is what you call an inter-dimensional entertainer.
JAKE	And is this his choir?
	JAKE points in the direction of the six QUEENS standing behind VERDI.
MISHA	Is his company.
	JOE SHMOE and his DARK SIDE enter, tied together. JOE cries out for Charlotte carrying a single red rose.
JOE	Charlotte?! Where is my Charlotte? *(asks JAKE)* Have you seen my Charlotte?
JAKE	*(sarcastically)* No, but I have seen Shakespeare, and the conqueror, and as you can see, the singing dude and his choir.
JOE	Charlotte?! *(turns to MISHA and SANJAY)* Oh good sirs, have you seen my Charlotte?
DARK SIDE	*Your* Charlotte?
MISHA	Sorry Joe, not today.
JOE	Oh Charlotte, my beautiful Charlotte!
DARK SIDE	Ugliest broad I've ever seen.
JOE	Why have you left me?
DARK SIDE	I would've left you sooner even if I was that ugly.
JAKE	You know if you're that torn up by it, you can have my fiancée. She left me this morning.
QUEENS	*(sadly)* Awww…
JAKE	And then I got hit by a car.
QUEENS	Oooooh. *(as if to say, "That must've hurt.")*
VERDI	Ah… *(as if to say, "Now I get it," or "That explains it.")*
JAKE	At least that's what this Russian dude tells me.
SANJAY	Oh come on. Joe, she left you a century ago.
MISHA	Vun hundred and tvelve earth years to be exact.
VERDI	Si si, la donna è mobile.
QUEENS	*(get really excited)* Haaah!!

They sing a few lines of VERDI's "La Donna è mobile" from the opera Rigoletto. *Duration: about ten seconds.*

La donna è mobile
Qual piuma al vento,
Muta d'accento—e di pensiero.

VERDI stops them after these lines.

SANJAY   Forget about her. She remarried, had children, grandchildren, and died fifty years ago.

JOE   *(angry)* What are you talking about? Yesterday! She left me yesterday. *(DARK SIDE howls.)* I don't need this. Charlotte?!

Scene Four

GABRIEL walks in with bargains for memories.

GABRIEL   Memories here! Get your memories. Unhappy with your memory? Nooo problem. Trade it in for a new one. On special today, two for one. Oh hey there, Jake, how you doing?

JAKE   Who are you? How do you know my name?

GABRIEL   Hayllo. *(points to her halo)* It's my job to know.

MISHA   Hi Gabriel.

GABRIEL   Oh hi Misha, Sanjay. Good to see you.

SANJAY   Any new developments in the Triangle?

JAKE   What triangle? *(JAKE is ignored.)*

GABRIEL   Naah, not since Shakepeare left.

JAKE   Left? He was just here. *(still ignored)*

MISHA   *(addresses GABRIEL)* So vat have you been up to lately?

GABRIEL   Just had coffee with the Big Guy.

SANJAY   *(all excited)* Here? In the Triangle?

GABRIEL   No, not here. Up there. *(points up)*

JAKE   *(impatient) What* triangle? Hellooo? Is anyone listening to me?

GABRIEL   So how are the wife and kids, Sanjay?

SANJAY   Oh she's complaining: *(imitates his wife)* "Sanjay, I need new house. Sanjay, I need new car. Sanjay, I do not have the arms of Vishnu.

Get me a new maid. Sanjay this, Sanjay that…" Uhht, woman, I'm not made of money! Get it yourself.

MISHA   I tyold you not to get married. "Be like me," I syaid, "the lone volf." But nyeeet. Sanjay vant family, Sanjay vant little Sanjays, and now look vat Sanjay got.

GABRIEL   *(breaks out in laughter)* Ha ha ha! Ohhhh beautiful earthly problems. How lucky you are! Isn't that right, Jake?

JAKE   *(extremely wound up)* All right, that's it. I want out of this mental hospital. *(Now he looks away from GABRIEL and the explorers in search of someone else.)* Shakespeare? Alexander? Where are you? Help me get outta here. Where's the exit?

GABRIEL   Jake, you really oughta relax.

A janitor comes in and shakes a box of Tic Tacs to offer it to JAKE. He says nothing.

Here, have a Tic Tac.

JAKE looks at the man offering a Tic Tac.

Oh, this is our inter-dimensional janitor.

MISHA   Oh hyello, old friend. How are you today?

The janitor says nothing, just nods with little emotion and leaves.

GABRIEL   Unfortunately he's a mute. But Jake, you really should enjoy your time in the Triangle. *(JAKE begins to say, "What triangle?" but GABRIEL knows this and stops him.)* Uh uh uh, now don't you say "What triangle?" because it's not important. Enjoy your visit. When it's the right time, Misha will explain it to you.

JAKE   And what *time* is it now?

GABRIEL   Temple of Gloom time.

Trumpet call. QUEENS say: "Ta ta da daaa!" each time there is a trumpet call for the Temple of Gloom.

Scene Five

SHAKESPEARE and JOE march in, led by ALEXANDER. VERDI and the QUEENS follow.

ALEXANDER   *(determined, in the voice of a commander)* I am the leader who has been chosen to speak for us and to negotiate on behalf of our cause.

SHAKESPEARE	Our cause be the hasty return of our memories.
ALEXANDER	Silence, William! *I* am the leader. *(turns back to GABRIEL)* Now, we have decided we want all our memories back.
VERDI	Si, all our-a memories.
GABRIEL	But Verdi, you have all your memories.
VERDI	Oh yes, yes of course. But as an entertainer, I try to belong. Come along ladies, we have to see this. *(QUEENS giggle.)*
QUEENS	Of course, Giuseppe. We're coming.
VERDI	Gabriel-*e*, iz-a okay with-a you if I come along, yes?
QUEENS	Oh yes, Gabriel, let us come. We'll be good. We promise.
GABRIEL	Why not?
ALEXANDER	Well?! Are you going to address my cause or must I be forced into battle?
GABRIEL	Oh always the same with you, Alexander. You never learn.
JOE	Well?
GABRIEL	All right, you want your memories back? Then you must travel to the Temple of Gloom.
ALEXANDER	To the temple!
	Two trumpet players enter from one side of the stage, holding their trumpets high up, and play "The Triumphal March" from VERDI's Aida.
	ALEXANDER turns with his sword to march out the wrong way. Everyone but the explorers and GABRIEL follow.
GABRIEL	Uh, Alexander?
ALEXANDER	Quiet, I am searching for the Temple of Gloom.
GABRIEL	It's that way. *(She points in the opposite direction.)*
ALEXANDER	Yes, of course. *(He turns and marches the other way.)* Follow me!
	Trumpet players (still on stage) again play "Triumphal March" from VERDI's Aida.
	SHAKESPEARE and JOE march out, following their leader. The trumpet players also march out.
VERDI	Ahh gentlemen, I will see you in the temple.
QUEEN ONE	See you later, Jake.

> QUEEN ONE winks and giggles. VERDI and the QUEENS begin
> to leave, when suddenly a man dressed in a red Zorro outfit rushes
> in from the same side from which VERDI was leaving. He gives
> VERDI a scare. VERDI screams. The QUEENS scream. MISHA
> pushes JAKE back as they are also scared. It's a ricochet effect.

DON JUAN   Ah! *(theatrically)*

> Everyone on stage reacts in shock, and GABRIEL, MISHA,
> SANJAY, and JAKE back out to make room for him. VERDI
> screams and falls backwards. The QUEENS scream also and
> move backwards. VERDI then gets up, checks the state of his
> heart and buttocks, and signals to the QUEENS to stop screaming
> because he's okay.

VERDI   Who are you? You almost gave me a heart attack.

DON JUAN   *(Heavy Spanish accent. He does fancy sword moves while making the swoosh sounds of the sword himself. He stops halfway, and does a martial arts pose.)* Excuse me, do you know where the Hart House *(replace "Hart House" with name of theatre)* washroom is? *(His sword points outward toward the audience. He pulls it back.)* What, this? No, I'm not going to hurt you. *(thrusts the sword forward)* No, I'm kidding, you're dead, hwah! *(fancy movements again)* I am Don Juan Manuel Fernandez Del Toro Escobar Taco Bell Rivero... *(Spanish music)* the two hundred and seventy-fifth best conquistador of all time. *(Spanish music)*

VERDI   Congratulations! *Eccellente!* Forgive me, but I am in a rush.

DON JUAN   No, I do not think you understand. I am here to challenge you.

VERDI   Challenge me? For what?

DON JUAN   For your ladies. *(QUEENS giggle.)*

VERDI   My queens?

DON JUAN   Si, your Queens. You see, I am chealous of your company. You have six queens, and I, a prisoner of love, have none. I ask, what decent man has six queens? Four or five maybe, but six is just too much. *(turns to QUEENS)* Ladies, I am here to offer my services. Who shall I save first?

> The QUEENS face away from audience and each quivers
> as DON JUAN approaches her, looks her up and down, and
> comments something like, "No, what is wrong with you?" and
> "Oooh, nice makeup but no," in a heavy accent. After going to
> each of them, he goes back to QUEEN FIVE.

Dona Katherina? *(He kneels before her and reveals to the audience. He reaches out to QUEEN FIVE.)*

QUEEN FIVE   Oh *(giggles)* not me, signor, I already lost my head.

QUEEN TWO   It's true, I did too.

VERDI   *(anger building)* Now wait a minute, these ladies are already spoken for. They are not my wives. They are my company, my choir. Who are you, Don Juan, in your tightey-whiteys and my grandmother's tablecloth, to say I am not decent?

DON JUAN   What, are you crazy or what? Signoritas, I seek one queen for my kingdom.

QUEENS ONE, TWO, & THREE
   (coquettish) And where is your kingdom? *(They squish together and QUEEN ONE lifts her foot up.)*

DON JUAN   It is, it is… *(searching for answer, reveals to the audience)* it is… lost in time. *(QUEEN ONE's foot goes down immediately.)*

VERDI   *(laughs, dismissive)* Ah, you have nothing to offer them!

DON JUAN   I say we let the ladies decide.

QUEEN ONE   *(slowly raises hand)* I like Giuseppe.

QUEEN TWO   Me too.

QUEEN THREE   Me three. And you ladies? *(referring to QUEENS FOUR, FIVE, and SIX)*

QUEENS FOUR, FIVE, & SIX
   We like Giuseppe.

DON JUAN   *(mimics them)* "We like Giuseppe." *(fake spit)* I spit on you!

QUEEN ONE   Can *you* sing?

DON JUAN   No, but I can dance the flamenco. *(He dances a few steps of the flamenco for four or five seconds while a guitarist plays alongside him.)* As well as the cha-cha-cha. *(does action with sword)*

QUEENS   But you can't sing.

VERDI   There you go. Ladies, let's go. *(They start to leave.)*

DON JUAN   No, wait!

Music: pianist plays the theme from Beethoven's Symphony No. 5. Duration: ten seconds. VERDI immediately gets upset because he's being upstaged.

VERDI	*(turns to musician)* Beethoven? I Giuseppe Verdi and you play Beethoven? *(says something angrily in Italian)*
DON JUAN	We shall meet again. You have not seen the last of Don Juan Manuel Fernandez Del Toro Escobar Taco Bell Rivero… the two hundred and seventy-fifth best conquistador of all time. *(Spanish music)* Hey, you, Mr. Adjudicatooor, *(then name of adjudicator or any authority figure like a teacher, principal, counsellor etc.)* you're next! Hwah!

> *He waves his sword around and makes whooshing sounds after the threat. DON JUAN leaves theatrically and falls as he leaves on the opposite side that VERDI left.*
>
> *GABRIEL, MISHA, SANJAY, and JAKE come downstage. GABRIEL comes in flapping her wings. Music.*

JAKE	Whoa?! What was that?
SANJAY	Oh, that? That was a disturbance in the force.
MISHA	A so-called dimensional rift.
JAKE	And the Temple of Gloom, what's that?
GABRIEL	It's a theatre for the arts, drama, and music, showcasing the world's worst productions.
JAKE	And is that in the part of the cuckoo house you call the Impressionist Wing?
MISHA	Is not cuckoo house. Is Zoominverse Triangle.
JAKE	Zoomy what?
SANJAY	Hrmm. *(clears throat loudly)* The Impressionist Wing is located in the Zoominverse Triangle. "Zoom-in-verse" because you *zoom* in on one memory which becomes one impression. That's why it's the Impressionist Wing, you understand?
JAKE	*(sarcastic)* Suuure, I get it.
MISHA	Really, do you? You see, Jacob, the Temple of Gloom is portal bitveen Zoominverse Triangle and the Smoothie.
JAKE	*(excited)* What's that about a smoothie?
SANJAY	Not *a* smoothie, *the* Smoothie.
MISHA	The Smoothie is everything that has or has not happened and will or will not happen.
JAKE	So what you're saying is that the Smoothie is our universe?
GABRIEL	No, our universe is called the Lobby.

MISHA	Vich is contained vithin the Smoothie.
JAKE	The Lobby? You mean to say that our universe is very small? *(shows "small" with hand)*
MISHA	Yes. Very small. *(He makes JAKE's hand even smaller. Then JAKE looks at it.)*
JAKE	And you know this how?
MISHA	Ve are vat you call inter-dimensional explorers.
JAKE	Oh, so you're an explorer?
MISHA	Yes.
JAKE	And you're a scientist?
MISHA	Yes.
JAKE	You're a crazy Russian scientist? *(mocks him)*
MISHA	Yes. No.
JAKE	You said yes.
MISHA	No. No, I did not.
JAKE	Yes, you did.
MISHA	*(makes a funny sound)* No. Be quiet, Jake. Do not ask such questions. They are beyond the scope of your measly understanding.
GABRIEL	Boys, come on, I don't have eternity to waste on your explanations.
SANJAY	*(irritated)* Of course you do. You *do* have eternity. What are you talking about? You live forever.
GABRIEL	I know, but I feel so human when I say that.
JAKE	Okay, so are we gonna go to the temple or what?
SANJAY	Yes, let us go.
GABRIEL	This way, boys!
QUEENS	*(from backstage)* Ta ta da daaaaa!

Change of lighting. Drums. GABRIEL, MISHA, SANJAY, and JAKE turn and are now in the Temple of Gloom.

Scene Six

> SHAKESPEARE, JOE, VERDI, and the QUEENS march on stage from the opposite side from which they went out, led by their leader, ALEXANDER. GABRIEL and the explorers are already in the temple.

ALEXANDER To the temple!

SHAKESPEARE, JOE, VERDI, & QUEENS
To the temple!

ALEXANDER *(addressing GABRIEL)* Well, what do we do now, tradesman?

GABRIEL Excuse me one moment

> *Claps hands. All freeze. Music plays to indicate wings flittering. Then music plays as GABRIEL transitions into a wizard. She turns around, puts on a wizard's hat and a mask with wizard glasses, and claps hands to unfreeze everyone. Then she clears her throat and speaks slowly and theatrically.*

> Hr hrmm. I am the keeper…

JAKE Of what?

MISHA Patience.

GABRIEL I am the keeper of… *(music)* the sacred memory box. You have entered the Temple of Gloom and I am the Wizard of *Glooooooom.*

SHAKESPEARE Forgive me, *mighty* wizard, but are you not also the Tradesman of the Wing of Impressionism?

GABRIEL Oh yes, that too. *(normal voice)* I'm a multi-tasker, *(goes high with body and high-pitched voice)* multi-tasker, *(goes low with body and low voice)* multi-tasker.

ALEXANDER All right, wizard, what is this memory box you speak of?

GABRIEL It's a box that contains all of your memories, the so-called key to the fountain of the past.

ALEXANDER And are you going to give us this box, or we have to fight for it?

GABRIEL No, *(knocks him back)* you must answer one question.

ALEXANDER That's it? Just a question? *(excitedly)* Well, on with it!

GABRIEL Not just a question but a question of a most trickular nature.

VERDI Oh Gabriel-*e*, just tell them the question already.

ALEXANDER	Yes, tell us.
GABRIEL	Very well then, Alexander, William, Joe. *(points to the six QUEENS)* Which of these six was the true love of the eighth?
ALL	What?
ALEXANDER	Sixth?
SHAKESPEARE	Eighth?
JOE	Who's the eighth?
GABRIEL	Well that's just it. You have to figure it out.
SHAKESPEARE	Pish-posh.
JOE	That's ridiculous.
DARK SIDE	You're ridiculous.
ALEXANDER	How do we figure it out if we have no memories?
GABRIEL	That's the trickular part.
JAKE	Whoa! Whoa! Stop everything. I'm confused.
	So to get their memories back, they have to use their knowledge of the past to answer Gabriel's question?
MISHA	Is correct.
JAKE	Sorry, *wizard.* Don't you think you're being a little mean to these guys?
ALEXANDER	Yes, I agree.
GABRIEL	What's the difference? They won't remember anything tomorrow. They have no ability to retain memories.
JAKE	Are you saying you play the same joke on them every day?
GABRIEL	Nooo, I have a new question each time they come to the temple.
JOE	Hey!
DARK SIDE	What's the idea?
SHAKESPEARE	Excuse me, mighty wizard. I've given a lot of thought to this question and have concluded… *(He pauses and everyone curiously leans in, awaiting his answer.)* I do not know the answer.
VERDI	Oh signore, let me be of some assistance.
QUEEN TWO	Oh please?
QUEENS FIVE & SIX	
	Please?

QUEENS ONE, THREE, & FOUR
Let us help.

GABRIEL   Very well then.

QUEENS   *Ohh. (They giggle.)*

QUEEN ONE   So kind of you.

GABRIEL   You can help them, Giuseppe, but if you do, and in the event that they answer correctly, I will grant them their memories only for today.

JOE   Just for one day? You mean it won't be permanent?

DARK SIDE   Like your brain damage.

GABRIEL   That is the penalty for cheating. If you want to talk about forever, you have to find the answer on your own.

VERDI   Well, gentlemen, it's-a your choice.

QUEENS   Your choice, gentlemen. Come on now, let Verdi help you. Put a little love in your heart.

> QUEENS ONE through FOUR start to sing "Put A Little Love in Your Heart."

> QUEEN FIVE starts off solo and then all QUEENS join in.

VERDI   *(stomps with stick)* One, two, three, four, hit it!

> Music: QUEENS now fully break out in song, very energetic, sung like gospel music. Option one: they sing short excerpts from "Put A Little Love in Your Heart," music and lyrics by Jackie DeShannon, Randy Myers, and Jimmy Holiday.

> Alternatively, the QUEENS can sing a different song with original music and lyrics. The song should be upbeat and happy with a theme of filling your heart with love and joy so as to allow the QUEENS to convince the gentlemen through song to let VERDI provide assistance. The song should last one to two minutes and the actors on stage must dance to it, as indicated below.

> Each queen has a different hat at this point while singing in gospel style and each still has her own item—a fan, nail file, or mirror. The rest of the characters break out in dance starting off with GABRIEL, who sprinkles ALEXANDER with dance powder to get him started. SHAKESPEARE dances with his skull, asking it to dance, and VERDI goes around poking people with his stick and getting them to dance. Finally, during the ending of the song, VERDI performs what looks like some magic ritual on JAKE to get the dance spirit out of him. This revival happens while the

> *QUEENS are ending the song by repeating whatever the end line is a few times.*

ALL   *(look at each other and then back to VERDI)* Go ahead, Verdi, help us.

Scene Seven

VERDI   All six of these ladies are queens of the same king.

ALEXANDER   Impossible!

SHAKESPEARE   Pish-posh.

JOE   How can that be?

DARK SIDE   Who cares?

QUEEN ONE   Don't ask me, I'm number one.

QUEEN SIX   Always rubbing it in, aren't you?

VERDI   Ladies, please.

QUEENS ONE & SIX
    Sorry, Giuseppe.

VERDI   Where was I? Oh yes, well, Henry VIII of England had six wives. Their fates were as follows: *(Each queen does her own actions to symbolize her fate.)* Divorced. Beheaded. Died. Divorced. Beheaded. Survived.

GABRIEL   Now think about it boys. Which of these six was the true love of the eighth?

ALL   *(murmuring while music plays)* Divorced... Beheaded. Died. Divorced. Beheaded... Survived.

ALEXANDER   Number six! His true love was number six, the survivor!

SHAKESPEARE   Noo, 'twas the second. The one he doth first beheaded. Ohh, what tragedy befell this tale of love.

JOE   Number three.

GABRIEL   What's that, Joe?

JOE   Well it can't be the ones he divorced or beheaded. *(Complete turn. Because they're tied back-to-back, whoever is speaking turns towards the audience.)*

DARK SIDE   Good thinking, Sherlock.

QUEENS ONE, TWO, FOUR, & FIVE
               (angry, with hands on hips) And why not?

JOE   *(DARK SIDE mimics him. We only see DARK SIDE's face.)*
               Sorry ladies, but that leaves number three, the one who died,
               and Alexander's choice: number six, the one who survived.

ALEXANDER   Ha ha! The survivor! *(thumps chest)*

JOE   But if number three died before he had a chance to divorce or
               kill her...

DARK SIDE   Yeees, continue.

QUEEN THREE   *(angry)* Oh!

JOE   Then it *must* be number three.

DARK SIDE   Number three!

QUEEN THREE   *(happy)* Mm hmm.

QUEEN ONE   Outrageous!

QUEEN SIX   Do you believe this shmuck?

QUEEN TWO   Absolutely not!

JOE   What can I do ladies, his true love is three. Am I right?

DARK SIDE   You're always wrong but in this case you might be right.

GABRIEL   You have chosen *wisely*, Joe Shmoe.

               GABRIEL claps her hands once in front of JOE.

               Memory music.

JOE   My memories! They're back!

DARK SIDE   Hallelujah! *(sarcastic)*

QUEENS   *(They sing "Hallelujah" from Handel's* Messiah *like an angel choir.
               Singing should last about eight seconds.)* Hallelujah, hallelujah,
               hallelujah, hallelujah, hallelujah.

GABRIEL   Remember now, because Verdi helped you this is temporary.
               It's only for one day. You'll lose them again tomorrow.

JOE   Oh no, what do I do?

DARK SIDE   Write 'em down, genius.

JOE   With what?

DARK SIDE   Ummm, a pencil?

SHAKESPEARE	Or a quill and some ink? *(takes out a white feather from his pocket)*
JOE	*(JOE runs out shouting for a pencil.)* Pencil?! Does anybody have a pencil?!
DARK SIDE	Not like that, fool. Let me show you how it's done: *(turns to the audience)* Give me a pencil! I demand you give us a pencil… *(As he runs off stage, he drops his rose and JAKE picks it up.)*
GABRIEL	*(shouting after JOE)* Good luck finding a pencil in the Temple of Gloom! Ha ha ha! Well that was fun, wasn't it boys?
ALEXANDER	*(in anger)* All right, now you listen to me, wizard, tradesman, whatever you call yourself. You give us back our memories right now!
GABRIEL	All right then. *(She takes off her wizard's hat.)* I'll offer you the same deal I offer you every day. Trade in your existing memory and you'll remember your life.
ALEXANDER	Give up Bucephalus?
GABRIEL	No, you don't have to give him up. If you agree to my deal, I'll not only give you back your other memories, I'll give you your memory of Bucephalus back as well.
SHAKESPEARE	And are we to believe you?
GABRIEL	That's the point.
ALEXANDER	What trickery!
SHAKESPEARE	Pish-posh!
GABRIEL	Would I lie?
MISHA & SANJAY	
	Yes!
ALEXANDER	You mean to tell me that all I have to do is give you my memory of Bucephalus and you'll give me back all of my other memories?
GABRIEL	Including the one of Bucephalus.
ALEXANDER	And I, Alexander the Great, am supposed to believe you?
GABRIEL	Hey hey, don't shoot the messenger.
SHAKESPEARE	Pish-posh! Trickery I sense.
GABRIEL	Well take a moment, think about it.

They make their decision immediately

SHAKESPEARE & ALEXANDER
(firmly, while looking at each other) I don't believe it.

MISHA	You're making a terrible mistake.
GABRIEL	And you'll make it again tomorrow.
SANJAY	You must have faith in this tradesman. It is the only way to break the vicious cycle of entrapment.
ALEXANDER	William, let's go! *(snaps his fingers)*
SHAKESPEARE	*(snaps fingers in reply)* Indeed.
QUEEN FIVE	Goodbye, boys! *(They call out.)*
MISHA	Dosvidanya *(pronounced "Dosveedanya")* gentlemen.
	ALEXANDER leads the way out. SHAKESPEARE and ALEXANDER exit the stage.

Scene Eight

VERDI	Well, that's my cue. Shall we, ladies?
QUEENS	*(giggle)* Of course, Giuseppe, we're coming.
	They begin to sing but VERDI stops them and bangs the ground with his stick to cue the pianist to play the music for them. The pianist wakes up abruptly and begins to play. VERDI smiles in approval.
VERDI	*(They sing on their way out.)* Libiamo, amore, amore fra i calici più caldi baci avrà.
QUEENS	I calici più caldi baci avrà. I calici più caldi baci avrà.
JAKE	Wait a second, where's Verdi and his choir going?
GABRIEL	Jake, you gotta understand something. Verdi stays here because he wants to. He can leave the Impressionist Wing whenever he wants. He *has* all his memories but you see, Joe here needs a little company.
JAKE	What do you mean *Joe*? What about Shakespeare and Alexander?
GABRIEL	Why would they need company? They left a long time ago. The Impressionist Wing was a passageway for them to another part of the Smoothie. You see, they let go of their memory a long time ago. The people you were talking to are only impressions of Shakespeare

and Alexander. You see in this world pictures are alive. *(They tilt their heads.)*

JAKE   Huh?

GABRIEL   Think of it this way. You know when you're walking in the sand and you leave footprints behind? *(JAKE nods.)* Well, William Shakespeare and Alexander the Great once walked through the Impressionist Wing. Only instead of footprints, they left impressions.

JAKE   So Shakespeare *was* stuck here?

GABRIEL   Was. Is. Tense has no meaning in this place.

JAKE   And he moved on…

GABRIEL   Recently.

JAKE   And how long…

GABRIEL   Time also has no meaning here. But take Alexander for instance. He focused so long on his memory of Bucephalus—

JAKE   His horse?

GABRIEL   Yes… that it left a lasting impression.

JAKE   Like a footprint.

                GABRIEL points as if to tell JAKE that he's missing something in his analysis. JAKE catches on.

                A 3-D footprint. A 3-D mould! Misha, I understand!

MISHA   Is about time.

SANJAY   I knew you could do it.

Scene Nine

                Drums. Music. Rumbling. The Temple of Gloom is shaking.

JAKE   Whoa! What was that?

                SANJAY falls backwards because of the shaking.

MISHA, GABRIEL, & JAKE
                (in slow motion) Whaaaaaaat's gooooiiiiing on?

                Slow motion ends.

GABRIEL	It's just a little remodelling. Nothing to worry about. *(loud rumbling sound)* Well that's faster than I expected. On the other hand, we should probably evacuate, right now.
JAKE	What do you mean? What's happening?
GABRIEL	Well this temple is kind of unstable at the moment.
MISHA	Do nyot panic, Jacob.
JAKE	Unstable?!
GABRIEL	The last of the pillars is falling. That pillar behind you is Joe's memory. The moment Joe lets go of his memory, that pillar will fall and the Temple of Gloom will collapse... temporarily, until another visitor comes along.

> *Rumbling.*

| SANJAY | *(after looking into the distance, listening to something, or someone)* Well, time for me to take Little Raj to soccer practice. Misha, see you tomorrow in the Impressionist Wing. Jake, until we meet again. *(He leaves.)* |

> *Pianist plays theme of Exodus in background. Any classical, dramatic music like a Chopin piece will do.*

JAKE	*(yells out to SANJAY, who does not respond)* Meet again? Where?
MISHA	Who knows? *(rumbling)* Vell, that's it for me.
JAKE	Where are you going?
MISHA	The laboratory calls. There is much vork to do. Ve shall meet again, Jacob. Dosvidanya. *(He leaves.)*

> *Three Dancers of Destruction come in and do a hip-hop dance to represent destruction.*

> *Piano is still playing the exit music. The janitor comes in and signals angrily with his hands for everyone to leave.*

| JAKE | *(yells out to MISHA)* Misha?! What do you mean *meet* again? You live in Russia for Pete's sake. |

> *MISHA does not respond as he leaves.*

| GABRIEL | Jake, I hate to tell you but we really gotta go. *(rumbling)* NOW! *(They leave.)* |

> *Loud drums play while they run offstage. The last pillar falls and the temple is destroyed. Quick lighting change.*

ANNOUNCEMENT
(said by the pianist in a woman's voice and a mocking tone)
Code Blue. Code Blue. Dr. Brown to Emergency, Dr. Broooown.

FEMALE NURSE (She brings in man in a wheelchair. This nurse is cute and very flirtatious. She likes JAKE a lot.) Oh you're awake! You've been asleep for quite a while. I'll get Dr. Bains to see you now.

A doctor who looks like GABRIEL comes out.

Oh. (startled by the doctor) There she is. (FEMALE NURSE looks back at JAKE as she leaves.)

DOCTOR Jake, nice to see you awake. How are you feeling?

JAKE Gabriel? Are we still in the Impressionist Wing?

DOCTOR Who's Gabriel?

JAKE Oh I'm not falling for that one again, wizard.

DOCTOR I see you still haven't fully recovered from your shock. We'll keep you here a few more days for observation. I should mention that you have had calls of concern: one from a Dr. Misha in Moscow, very respected in the medical world, and one from a Dr. Sanjay from the Calcutta Institute. Impressive, I must say.

JAKE looks bewildered. A jolly MALE NURSE in a purple nurse outfit and pigtails comes rushing in. The nurse has an Italian accent and looks and speaks exactly like VERDI. The same actor who plays VERDI should also play MALE NURSE.

MALE NURSE Doctor, doctor, it's time for his medication?

DOCTOR (now turns to JAKE) Jake, the nurse here is going to take care of you. I'll be back later to check up on you.

She leaves. The nurse starts humming "Libiamo ne'lieti calici."

JAKE Verdi?

MALE NURSE Me? No. I like very much but it's not me. I'm Nurse Bellissimo. Oh, you still a little bit funny from the car crash. Don't worry, I take good care of you. Oh! I know just what you need. (looks at clipboard) I'm a gonna give you some zenker amino phylic tetra zanthate. See, look at this big needle (takes out a giant needle). Oops! Oops! Oops! (With each oops, he squirts the audience with water from the needle. Searches pockets and around.) Oops, I forgot something, the rubbing alcohol. (As he starts to leave, the six nurses hum "Libiamo" from backstage.) Ahh look at this, here come my student nurses to help you, I be right back, Blakey, Flaky, (now remembers his name and pinches his cheek) Jakey!

As he leaves, the six student nurses who look exactly like the six QUEENS, only not tied together and wearing nurse outfits, check up on JAKE. When they get to his wheelchair, they don't hum anymore but start singing the actual words. Three of them come in carrying glasses filled with strange coloured liquids—e.g. bright orange, blue—which they start drinking and shoving down JAKE's throat as if it were his medicine. The other three check his heart rate, his temperature, massage his head, fluff his pillow, and such, the whole time singing "Libiamo." Length of song is approximately fifteen seconds. Then JAKE breaks free.

NURSES   *…Libiamo, libiamo ne'lieti calici*
che la bellezza infiora.
E la fuggevol, fuggevol ora s'inebrii
a voluttà

JAKE breaks free and stands up.

JAKE   This has got to end! *(QUEENS giggle.)* Now!

The lights go out quickly.

The end.

Giuseppe Verdi (Gaspare Bellissimo) accompanied by a choir of six queens in tutus (Melanie Costa, Monica Serodio, Alessia Lalomia, Stefania Macchiocchi-Lancia, Jessica Cuello-Gatica, Erica Parisi) and Don Juan (Tiago Abreu) compete for attention.

Photo by Marianne Yugo.

Leaving Hope

by BJ Castleman

In the Bypass Café, Matthew Lee (Jason Stroud) is threatened by his big brother, Deputy Roy (Phil Hatton), for mouthing off while Jamie (Andrew Cockburn) and Joyce (Devon Muhic) look on.

Photo by BJ Castleman.

Leaving Hope was first produced by the students of Cedarbrae Collegiate Institute Drama Collective, Scarborough, at the 2001 Toronto District Festival and at the Toronto Regional Showcase of the Sears Ontario Drama Festival at Hart House Theatre in Toronto, in the spring of 2001.

Joyce Dequasie
Jamie Phillips
Corrie Henderson
Matthew Lee Preston
Roy Preston

Devon Muhic
Andrew Cockburn
Carrie L. Neales
Jason Stroud
Phil Hatton

Directed by BJ Castleman
Assistant Direction by Shelly Meichenbaum
Infrastructure by Katie Martin
Stage Management by Mark Hastings and Megan Tate
Assistant Stage Management by Laura Hyde and Assumpta Uzaka
Props Management by Ashley Russel
Lighting by Simon Buchan and Danny Collins
Backstage Crew: Sweta Brahmbhatt, Sanjay Singh, and Michael Thompson

BJ CASTLEMAN

BJ Castleman has been involved in theatre since the first grade, when he played a daffodil who summoned all the second grade roses to dance. He has been a performer, director, producer, and teacher. The high point of his performing career was playing George in a Toronto production of *Who's Afraid of Virginia Woolf.* He has directed a variety of productions, from *Mary, Mary* for the Stardust Dinner Theatre to *Jesus Christ Superstar* for Broadway North and *Chess* for Applause*Applause. He is the retired Head of Drama and Film at Cedarbrae Collegiate Institute in Toronto. His play *Wilderness* was featured on TVOntario in the mid nineties. Another, *And think of me...* was filmed for Citytv. He has written over forty works for stage. He continues to be an active director and writer.

characters

JOYCE
JAMIE
CORRIE
MATT
ROY

Scene One: Jamie

It is Sunday morning at the Bypass Café and Bus Stop in Hope, Texas, in the early sixties. JOYCE, the waitress/manager, has been open for several hours, serving customers on their way to church and others departing on the infrequent bus that comes through the small town on its way to Amarillo. There is a short counter with three or four stools, a couple of booths, and a large window looking outside (upstage). The cash register is right in front of the entrance. There is a large schedule of Greyhound arrivals and departures. The place is empty. JOYCE is wiping down one of the booths.

Note: The accents are southwest US, not the heavy diphthongs of the Deep South, which might make the characters seem humorously sluggish. There is an easy clip in the speech, forcing words together, accounting for many of the speech patterns. Some indications of the dialect have been written into the script—pronunciation as well as vocabulary. These are by no means definitive. The aim is to keep it real, and less is always more on stage.

The phone rings. JOYCE goes behind the counter and answers.

JOYCE   Hope Bypass and Bus Depot... Oh hi, Mr. Montoya...

JAMIE Phillips enters. He carries a lumpy duffle of clothing and an empty cat cage. He is dressed in a sports coat, slacks, and a tie. He looks around for a moment then focuses his attention on the A & D chart on the wall.

JAMIE   I wanna get a ticket.

JOYCE   *(motioning him to hold on)* It's straight through to Denver: no transfers... 'cept Amarillo. 'Bout six or seven tonight... You're welcome, Mr. Montoya. Adios to you, too.

JAMIE takes out some money and waits impatiently. Something is obviously bothering him. He checks behind to see if he has been followed. He acts like a person who has left in such a hurry, he's not sure he's remembered everything.

Well, look at you. All dolled up in your Sunday-go-to-meeting duds? 'T's barely ten o'clock. What're you... oh yeah, this month's ad. Just put in the regular stuff about the Bypass. Like last month. I'll give Matthew a cheque for you later.

JAMIE   No, I want a ticket.

JOYCE   A ticket? Oh… Thought you wanted the ad for the *Herald*.

                 Getting the ticket and a cash box.

                 That'll be four twenty-three.

JAMIE   Not Amarillo. A ticket for Dallas. One way.

JOYCE   Dallas is more. Gotta look that one up.

JAMIE   Matthew Lee in yet?

JOYCE   Said he couldn't work today. Had to get LaWanda, but she won't be here till… Let's see… The five twenty-eight or the eight twenty-eight.

JAMIE   There one this mornin'?

JOYCE   'Leven twenty-eight. One way. Your folks *know* you're goin' to Dallas?

JAMIE   Any law you can't sell a bus ticket to a seventeen-year-old?

JOYCE   Not as long's you got twenty-three dollars…

JAMIE   And sixty-six cents. I got it. *(fishing coins from his pocket)*

                 What time's Matt supposed to be here?

JOYCE   Usually gets here 'bout 'leven forty-five. His shift starts at 'leven thirty but he barely gets here in time to throw on the patties before the holy rollers hit the doors. But if y're waitin' for him, y' won't make it. Bus leaves 't 'leven twenty-eight on the dot. Twenty-three sixty-six.

JAMIE   Yeah. Yeah. Sixty, sixty-five, sixty-six.

JOYCE   One-way Hope, Texas, to Dallas, Texas, comin' up. *(notices cage)* You takin' a pet? 'T's gonna cost you extra.

JAMIE   Uh, no. I was gonna leave 'im with a friend. But he's out roamin' somewhere. The cat… not the friend.

JOYCE   One-way to Dallas coming up. *(finding the envelope in the box)* Hey! Look at this. Your name's on it… and two tickets inside. So take your money. From the looks of your wallet, you'll need it.

JAMIE   How'd they get here?

JOYCE   Someone must've bought 'em yesterday.

JAMIE   *(distracted by the envelope)* Matth… what was he thinking.

                 Crosses to the window and checks in each direction.

                 Could I get a coffee?

JOYCE	*(pouring the coffee)* Twenty-five cents… *if* you can afford it. And I guess you can. That's twenty-three sixty-six refund.
JAMIE	What was he thinking?
JOYCE	*(putting the coffee near his bag)* Well, sit down. The bus ain't due for a while.

JAMIE is preoccupied. He spills the coffee.

JAMIE	*(sotto voce but strong)* Fuck!
JOYCE	What is the matter with you?
JAMIE	Nothin'!
JOYCE	That's one nothin' I don't wanna be in front of when it comes barrellin' down the freeway…
JAMIE	Let's just say it hasn't been a good day.
JOYCE	Let me guess. Your little disaster at the Harvest Moon Ball the other night.
JAMIE	News travels fast.
JOYCE	Only thing'at travels faster 'n news 'n these parts is bad news.
JAMIE	Two days 'n' the whole town knows.
JOYCE	Look, sugar, there's hardly an after-school or a weekend goes by there ain't pack of you kids in here chompin' down fries and guzzlin' Cokes. And most o' ya's got pretty big mouths.
JAMIE	Specially that Ginger Evans.
JOYCE	Her's is one of the biggest. Genetics, I reckon. Gets it from her mom. *(beat)* 'N' yesterday she was here all day. Holdin' court like she'd just made a breakthrough in medical research or somethin'.
JAMIE	Matthew Lee didn't say…
JOYCE	He left as soon as they got here. Good thing, too, 'cause by noon that Evans girl had let all the sordid details carefully "slip" out.
JAMIE	And she saw a lot of details.
JOYCE	The graphic portrayal of your particular transgression was especially colourful. In the washroom at the school?! Really, Jamie, not even I was that stupid.
JAMIE	Sometimes you get carried away; there's no time to think.
JOYCE	Granted, the removal of clothing while writhing on a bathroom floor don't require much thought.

JAMIE   And not thinkin' has major consequences.

JOYCE   Everthing has consequences.

JAMIE   I've never had no consequences as big as this.

JOYCE   *(beat)* So you're gonna make all the tongue-flappin' and jaw-waggin' go away by goin' away yourself. Take Joyce's advice: just wait. Next week there'll be another scandal 'n' everbody'll forget all about you.

JAMIE   I don't think so. Last night the principal came by the house and informed my folks I was gonna be transferred to another school. They went on and on like I wasn't in the room. 'N' I sat there. I just sat there sayin' zip! I thought that was the worst of it; then this morning the deacons came 'n' told my dad he couldn't preach today. They arranged for some replacement from over't Pampa to step in.

JOYCE   Because of you?

JAMIE   Bible says the sins of the fathers shall not be visited on the sons. Guess it don't say nothin' 'bout sins of the sons bein' visited on the fathers. He just sat there and took it. He looked so... humiliated. Then this morning at Bible class... Fuck! I'm gettin' outta these church clothes, Joyce. I'm gonna burn 'em.

JOYCE   Sorry, Jamie. I gotta get the potatoes mashed before those Baptists get here. They get pretty riled 'f their taters ain't just so.

             Exiting to kitchen, but turns.

             If ya take the four twenty-eight, you'll have plenty of time to settle things with Matthew.

             JOYCE exits to the kitchen. JAMIE starts to remove his Sunday clothes. He raises his voice to continue.

JAMIE   I was plannin' to go later... this evenin'. But Jack Bell and Leon Haney started in on me during the invocation this mornin'.

JOYCE   *(re-entering)* What happened this morning, sugar?

JAMIE   Before Sunday school everthing seemed normal... Then I noticed people weren't look at me quite the way they used to. Lots of whispers, y'know.

             JOYCE notices JAMIE is only in his underwear.

JOYCE   Jamie!

             He moves around behind a booth or table and begins to put on jeans, a shirt, and black Chucks.

JAMIE   'Snot like it's nothin' you never seen before.

JOYCE	Go in the back room… If any of those holier-than-thous see you droppin' yer drawers around here. Well, that's somethin' neither one of us needs. Oh, they won't say nothin'… not to yer face. They just stare. *And* whisper. Gives me the heebie-jeebies.
JAMIE	Like this mornin'. Now when they look at me, they're really lookin' at me, not that is-there-someone-standin'-behind-you kind of look I used to get. I'm like someone they know somethin' about.
JOYCE	That's the nature of sexual indiscretion, honey, makes you turn suddenly visible.
JAMIE	Just as I thought I was gettin' invisible again after that water tower thing. But when that visitin' preacher saw me, his hallelujah hackles set right up and vibrated, and I became the impromptu lesson of the mornin': a perfect example of the mark of Cain. The legacy of Sodom.
JOYCE	He actually said "legacy of Sodom."
JAMIE	All he needed was slides to make everything crystal clear.
JOYCE	What did you do?
JAMIE	All I could do was stare at my dad, sittin' there while someone else was doin' his job… with his eyes lookin'… like they wasn't focused on anything. Not even me. Then the evangelist went on 'bout the wickedness of rock 'n' roll and television. Don't know what that had to do with anything.
JOYCE	*(exiting to the back room)* That's those Southern Baptists. They had their way, we'd still be ridin' dinosaurs to work.
JAMIE	'F this one had his way, I'd be *under* one of those dinosaurs.
JOYCE	You oughta stay and face the music. You're too young to go runnin' away from home. Nobody does that anymore.

He sits on one of the bar stools to tie his sneakers.

| JAMIE | I won't be the first Phillips to hit the road, y'know? My uncle Bert left home at sixteen. A quarter in his pocket, the shoes on his feet, and a guitar slung on his back. Carried that guitar for years. Didn't play a lick. Well, one chord, one chord some zonked-out boozer taught him at a church social one Saturday night. One chord. That's all he started with. And that's all he ended with. Never learned to play. Told me once he hated that guitar. And when I asked him why he carried it around for so long, know what he said? |

Waits for a response.

Well, I'll tell you anyways, seein' as how you're so conversational and all. He said he could play that one chord real fine, perfect almost, and he never learned any more 'cause he'az afraid he'd never measure up to that first chord. Like a writer whose first novel's a big hit then fizz. He didn't want to go through life downhill. *(beat)* What I did, what we did, was not wrong. Nobody was hurt…

JOYCE   Then why not stay?

JAMIE   'Cause not everbody sees it the way I do. And they're all up in arms. I don't know why. Hell, we're just kids.

JOYCE   You are not, by any stretch of the imagination, just kids.

JAMIE   No, we knew what we were doin'.

JOYCE   So does everybody else in town thanks to that loudmouth Evans girl. But just because life is a little uncomfortable…

JAMIE   Understatement. Twice this morning at church, Jack Bell smashed me up against the wall. While his pal, Leon, was yellin' "'Scuse us," Jack was whisperin' "homo" in my ear.

JOYCE   So you're leavin'?

JAMIE   'Bout the size of it. 'F I don't, my dad'll have to move some place where they don't know about me, 'cause now he's a failure as a father. They already brought in somebody to take his place this morning. I'm sure there's some tryin' to make it permanent. I heard them talking last night, like they always do. I'm in bed—not sleepin' as usual. They're in the kitchen drinkin' coffee and talkin'… Mom loves it here. Caroline and little Robert's got so many friends.

JOYCE   So you're gonna vamoose with…? Who's the other ticket for?

JAMIE   I'm sure Ginger announced that one loud and clear.

JOYCE   I got an idea but the horse's mouth'd be more reliable?

JAMIE   It's not my place.

JOYCE   Playin' it cool, hunh?

JAMIE   I'll put these things in the trash out back. I wouldn't want you to get in trouble. *(stopping on his way out)* If you want, Joyce, you could refund our money and we…

JOYCE   We bein' you and…?

JAMIE   We could pay the driver. That way there wouldn't be any questions.

JOYCE   I can take care of myself, kid.

JAMIE	I'm sure ya can.

JOYCE watches him leave. She quickly takes out the small phone book and looks up a number. She picks up the phone and dials.

Scene Two: Corrie

She is listening to the rings when CORRIE enters. JOYCE puts the receiver back on its cradle. CORRIE is seventeen and tentative, not completely sure of herself, but sure of the role she has chosen in life. She is looking for someone.

CORRIE	Hi, Mrs. Dequasie.
JOYCE	Hi, sugar. Have a seat. There's plenty of room... Corrie, right? Sally Henderson's girl? Baptist service out already? I better get a move on.
CORRIE	Not for a while yet. Jamie Phillips here?
JOYCE	No suitcase, no duffle bag. Guess you come to say goodbye?
CORRIE	Then he *is* leavin'. For sure.
JOYCE	Seems pretty sure to me. Makes absolutely no sense. But I guess you young folks see things different.
CORRIE	Did he buy a ticket?
JOYCE	Actually he's got two. *(quickly)* Look, the smartest thing you could do is talk him out of it.
CORRIE	I don't know if I can. *(beat)* I don't know if I want to.
JOYCE	Runnin' away never did anybody any good. He's takin' some trash out. Coffee?
CORRIE	Could I have a Dr. Pepper?
JOYCE	A woman after my own heart. Here. *(refusing her money)* No, no. That's okay.

ROY Preston, the deputy sheriff, enters. He crosses to the counter and fishes for change.

ROY	Mornin', Joyce.
JOYCE	Mornin', Roy. How's business?
ROY	Like ever other Sunday mornin'.
JOYCE	Black. Right?

ROY	Corrie. Church out already 'r you playin' hookey?
CORRIE	No.
ROY	How's that pinch hitter they got preachin' over there this mornin'?
CORRIE	All right, I guess.
ROY	Guess Reverend Phillips's not too happy 'bout that. I told 'im ages ago, that son o' his had a leash way too long. He didn't listen. Par for the course. Now he knows. Guess him 'n' that brother o' mine're in...
JAMIE	*(entering)* I put those things inside an old paper bag, don't think... Corrie.
ROY	Well, if it ain't the little pervert in person. Corrie not bein' in church's one thing, but the preacher's kid. You goin' for a triple play, boy?
JAMIE	I'm not goin' for nothin'.
ROY	You two, the bus depot. I'd say that shows signs of eloping... 'cept I don't think it'd be with her.
JAMIE	Shut up, Roy.
ROY	What's the matter, sissy-boy? I hit a nerve?
JOYCE	*(interrupting)* That was black coffee, Roy? Black? You leave these two kids alone. They got enough trouble without you addin' y'r two cents.
ROY	Don't know how your daddy c'n hold his head up in front of all those people.
CORRIE	*(taking the focus off JAMIE)* You seen Matthew, Deputy Preston?
ROY	S'posed to be cleanin' out the garage. *(to JAMIE)* You watch yourself, kid. 'Cause I got my eye on you. I don't like your influence on my kid brother one bit. And I wouldn't put anything past you. I caught ya fer lettin' the air outta the patrol car and fer paintin' the water tower. I got my eye on you.
JOYCE	Don't you think you better get back out there 'n' keep those highways safe for the citizens of Hope?
ROY	*(to JAMIE)* Ever vigilant. That's what the sheriff says. Ever vigilant.
	ROY exits. JAMIE and CORRIE are relieved. JAMIE becomes a little awkward.
JOYCE	He don't even know what "vigilant" means, I bet. *(after a moment of awkwardness)* Well, those potatas aren't gonna mash themselves.

She exits. There is a long moment of silence. CORRIE just stares at her pop, not speaking.

CORRIE Jamie, you can't let somebody like Roy Preston run you outta town.

JAMIE That's the least o' what I gotta put up with. Ya can't talk me out of it. Like that drag race on the Farm-to-Market last summer. You were sure we'd be killed; come to think of it, I was sure we'd be killed. I wanted you to talk me out of that one, but this time... I've made up my mind.

CORRIE You are so pig-headed...

JAMIE I mailed you a letter on the way over. *(pause)* How'd you find me?

CORRIE When we went down to Sunday school, I saw Jack 'n' Leon trip you on the way to teen class. Then you disappeared during the sermon.

JAMIE Didn't feel very welcome.

CORRIE Guess not. After what that preacher from Pampa said.

JAMIE I can imagine what he's rantin' about right now. 'N' my family sittin' there. He's probly heatin' the deacons up for tar 'n' feathers.

CORRIE No.

JAMIE They're gonna fire my dad.

CORRIE They wouldn't do that.

JAMIE Corrie! 'Course they would. You think everybody's so pure 'n' honest 'n' goin' through life doin' the right thing like you. They'll get all heated up over this—all self-righteous, all puffed 'n' proud— 'n' the decons'll announce it's for the protection of their children. Who can fight against that. They'll fire him for sure.

CORRIE *(silence)* I went over to your house. Then down to the bandshell. Didn't know where else you'd be, so I went over to Matt's. His mom made him go to early Mass and come back to clean out the garage. I wanted to ask him lots o' things. I had a lot on my mind. I saw how you looked when the preacher said those awful things. I wanted to ask him— Matt—but he said I should talk to you. *(pause)* I was gonna ask you... *(pause)* I need to know. I was s'posed to sing a solo... with the choir this mornin'. Guess Mrs. Orr'll do it. She likes that song 'n' she's got a pretty good voice. Jamie, you gonna leave?

JAMIE nods.

Just go?

JAMIE This mornin'.

CORRIE	*(silence)* Matt knew that. I think. How'd he know that 'n' I didn't?
JAMIE	I talked to him yesterday.
CORRIE	You could've talked to me. Why are you doing this? So sudden?
JAMIE	You heard the minister. There's a time for plantin' and a time for castin' out demons. Well, I'm not hangin' around to be cast out.
CORRIE	That's preacher talk. It don't mean nothin'.
JAMIE	If it's not about you, it's nothin'. If you're the one with the demon, it *is* about you and everbody around you. They wouldn't let Dad preach this mornin'; my little brother got in such a bad fight at little league yesterday, the coach sent him home—a fight about me. The principal was over last night. I won't be in school tomorrow. I get the day off. While they transfer my papers to Panhandle.
CORRIE	That's miles. They can't do that.
JAMIE	If I'm a threat to the "well-being" of the school. Can't even go clear out my locker till Monday night. Tell ya, I'm not hangin' around.
CORRIE	It'll pass.
JAMIE	It's just starting. Remember what happened to that Tilson kid. Hubert. It's been two years and they still call him Vacuum Mouth. Jake threw his Levis up on the roof of the gym at the homecoming bonfire. Believe me: it's only the beginning.
CORRIE	Ginger Evans is a lying bitch. That's what I want you to tell me. Say that and I'll believe you. Say she made it all up. She's jealous and said she caught you with some other girl to get at me.
JAMIE	Some other girl?
CORRIE	*(not letting him get started)* She oughtn't make up stories like that about people just 'cause she's jealous.
JAMIE	Corrie... don't you know?
CORRIE	*(overriding again)* She's always shootin' off her mouth. Anything nasty about anybody. Most of what she says is stories she's heard her mother tell.
JAMIE	Most!
CORRIE	The rest is lies. Like this... 'cause I know you wouldn't...
JAMIE	Not like this.
CORRIE	Then you tell me. You go around tellin' everbody we're boyfriend 'n' girlfriend. You're supposed...
JAMIE	I don't say that. I didn't ever say that.

CORRIE	Well, I do 'n' you don't stop me. I'm not supposed to find these things out from Ginger Evans or Jennifer Toohey. You tell me. I haven't even seen you since you dragged me outta the dance. You didn't call yesterday. You always call Saturday afternoon. Why didn't you call yesterday, Jamie. I was expectin' to go to the drive-in. I waited all day. You didn't even call. Jennifer Toohey called. Beth-Ann called. Elaine and Victoria. Everbody I ever knew called. Then Ginger Evans called to apologize and tell me she considered it her civic duty to tell what she saw. What did she see, Jamie? You tell me.

JAMIE has moved away. CORRIE has followed and stands almost immediately in front of him.

JAMIE	If so many people called, you should know the truth by now.
CORRIE	I don't know anything. Nobody says anything... to me anyway. They're "so sorry." It's "so sad." Well right now it's so nothin'. What is it, Jamie? You tell me.
JAMIE	*(turning away)* Ginger wasn't lying. She caught us... *(He looks at his cup.)* in the washroom up on the second floor during the dance. She walked in. We weren't exactly dressed. The bitch must've stood there in the doorway five minutes before we heard her laugh. Fuck!
CORRIE	*(She begins hitting him on the back.)* Damn you, Jamie! Damn you! Damn you!

He turns and grabs her wrists.

How could you do this? How could you do this? All you had to do was tell me you were tired of me. It'd be hard but I could handle that. But all this talk 'n' I'm out in the cold. I don't know. It hurts, Jamie. It hurts.

CORRIE dissolves into tears. She continues to mumble as JAMIE helps her into a booth. JOYCE steps out of the back room.

JOYCE	Everything okay?
JAMIE	*(motioning her back)* Yeah. Fine.
JOYCE	If you need anything... uh...
JAMIE	No thanks.

JAMIE takes several napkins from the dispenser and offers them to CORRIE, whose face is still hidden. She pulls away from him. He sits for a moment and then slides out, standing awkwardly for another long moment.

JAMIE	'Ts nothin' I asked to happen. It just did. As big a surprise to me as anyone.

CORRIE	Was... was... that the first time? You were... unfaithful.
JAMIE	No.
CORRIE	But it was the dance. Our last Harvest Moon.
JAMIE	You want me to explain somethin' I don't understand myself. It *was* the dance, Harvest Moon Ball. All dressed up. The booze, the music. Just happened.
CORRIE	*(blowing her nose and preparing herself for the worst)* Who was it? *(silence)* Who was it? You could at least tell me that... so that I won't feel such a fool when I run into her in the hall. Who did Ginger Evans find you with, Jamie.
JAMIE	You don't know? You really don't have any idea?
CORRIE	Nobody'll tell me.

MATT enters and stands inside the door. CORRIE's back is to him. MATT is tall and attractive. He wears boots and a jean jacket; he is a Texas ranch kid. He has a large suitcase and a large soft bag that looks very full.

JAMIE	It was...

JAMIE stops when he sees MATT.

CORRIE	Who? Debbie Camp? I know for a fact she wouldn't hesitate if she had the chance. Or Lynda Pearson? Who did Ginger Evans catch you with at the dance? Who, Jamie?
MATT	It was me.
CORRIE	Matthew Lee? But Ginger said...

Scene Three: Matthew

MATT	It was me.

JAMIE nods as CORRIE looks at him. He does not look away from her.

It was program dance six. I signed her card earlier. She had me down for almost every program dance. So she came looking for me and found me... us. *(pause)* I told her I was drunk and didn't know what I was doing... *(pause)* but I wasn't drunk.

CORRIE looks to JAMIE for confirmation.

JAMIE	Neither of us was.
CORRIE	Oh my god! Oh my god! Oh my god! Oh my god!

She gets up and runs out the back door almost hitting JOYCE, who is entering. There is a moment of silence while all are fixed on the door where CORRIE left.

JOYCE	What's the matter with her?
JAMIE	She found out.
JOYCE	She didn't know 'bout you two?
MATT	You'd better go talk to her, Jamie.
JOYCE	You've done enough damage for today. I'll talk to 'er.

JOYCE exits. JAMIE and MATT stand for an awkward moment.

MATT	You get the tickets? I left two. I didn't want you leavin' without me.
JAMIE	We went through all that last night. I didn't think you were goin'.
MATT	I changed my mind.
JAMIE	Why? You're dad won't get fired. You don't have any little brothers or sisters that have to walk in the shadow of your reputation… a mother who's the recording secretary of the PTA. You've got the basketball team, the student council, the scholarship, college…
MATT	I've also got you, which I won't, if you leave without me. *(waits for reaction)* I thought you'd be happy when you saw the two tickets. *(pause)* Don't worry. It'll be great. Just the two of us. We'll get a place… an apartment or somethin'. My uncle Will, down at Fort Worth, has an apartment out near White Rock. Hey! Maybe we could stay with him for a while. It'll be a cinch. Two can live as cheap as one, ya know. We'll be roommates, livin' in the same house. No sneakin' off to my garage… 'r the boys' washroom. I thought about it all last night. When I said you should leave, I was only thinkin' of how much better it would be for you. I wasn't thinkin' how much worse it'd be for me. But if I go too…

He waits for JAMIE's assent.

JAMIE	What about the Kiwanis Citizenship Prize? That's a lot of money.
MATT	Doubt 'f they let me keep it now anyway.
JAMIE	No, no, no. You had it right last night. I been thinkin' about it, too. I'll ditch. I'll be blamed. They'll say hundreds of prayers for me at church… 'n' maybe they'll let my dad stay outta pity. You'll be the lamb that was led astray but found the path again. Everbody'll love ya.

MATT	Bullshit!
JAMIE	No shit! I'm serious. Things're are already pretty ugly.
MATT	Besides havin' ta change schools? What?
JAMIE	You didn't hear about church this mornin'.
MATT	Corrie told me. And Jake and Leon came by after Sunday school.
JAMIE	Came by?
MATT	Sometimes we throw the ball around.
JAMIE	They didn't call you names 'r anything?
MATT	No.
JAMIE	See? They broadside me in the basement of the church 'n' go over 'n' have Sunday tea 'n' cookies with you.
MATT	Why shouldn't they?
JAMIE	Exactly! Everbody knows what happened. Everbody knows it takes two to tango. But you, thanks to Ginger, have an alibi. You were drunk and I'm the "Tool of Satan." Why? 'Cause I'm the one with the reputation. The preacher's wild kid. Ditchin' class. Hauled in for paintin' the water tower, puttin' marbles in the sheriff's hubcaps. Always in trouble. 'N' you're the lamb led astray, could not possibly be you had any part in this. Just a drunk kid, gettin' his rocks off.
MATT	They're not gonna be that stupid.
JAMIE	What else? I haven't gotten anything but flack since program dance number six on Friday night. And you? It's like nothin' even happened.
MATT	I had to clean out the garage.
JAMIE	Oooo!
MATT	And I had to go to confession this morning.
JAMIE	And did you? *(beat)* Confess?
MATT	Couldn't help it. Father Scanlun already knew. I was gonna just do the usual self-abuse and swearing, but he knew...
JAMIE	Everything?
MATT	'Zactly what Ginger's told everbody. I didn't add any details. I didn't tell him about your birthmark, if that's what you're worried about. He told me to say some Hail Mary's and be careful about drinking too much.
JAMIE	There. Exactly what I was talking about. You're home free.

MATT	Don't say that. I'm here. I got my stuff. I bought the tickets. I even thought to get some cash. *(long pause, slowly)* So? Are we gonna do this?
JAMIE	I guess.
MATT	You and me, off into the sunset? Pretty big step.
JAMIE	Having sex in the unlocked washroom was a pretty big step.
MATT	As I recall, all I did was kiss you. You looked so great in your dinner jacket and that white rose. I wanted you to know you looked really... what's a little kiss between friends.
JAMIE	It went a lot further than a kiss.
MATT	Always does. *(beat)* Think, Jamie, it'll be incredible, you'll see. We'll be on our own, doin' whatever we like, when we like. You know? I never thought up there in Colorado that time, that first time... I never thought we... God, was I scared.
JAMIE	You're always scared. First in the pool, then first to yell "Shark!"
MATT	I'm not yellin' shark this time.

> Turns JAMIE to face him.

> We are going. Both of us. You won't have to head out all by yourself.

JAMIE	Matt...
MATT	We like the same things, get along well, don't we?
JAMIE	Yeah.
MATT	Then it's the logical thing to do.
JAMIE	Sure.
MATT	Lost in the big city. *(quickly adding)* Not the centre of attraction like "Hickville" Hope here. Nobody'll know anything about us.
JAMIE	That's the idea.
MATT	Nobody'll care what we do. I hope you can cook, 'cause I can't boil water.
JAMIE	I learned that in Scouts.
MATT	And to be honest and true and do a good deed every day.
JAMIE	Depends on what you mean by "good."

> MATT raises JAMIE's face and starts to kiss him. But...
> JAMIE is distracted by thoughts of CORRIE.

MATT	What's the matter? There's nobody here.

JAMIE	*(breaking away)* That was bad, Matt, what I did… what I did to her. Wouldn't blame 'er 'f she never spoke to me again. Think she's okay?
	MATT, to distract him and lighten the moment, picks up tags from the counter and gets JAMIE's bag.
MATT	Here. You should put a tag on your duffle.
	He looks around for another.
	Is this it? All you're bringin'?
JAMIE	Want my getaway to be clean and quick. You, on the other hand, probably have the kitchen sink.
MATT	Do not.
JAMIE	*(looking at the large bag)* That's almost as much as you took up to Colorado last spring.
MATT	Never know what you're gonna need.
	MATT is looking through his bag and pulls out…
JAMIE	Your blow dryer?
MATT	Course.
JAMIE	You're gonna have to lug that thing everwhere we go.
MATT	Just in case.
JAMIE	Isn't a weekend at Palo Duro, Matt. Or whitewater rafting for a day or two. We're leavin' and not comin' back…
MATT	That's why I brought the dryer.
JAMIE	I've seen what you look like in the mornin'. We'll call it "essential equipment."
MATT	You… are a rat!
JAMIE	And you're a weasel.
	Sudden thought.
	What'd your folks say?
MATT	They don't know. Do yours?
JAMIE	I wrote them a letter. Dropped it in the mailbox on the way over here. They'll probably get it Tuesday or Wednesday.
MATT	I didn't think.
JAMIE	You can't walk out without a word. They'll have the law on us— missing persons.

MATT	Joyce's got some paper around here somewhere.
	He gets paper from under the counter.
	What do I say?
JAMIE	You say goodbye.
MATT	Is that it?
JAMIE	There's not much more. You'll see 'em sometime. Say you'll phone when you get settled.
MATT	They're gonna wonder 'bout my graduation. What're we gonna do about that?
JAMIE	You haven't thought about this at all.
MATT	Yeah, sure… well…
JAMIE	You never do. You get an idea. Good ideas usually. Dream up some whitewater adventure, but you don't think about the details, about the rapids, about the bumps in the road. Well, those rapids are there. They're what it's all about. And the trip may seem romantic, but no one on that boat screamed louder 'n you.
MATT	You would, too, if you'd felt the boat flip out from under you. I was treadin' water; nothin' between me 'n' death but those two little ropes.
JAMIE	I'm the one had to pry your fingers off those ropes.
MATT	*(sees cage)* You bringin' Captain?
JAMIE	I was gonna leave him with Corrie, but… now? I couldn't find him anyways. He's out on the prowl somewhere or asleep in a warm cozy place. That's the life. But we'll be fine. Dallas. We'll get jobs…
MATT	You know? I lived in Hope all my life, Jamie. Born up at the hospital. Far's I been's Oklahoma. That time to Juarez with you 'n' Frank Harper. I was gonna go to Texas Tech next year… but that's not even far.
JAMIE	Then back to your dad's law firm.
MATT	Guess.
JAMIE	Road map already laid out start to finish.
MATT	Talk about scary.
JAMIE	Truth, Matt?
MATT	Always.

JAMIE	I wish I could stay… Both of us. I wish it'd never happened—not us. I mean I wish we'd never got caught. That was stupid. We could stay here in Hope. Finish school and all. You'd still have basketball practice. I'd be workin' on this week's editorial.
MATT	If wishes were horses…
JAMIE	But since I have to go, havin' you along'll be like takin' the place with me—part of it anyway. And you are good company… or would be if you'd improve your King's Gambit.
MATT	And you'd learn to shoot a basketball.

Scene Four: Corrie's Goodbye

CORRIE enters and stands just inside the door watching them.

JAMIE	I will. I make you that solemn promise. I will practise and practise till my knuckles are raw.
MATT	You don't use your knuckles.
JAMIE	I'll practise with whatever part of the anatomy you want me…

CORRIE goes to the booth for her purse and sweater. MATT notices her and JAMIE, taking the cue from him, turns.

Corrie.

Silence.

MATT	Corrie.

Slipping the sweater over her shoulders.

You okay?

CORRIE starts for the door.

JAMIE	You just gonna walk out?
MATT	Corrie?
CORRIE	That's what you're doin'. The two of you.
JAMIE	Nothin' to say?
CORRIE	*(stops)* No, Jamie, I don't have anything to say. I might have had, if I'd known anything, if you two hadn't kept me in the dark right up to the last moment. *(collects herself)* Mostly I don't understand it. You two. So I don't know what to say. Because to have something

to say, you have to have something to think. And when I think about the two of you... together—what the two of you did—then the only thing that comes to mind is what I've always been told to think. What everybody around here's always been told to think. That you're sick. Both of you are sick people. That's what I would think, should think.

How'd you even think of something like that? One old lady at church this morning said the umbilical must've got wrapped around your neck and starved your brain of oxygen. And worse.

But I know you to be decent 'n' everbody says you're not. I know you're kind 'n' people say you're the devil's tool. I thought you was honest with me 'n' folks say you... Everybody's so riled up. When I look at it, when Corrie Lynn Henderson takes a close look at you two, it hurts like hell, Jamie. But on the other hand it seems so... so... I don't know... so nothin'. So if I gotta say somethin', it's gonna be really hard 'cause nothin' makes sense.

JAMIE	Sorry I didn't say anything. I should've.
MATT	We both should've...
JAMIE	Matt, could I talk to her?
MATT	Sure. Joyce, you help me with this letter, 'n' I'll help you get ready for the Baptists. Deal?

He joins JOYCE in the kitchen. From time to time we can see them through the pass window. CORRIE and JAMIE are alone on stage.

CORRIE	Hubert Tilson's a little slow, Jamie. He does those things 'cause he don't know any better.
JAMIE	And look how they treat him. Me? Already it's no Texas Tech. Mom's already filled out the papers; they're sendin' me off to Abilene Christian. Otherwise known as Alcatraz.
CORRIE	So you decided to run.
JAMIE	Matt said it would be... easier.
CORRIE	Yeah, it probably would be. *(jumps to what she wants to know)* Was it all just talk? Everthing. You... me. All window dressing?
JAMIE	I didn't intentionally try to keep anything from you. It just happened. We've been friends for so long...
CORRIE	Did you mean any of it? With me?
JAMIE	At first I did. In the beginning. I meant to mean it. I wanted to mean it. And as things got more intense... I had no idea anything

was gonna happen with Matt. We were a couple, you and me…
Normal, I thought. Then Matt and I took that trip to Colorado,
things happened I didn't expect to happen. Suddenly the dam
broke open 'n' all this stuff I never let myself even think about
came floodin' out. I didn't know how to tell you. Tellin' anybody
was absolutely out of the question.

CORRIE   And I was convenient… so they wouldn't treat you like Hubert
           Tilson or put you in jail. A convenient disguise.

JAMIE   It wasn't because I didn't want to go out with you. Do things.
           It was good. I like being with you.

CORRIE   I thought I was so lucky to have someone that wasn't putting
           pressure. I'd hear how the other girls' boyfriends were always after
           'em. I thought it was because you were a preacher's kid.

JAMIE   Have I ruined it all? Is there anything we could…

CORRIE   Half of the fun of us together was lookin' at the prospect of more
           'n' more 'n' better 'n' better as time goes by. That's what love is…
           havin' 'n' knowin' it'll last, knowin' it'll grow… Knowin' they're
           there with you 'cause they want to be. Knowin' there's someone
           special waitin' to see you, to talk to you, to put his arms around…

           *In the kitchen, MATT laughs. CORRIE notices JAMIE's focus
           has long ago moved to MATT.*

           But I don't have that anymore, do I? Your future's somewhere else,
           isn't it?

JAMIE   I kept lookin' for the right time to say somethin'. There never
           seemed to be one, but now… This… everbody knowin', everthing
           out in the open. It's right, not easy, but right. Something I gotta
           do… for myself?

CORRIE   And for Matthew? *(beat)* You sure 'bout this, Jamie?

JAMIE   There's no future, no hope… nothing left here.

CORRIE   Not even… *(stops herself)* Be happy, Jamie. Both of you. I mean it.
           I understand him. More than I understand you. If you're lookin'
           from my viewpoint.

JAMIE   You be happy, too.

           She kisses him, backs away, then looks at kitchen.

CORRIE   Say goodbye to Matthew.

           *She turns and walks toward the door. Outside she passes the
           window and without looking back, holds her hand up in a
           final goodbye.*

Scene Five: Leaving Hope

> *JAMIE is a bit overcome and sits quietly for a moment. MATT enters, taking off a soiled bib apron. He has the unfinished letter in his hand.*

MATT   Is she gone?

JAMIE   Yeah.

MATT   I didn't get to say goodbye. C'mon, Jamie. You're the writer; you gotta help me with these. The bus'll be here any minute and I only got this one done. Here. You write the one to Coach Willard. I'll get the Kiwanis.

JAMIE   Your farewell letters shouldn't be in somebody else's handwriting. Specially mine. 'Nless I wanna end up on the post office wall with a price on my head.

MATT   They'd never. I said in my letter it was my idea, not yours. And old Mrs. Tweed, I oughta let her know I can't do her lawn this summer. And the Cogdales. *(short pause as he writes)* Where we gonna stay, Jamie?

JAMIE   We can stay at the Y, only a couple a dollars a night. You're not tellin' 'em that?

MATT   I brought a towel… and some soap. *(beat)* But I didn't bring any for you.

JAMIE   I'll be fine.

MATT   I shoulda brought more underwear and socks. Don't know when we'll get to do laundry and I hate dirty socks. And an iron. I took mom's travellin' one that folds up.

JAMIE   Is there anything you didn't bring?

MATT   Maybe lots of things. I don't know where we're goin'. I don't know what they're gonna have or not have.

JAMIE   Enough, Matthew. You brought enough. Look at this: my journals, a spare pair of jeans, a couple of shirts, and some underwear. What else do I need. I'm leavin' it all behind. All of it. Everything. And it's not easy. It's not easy walkin' away. I never did that in my life. I don't always start things, but I usually finish 'em. 'N' last night I just sat there while my mom filled out those applications for Abilene Christian. You think I want that? I'm gettin' out and leavin' it all behind.

MATT	I'm worried. That's all.
JAMIE	You're always worried, Matt. On the whitewater trip... which was your idea, you worried. Paintin' "Seniors '61" on the water tower was you're idea. You panicked. You're the one decided we should light bales on the road Halloween. You spent the whole night waitin' for the cops to arrest us. You worry. That's what you do. You want everthing to turn out right, so you worry. Maybe this time...
MATT	I need to know exactly what I'm in for.
JAMIE	For god's sake, Matthew. If you don't want to go, you don't have to. I never said you did. Just because leavin' town was your idea doesn't mean you have to leave, too. I'd like it, sure. I'd like it a lot, but I can't give you a road map of the next five years or a list of every goddamned thing you're gonna need. I'm not your mother!

ROY enters.

ROY	Well, if it ain't the two weirdos.
MATT	Can it, Roy.
ROY	Look, ya little J.D., I ran into our mother down at the A&P. She said you were supposed to be cleanin' the garage, but I swung by 'n' guess what? The little fairy had flown the coop. So I put two and two together...
JOYCE	*(peeking out then entering)* Coffee, Roy? Doughnut?
ROY	So you get yourself back to that garage.
MATT	'N' what if I say, "Go shove your head up your..."
ROY	Hey! You're lucky I don't cite you both for violatin' section four hundred twenty-six of the state penal code.
MATT	You gotta have proof for that, Roy. 'N' all you got's a pack of gossip.
JOYCE	Your coffee.
ROY	Some day that mouth's gonna get you in big trouble, Matt.

ROY exits.

MATT	Sorry, Jamie.
JOYCE	Don't know why folks have to be like that. But this town's got more 'n its share.
MATT	Don't matter. We're out of here.
JOYCE	Then you'd better get a move on. That Greyhound'll be here any second. *(taking out a couple of boxes from under the counter)* I gotta

put the parcel post out. There any in the back wouldn't fit under the counter?

She exits.

MATT	I know what you're tryin' to do.
JAMIE	What's that?
MATT	You're tryin' to make me stay. To make me mad at ya so I'll tell ya to fuck off. I'm not lettin' you leave me. Things're not gonna be so great for me around here either. Know what Ginger Evans told Jack? She said she didn't know why I had to go to you to get my rocks off. That's what I gotta face. Maybe they will blame it all on you, but that don't mean they aren't gonna look at me funny when I walk down the halls. There'll be doubts.
JAMIE	That's all they'll be… doubts. If I leave, it gives 'em an easy way out. 'N' people always want the easy way out.
MATT	Like you?
JAMIE	Look, you're mother's already worried 'bout you. And your dad, too, probly. You're their baby. My family wants to ship me south.
MATT	I gotta mail that letter… or I could phone. She's worried about me?
JAMIE	'Course she is.

JAMIE turns and takes a moment walking away from him. He faces the audience.

She'll be even more worried after we go. So…

Long pause. This is not easy for JAMIE to say.

Go talk to her.

MATT	What?
JAMIE	*(turns, emphasizing)* Go talk to her.
MATT	There's no time.
JAMIE	There's all the time in the world.
MATT	All right, let's go talk to her.
JAMIE	No, Matthew. You. You go talk to her. I got places to go.
MATT	But…
JAMIE	I know you wanna come, too, Matt. 'N' it wouldn't be bad for me. I know that. I'd give anything… But… There are times when the circumstances are against you. When you got somethin' to do 'n'

it's *not* your choice. We get pushed to a point where we can't choose between what we want 'n' what we don't want. There is no choice.

MATT   It was my idea...

JAMIE   For me to go.

MATT   Without me?

JAMIE   It's gotta be.

MATT   I haveta stay? I don't know 'f I can. They'll say terrible things about you.

JAMIE   Maybe. Probably. But I'll be somewhere else. Ridin' other rapids 'n' gettin' in more trouble 'n you can imagine. *(getting the cage)* Here. Find Captain. Take care of him. I'll sleep a lot easier.

MATT   Captain?

JAMIE   My brother 'n' sister don't care about him. I always looked after him. And he likes you. Okay?

MATT   Of course. *(beat)* I wasn't ready... I'm not ready for this.

JAMIE   What was between us is nobody else's business, Matthew. Whatever they say. Whatever they think. What was between us was between us.

MATT   Is.

JAMIE   Is.

JOYCE walks through quickly with some parcels and grabs those she left on the counter.

JOYCE   Oh, would you two just kiss before all those Baptists come rushin' in here and ride you out of town on a rail.

She goes out the front door and off.

JAMIE   I can't stay.

MATT   I oughta be goin', too.

JAMIE   When you wake up tomorrow, it'll all make perfect sense.

MATT   When will you be back?

JAMIE   I... I don't know.

MATT   Jamie...

The sound of the bus's air brakes fills the stage. JOYCE sticks her head back in.

JOYCE   Come on. Get a move on if you're going.

JAMIE   I gotta go.

MATT   *(handing him his bag)* I know. You don't wanna miss that bus.

> *They clasp each other—a brief but very intense moment. JAMIE goes. But he stops at the door and comes back. They kiss a big, warm kiss. JAMIE turns quickly and grabbing his bag at the door hurries off. We see JOYCE outside. MATT stands with his back to the audience. There is the sound of the bus departing. Silence. JOYCE watches. CORRIE is seen across the street. There is the sound of a sniffle from MATT. He wipes his nose on his sleeve and picks up the cat cage and hugs it close as the lights fade.*
>
> *Curtain.*

Matt (Jason Stroud) tries to reassure Jamie (Andrew Cockburn)
that everything will work out in the long run.

Photo by BJ Castleman.

PIe IN THe SKY

By Livia Berius

Pie in the Sky cast from left to right: Morgan MacDougall-Milne, Madeleine Cohen.
Photo by Livia Berius.

Pie in the Sky was first produced by the students of Northern Secondary School, Toronto, at the 2002 Toronto District Festival of the Sears Ontario Drama Festival and subsequently at the Toronto Regional Festival at Hart House Theatre in April 2002. The production received four awards of excellence: one for student playwright Livia Berius, one for student director Morgan Norwich, and two for performers Madeleine Cohen and Morgan MacDougall-Milne.

Marilyn	Madeleine Cohen
Rita	Morgan MacDougall-Milne
Voice of Evelyn	Stephanie Atkins
Voice of Marguerite	Katie Zulak

Directed by Morgan Norwich
Stage Management by Katelin Cook
Produced by Chloe Wolman
Staff Advisor: Victoria Dawe
Set Construction by Adam Lennox
Sound Operation by Andre Gordon
Technical Crew: Aaron Feldman, Sara Jane LaRocque, James Macdonald

Livia Berius

Livia Berius loved to write from a very young age. *Pie in the Sky* was her first play, written when she was a drama student at Northern Secondary School. After graduating from high school, Livia was accepted into the prestigious playwriting program at the National Theatre School of Canada, which she graduated from in 2005. Her play *Blue Heron* was produced as part of the school's New Words Festival in 2005. Livia continues to pursue the arts. She is a member of Pink Jellybean Productions, an all-female theatre company. Her play *A Girl Named Graceland* was produced by the company at the SummerWorks Theatre Festival in Toronto in 2004, and toured to Winnipeg for Femfest in 2006. Livia is also a member of the Maboroshi Orchestra, a shadow-puppet company. The company has toured productions and puppet-building workshops across Toronto and to Labrador for the 2007 Labrador Creative Arts Festival. Livia is excited to introduce *Pie in the Sky* to a new generation of young theatre artists.

characters

MARILYN
RITA
EVELYN
MARGUERITE

Scene One

Time: August in Toronto during the mid-1950s.

Scene: The exterior of one of those semi-detached affairs on Annette Street in west-end Toronto. Both homes have a single door and a large front-room window. A porch embraces the two residences, uniting them together. Originally, the two abodes were identical. However, over the years, the semis have been restyled to suit the individual tastes and lifestyles of their owners.

One half of the house is somewhat shabby in appearance. The paint has peeled in places to reveal the brick beneath, and the drainpipe is rusting. There is an unkempt appeal to the home. Undergarments blow in the breeze from a clothesline. Dandelions wilt in an old jam jar on top of a slightly askew welcome mat. The front-room window looks in onto a bright kitchen. A table with chairs and a Frigidaire are in view. This is the home of EVELYN Marysh and her daughter, MARILYN.

The other half of the semi contrasts heavily with its neighbour. Although in ship-shape condition, this home is stuffy and uninviting. The siding has been carefully painted. Flowers, of a shade that match perfectly with the colour of the home, line up at military attention in the window box. Sheer curtains hang over the window, obstructing our view of the living room. Inside there is a small television, a rug, and an armchair. A picture of the holy family hangs on the back wall. This is the home of MARGUERITE Lavoie and her visiting granddaughter, RITA Dennis.

From the door of each house, steps spill onto the front lawns. The Marysh yard is cluttered with curiosities. Hula hoops lie in the grass. A chaise longue style lawn chair relaxes in the middle of the yard amidst movie magazines, candy wrappers, and a portable radio. Save for the carefully mowed lawn, the Lavoie yard is empty.

At rise, MARILYN rushes out of her house. MARILYN Marysh is a colourful and spirited ten-year-old who envisions herself as a mature young woman, not a little girl. The clothing she sports obviously come primarily from her mother's stylish wardrobe. MARILYN also wears lipstick, imperfectly applied to her lips. She slams the door behind her as she beelines for the mailbox.

EVELYN   *(from interior)* Mar-i-lyn! Don't slam that door!

MARILYN   Sorry, Evelyn!

MARILYN reaches into the mailbox and pulls out a stack of envelopes. She hastily reads the address on each, letting bills drop at her feet and tossing away advertisements like Frisbees. She finally comes to a large brown envelope.

(reading) Miss Marilyn Marysh, Twelve Annette Street, Toronto, Ontario from… New York City… It came! I can't believe it came! He wrote back! *(She opens the envelope, pulls out a sheet of paper, and reads—stumbling over words.)* Dear Miss Marysh. Thank you for your k-kind letter. I am very lucky to have such won-wonderful fans like you. En-closed is an auto-auto-autographed! photo of myself. Love, *Love!* Your friend, *friend!* Paul Anka. *(She reaches into the envelope, pulling out a glossy eight-by-ten photo. She kisses the image, then exits through door, waving the photo triumphantly.)* Evelyn! Look what came in the mail!

The window at the Lavoie house starts to flicker and glow with light from the television set. The sound of channels being changed. RITA's shadow can be seen watching.

Pause.

(re-entering) Okaaaay…! Sheesh! Some people just don't appreciate sensational news. *(She mutters as she collects mail that has been thrown on the porch and lawn.)*

MARGUERITE   *(from interior)* Rita, tu deviendras aveugle à regarder autant de télé! You will go *blind* from watching so much of that television, ah…? Il fait beau aujourd'hui. Va prendre de l'air. Take some fresh air. Oh, ma chérie? Give me service please to take those *bouteilles vides* by the door *avec toi!*

Television off.

RITA begrudgingly exits the house. RITA Dennis is a nervous and quiet ten-year-old girl. She would be much more at ease watching television than interacting with real people. RITA wears simple play clothes, and her hair is slightly dishevelled. She appears on stage holding milk bottles in her hands, and carrying a cardboard shoebox tied with string under one arm. Pause.

MARILYN, in the midst of gathering mail, looks up to notice RITA, who is inconspicuously lining up milk bottles on her stoop.

MARILYN   Hi… gee, you must be Rita from Winnipeg, right? Evelyn told me you were moving in next door with your grandma.

RITA nervously glances at MARILYN, then away. MARILYN skips over to RITA.

Do you know French?

RITA nods slightly without looking up.

Oh wow! French is like the language of love. I'm learning it in school. But all I know is words like purple, cheese, and hotdog. That one's easy—*le hotdog*. It's the same in English. I don't know how to say anything romantic yet. Maybe you can teach me! Evelyn told me you're—what's the word? Like you speak English *and* French? Bilingual! *Bi-ling-u-al*. Wow. That sounds sooo romantic.

RITA looks up.

What's in the box?

RITA hides the box in her skirt, and looks at the ground.

Hey, that's okay… Oh, gee whiz! Where are my manners? I guess I should introduce myself. I'm Maude Marysh and I'm ten-*and-a-half* years old. *(offers her hand)*

RITA allows herself to shake MARILYN's hand, but then quickly pulls away.

(persisting friendliness) But *puh-lease* call me Marilyn. Only teachers and square kids call me Maude. See, I was named after my grandmother on my father's side whose last dying wish was to have a grandchild named after her. Can you imagine calling your child *Maude*? Evelyn says she almost choked on her mahi-mahi at Bill's Polynesian Palace when Daddy finally got up the nerve to ask her, but she just couldn't say no. I on the other hand, knowing the years of embarrassment which lay ahead of me at the expense of being called *Maude*, started to kick inside Evelyn's belly: No! No! No! Evelyn says she just thought the fish was bad.

RITA is somewhat intimidated, but continues to listen.

See, the thing of it is, I plan to move to Hollywood when I turn sixteen and an old-fashioned name like *Maude* just isn't going to make me a big rich film star. How many glamorous people do you know named Maude?

RITA looks at MARILYN blankly.

None, right? Absolutely! When I was six, I changed my name to Marilyn after my true idol and hero—Marilyn Monroe. Isn't she a dream? Now *you* are lucky. Rita is a simply sensational name… like Rita Hayworth! Say, have you seen any of her pictures? You should. They are simply di-vine! Anyways, I know you're thinking it's simply hateful of me to go against my croaked grandmother's wish… but after Daddy-O went out for a pack of cigarettes and never came back, I feel that I'm no longer obligated to keep his mother's lacy old name. That's fair, isn't it? I think so.

RITA stares at MARILYN in awe, clutching her box tighter.

You know… it's funny that we're only meeting *today* when you moved in a week ago Monday. I must apologize that Evelyn and I haven't been over to welcome you to the neighbourhood. We meant to bake you some cookies, but we're simply all thumbs in the kitchen… Hey! Why don't you come over now? Evelyn will fix us some milk and *store-bought* chocolate-chip cookies.

MARILYN begins to move toward the Marysh residence. RITA takes a few steps toward her in curiosity.

(building excitement) We can drink our milk out of wine glasses in the dining room like high-class ladies! Then we can stick our heads in the Frigidaire before Evelyn starts caterwaulin' about Freon.

Nervous, RITA slowly starts to retreat.

(running up the steps, expecting RITA to follow) I'm so glad you're here, Rita. It's gonna be great having a friend just next door, don't you think so… Rita?

MARGUERITE   *(from interior)* Ri-ta! Le déjeûner est prêt! The lunch, Rita!

RITA looks at MARILYN and then runs into the house.

MARILYN watches RITA exit. Disappointed, she enters her house with the mail.

Scene Two

The television flickers inside the Lavoie home. RITA can be seen watching. Television noise fades out as music comes in on MARILYN's radio.

MARILYN exits the house wearing a cute swimsuit, lipstick, red and green 3-D glasses, and high heels that are much too big for her. She is holding a fan in one hand and her portable radio in the other. MARILYN makes her entrance with a large flourish, like a star in front of millions of adoring fans. She blows kisses, signs autographs, mouths thanks, and winks to her imaginary entourage as she dramatically descends the stairs like a red carpet.

She reaches her destination on the lawn and pretends to take a microphone.

RITA hears movement next door and parts the curtains. She watches MARILYN's antics with intrigue.

Music fades out.

MARILYN   Thank you. Thank you. You're too much, really. Well, Mr. Sullivan, or… can I call you *Ed*? I tell you, I couldn't do it without the sensational fans who go see my pictures. Thank you. You're making me blush! And of course my manager, who is the love of my life and has the key to my heart, *Paul Anka*! *(blowing kisses to the audience)* Thank you. Thank you!

RITA has moved from the window to the front door. She quietly exits the house and continues moving until she is standing at the edge of the lawn, looking directly at MARILYN. She has the box wrapped in her skirt.

(stops the charade abruptly, embarrassed) Oh, hi Rita. I didn't see you standing there. I was just fooling around. Do you want to come over?

RITA considers.

Aw, come on. It will be fun. We can hula hoop to the top ten on the radio. Evelyn hoops with her friends after the fourth drink at our parties. Or so Fred tells me. I have to be in bed by eight. Ain't it a drag being ten?

She picks up a hoop and prepares to hula, turning on the radio. She hands RITA a second hoop.

A pop tune begins to play on the radio. MARILYN starts to hula like a pro.

RITA watches, holding the hoop in her hand awkwardly.

Don't you know how to hula? It's not that hard. You just have to move your hips like this. *(demonstrates)*

RITA considers.

(trying to take the box from RITA) Here, it will be easier if you put that down.

RITA tightens her grip and pulls the box away, hugging it protectively to her chest.

…Okay, I guess you can hold it. *(starts to hula)*

RITA cautiously mimics MARILYN's motions. She gets embarrassed and stops.

(understanding, turning off radio) Or we don't have to hula. We can do something else.

RITA looks down at the ground.

(gently) Hey. You don't like to talk much, do you?

RITA shakes her head slightly.

That's okay… I like to talk… *a lot!*

RITA smiles at MARILYN.

Hey, I've got an idea! Do you want to see a movie? *House of Wax* is playing at the Capitol. I already saw it last night with Fred, but I'll go again. I missed a lot 'cause I had my hands over my eyes for most of it. I simply screamed through the whole thing. I absolutely looove horror films! I'm totally hooked on the depthies. *(removing the glasses)* Have you ever seen a 3-D picture?

RITA shakes her head no.

You get to wear these celluloid glasses that magically make the picture come to life right before your very eyes! Come to life! Sensational!

RITA takes the glasses and examines them closely.

MARILYN watches RITA thoughtfully.

You can keep those. I'll get another pair the next time I go.

RITA looks up at MARILYN, smiling in thanks. She puts the glasses on.

EVELYN   *(from interior)* Marilyn, have you seen my new Bing-Bang Cherry lipstick?

MARILYN   *(pursing lips)* Uh-oh. *(to RITA)* See you later, alligator. *(exits)*

RITA runs into her house and eagerly turns on the television. She watches with the 3-D glasses on. Even though they don't help make the two-dimensional images come to life, RITA imagines that they do.

Scene Three

MARILYN is lying on the chaise longue reading Lady
Chatterley's Lover *by D.H. Lawrence. She is wearing EVELYN's
lingerie over her clothes, and has spike heels on her feet. She sips
on a strawberry milkshake dressed up to look like a cocktail.*

MARILYN *(reading aloud)* Inside herself she could feel the hum-ming of
pass-on pash-ion, passion, like the after-humming of deep bells.
(sighs deeply)

*RITA, still wearing the 3-D glasses, exits the house and walks
toward MARILYN. She is, as always, carrying her box.*

Listen to this. *(reads)* She fas-fascinated him helplessly, as if some
perfume about her int-intahh-intoxicated him. So he went on
help-lessly with his reading, and the throaty sound of the French
was like the wind in the chiminees to her. *(looks up from the novel)*
Isn't that romantic?

RITA nods, but doesn't really understand.

Lady Chatterley's Lover. I snuck it from Evelyn's night table.
(MARILYN puts her finger to her lips.) Shh. She just finished reading
it. She absolutely cried buckets over it and told me that it was
simply sensational. D.H. Lawrence is a *genius.* Have you read it?

RITA shakes her head no.

What do you like to read?

RITA shifts uncomfortably at the thought of having to answer.

Oh well. You should try this. It's very mature.

Pause.

Sounds of children playing.

*RITA looks up. Neighbourhood children are playing across the
street. RITA watches them with some interest.*

That's Sandra, Jack, and Donna Smithson. They go to St. Cecilia's
with me. Donna's our age.

RITA looks at MARILYN with question.

They won't talk to me. They're not allowed. Mrs. Smithson says that
I'm a bad influence.

RITA moves closer to MARILYN.

She says stuff like "Working mothers breed delinquent children," and all kinds of other bad things about Evelyn. Mostly because of Daddy, Mitch, and Fred.

RITA frowns, puzzled.

Pause.

(trying to distract) Hey, gee, do you…? Ah, do you want a milkshake? Fred just bought Evelyn a blender. She almost strangled him with the cord and told him she wasn't "that kind of woman." He showed me how to make really good shakes though. Almost as good as the ones at the drugstore. *(She runs into the kitchen where she pours a milkshake for RITA. She brings it down to her.)* Here we go! One milkshake for the young lady!

> *RITA takes the glass and sets it in the grass, continuing to gaze at the children playing. MARILYN notices RITA watching the kids. MARILYN nervously plays with her straw, tries to read her novel, and leafs through her magazines. Finally she gives up and looks over at the children too.*

EVELYN   *(from interior)* Marilyn! Baby, have you seen my purse? I'm losing my mind here…

MARILYN   No-o!

EVELYN   *(from interior)* Wanda and Ron are picking me and Fred up in ten minutes for stingers! We won't be late, baby. There's leftover chicken in the fridge if you get hungry…! Where is that purse?

> *Pause.*

MARILYN   *(to RITA)* Evelyn likes to go out a lot. She says you only have one life to live, so you might as well have fun doing it! Sometimes— most—a lot of people don't understand! But they don't know… it's kind of— *(stops, flustered)*

> *RITA turns her full attention to MARILYN. She nods encouragingly.*

> *Long pause. MARILYN looks away.*

Daddy was number one… He left when I was four. I was having my birthday party and he'd promised to get the cake on his way home from work. Chocolate fudge. My favourite. With big pink icing sugar roses and "Happy Birthday Maudie" written across the top in fancy writing; he'd crossed his heart and hoped to die. We waited and waited for him. People started to look uncomfortable and talked in quiet voices to each other. I knew what they were saying, but I didn't wanna believe them. *Daddy's coming, Daddy's coming,*

Daddy's coming, I kept repeating in my head. At eight o'clock, Evelyn had to run out to the corner store and buy Twinkies in little plastic wrappers for everyone instead. Mine fell apart when we tried to stick the candles in. I don't like vanilla anyways. Daddy finally showed up at eleven thirty after I'd gone to bed and all the guests had gone home. The shouting woke me up, so I went to sit at the top of the stairs to listen, but my eyes kept closing on me. When I woke up, it was still dark. I was cold and there was an itchy pattern on my cheek from the carpet. Evelyn picked me up and kissed me and tucked me in bed. Her face was all wet... *(pause)* I found my cake the next morning. It was lying in the garbage can outside the back door on top of eggshells and soup cans, where a raccoon was eating my pink roses.

RITA looks at MARILYN with sympathy.

Pause.

MARILYN's expression begins to change as she recalls the next memory.

Mitch was number two. He came when I was six and left when I was seven. He had a collection of sport coats and drove a red Corvette. Evelyn called him "The Weapon." But then he got a job in Calgary and asked Evelyn and me to go with him. Evelyn said no 'cause she didn't really love him.

RITA is listening attentively.

MARILYN grins.

After Mitch, Evelyn had loads of different boyfriends who would take her dancing at the Wedgewood or for pina coladas at the Kontiki Room. Evelyn had a wild time, but she was never serious about any of them.

RITA's eyes widen.

MARILYN is starting to smile.

Fred's number three. He came when I was eight. He doesn't have a red Corvette, but he brings me a bag of penny candy—"Sweets for the sweet"—every Friday when he comes home, and he never shouts at Evelyn.

RITA stares at MARILYN, thinking.

(smile fading) It's okay if you don't want to stick around.

Sounds of children playing fades out.

RITA shakes her head, taking MARILYN's hand and squeezing it. Distracted, she puts down the box, leaving it partially hidden under the chaise longue amidst MARILYN's movie magazines. MARILYN does not notice the box. She squeezes RITA's hand back in an expression of friendship. RITA makes a motion to speak, but then stops herself. MARILYN's attention is diverted to the house at the sound of EVELYN's voice, and she does not see RITA's attempt.

EVELYN   *(from interior)* Found it, baby! See you soon! Kisses!

MARILYN   Kisses!

Sound of side door closing.

RITA smiles at MARILYN.

(mischievous) I have a plan. Let's dress up! Evelyn has some real sensational numbers that I've simply been *dying* to try on.

MARILYN and RITA start toward the Marysh door.

You ever worn heels before?

RITA shakes her head.

Oh dah-ling, you haven't seen the world until you've seen it on top of four inches!

MARILYN races into the house, giggling with excitement. RITA follows.

Scene Four

The television flickers in the Lavoie home.

MARILYN exits her house and starts to run toward the Lavoie residence. She has dressed hurriedly today and looks less put together than usual.

EVELYN   *(from interior)* Baby, weather man said it might rain. Better pick up your magazines if you don't want 'em to get soaked!

MARILYN   *(annoyed)* I'm busy!

EVELYN   *(warning)* Marilyn!

MARILYN   Okaaay!

MARILYN detours to the magazines and hastily starts to gather them up. She discovers RITA's box. MARILYN puts down the magazines and slowly picks up the box, turning it around. She studies the exterior and thinks about opening it. Long pause. Television noise from next door. MARILYN decides not to. She grabs her magazines and throws them onto the porch. Holding the box under her arm, MARILYN runs over to the Lavoie house. She knocks until RITA answers.

RITA's face lights up at the sight of MARILYN. RITA is wearing her 3-D glasses.

Rita! Rita! Rita! Guess what? Oh, you'll never guess. I have sensational news!

RITA excitedly leans toward MARILYN for the news. She smiles with anticipation.

Evelyn and Fred are getting married and—this is the best part... *they're going to have a baby!* Isn't that sensational? I'm going to be a mother!

RITA's face falls. She notices the box under MARILYN's arm. RITA takes off the 3-D glasses, letting them drop. She frantically pulls the box away from MARILYN.

Oh. I found that mixed up with my magazines... Don't worry, I didn't open it.

RITA starts to shake, her lips trembling.

What's wrong? Aren't you happy for me?

RITA begins to cry, clutching the shoebox to her chest. She runs back into the house, slamming the door. MARILYN tries to stop her.

Rita, what's wrong? What did I say? Rita? *(She tries knocking at the door in vain. Then, dejected, she slowly starts walking home.)*

Rapid action. Television flickers and glows in the Lavoie house. Noise of channels being changed. RITA's shadow can be seen watching. She finds her 3-D glasses and puts them on. She goes up to the television and presses her nose to the screen. Frustrated, she takes off the glasses and throws them to the floor. Television off. From the Marysh house, salsa music begins to play softly. EVELYN's laughter. RITA sits in the darkness.

MARGUERITE   *(from interior)* Rita, I make this lovely *tourtière* for our *dîner*, ah? Wash please, *mon p'tit chou!*

MARILYN *sullenly enters her house, picking up the movie magazines on her way in.*

EVELYN   *(from interior)* Marilyn, is that you? Baby, get dressed! We're going out for Chinese to celebrate!

Music continues into the night.

Scene Five

RITA is seated on the steps hugging her box. MARILYN exits her home, not noticing RITA at first. MARILYN has stuffed a large lumpy pillow under her dress to make her look pregnant. Her hair is messy, but she still wears lipstick and high heels. She gingerly descends the stairs like a very pregnant woman might. MARILYN pats her belly affectionately and takes her time relaxing back into the chaise longue. She reaches up under her dress and pulls out the photograph of Paul Anka.

MARILYN   *(looking at photograph)* Oh, Paul. Look at me. Will you still love me nine months from now, when I'm big as a house? I don't believe you! *(She throws the photo aside. She fumbles around under the chaise longue and finds a bag of cookies, selects one, and takes a bite. She looks down and pats her belly lovingly.)* Hello in there little baby. I can't wait for you to come out and see me. I can't wait to take you roller skating, and teach you to put on lipstick without getting it on your teeth, and take you to— *(notices RITA)*

RITA and MARILYN exchange nervous looks. Pause. MARILYN is wary of speaking at first. She does not want to frighten RITA away. Slowly, she gets up and walks over to RITA with the bag of cookies. She holds them out, offering.

(gently) Hi Rita. Want a cookie? They're chocolate chip.

Pause.

RITA slowly takes a cookie from the bag.

(indicating belly) This is my baby. I'm naming her Tallulah. Isn't that a sensational name? I think it's a name fit for a movie star, don't you?

RITA looks at MARILYN with wide eyes.

Do you want to touch my belly?

RITA cautiously places her hand on MARILYN's belly.

(jerks) Whoa! Hey, Tallulah's dancing in there!

RITA draws her hand away with surprise.

She only does that when she really likes someone, and trust me, she doesn't like a lot of people. She kicks at Paul all the time.

RITA smiles a little. She stares at MARILYN's belly.

Babies are so itsy-bitsy and roly-poly, I just want to squeeze them! *(She takes a cookie from the bag and whispers.)* Do you know where babies come from?

RITA shakes her head no.

I do. Evelyn told me all about it! See, there's this store on Dundas Street where you can buy these special seeds. *Baby seeds.* You swallow them with a glass of milk. Then you start to grow a baby in here. But you've got to be careful not to leave them lying around, or else some hungry person might just eat 'em up as a snack, and then ZAP! Baby. Wild, huh? Did you know that babies live right inside your stomach? Well, they do! When I eat the cookies, the little pieces of spitty soggy crumbs fall all over the baby's head. So she has to run her noggin on the inside of my stomach to get the cookie goo off, *(laughs)* which tickles like crazy! Then she nibbles it with her gummy mouth. You wouldn't think that it hurts—ouch! —cause she doesn't have any teeth, but boy can that kid bite when she's hungry! And chocolate-chip cookies give her lots of energy. Now she's bouncing around in there. Come on, Rita. Tallulah wants us to dance with her! *(pulls RITA off of the steps and turns on the radio)*

RITA giggles as MARILYN starts to dance, her belly bouncing up and down. MARILYN grabs RITA's arm, bringing her into the dance. The girls dance around the lawn until they fall down laughing. MARILYN continues to roll around on the grass as RITA picks herself up and watches MARILYN, thinking hard.

(lying back, looking up at the sky) I can't wait for my baby to come.

RITA lets herself remember. She closes her eyes and silently mouths "Mathieu."

Scene Six

Evening. RITA exits her house and walks toward the Marysh home, nervously clutching her cardboard box in one arm. She walks up the steps and knocks timidly on the door. MARILYN answers wearing a pillow under her dress, and a bride's veil.

RITA   *(very softly)* Marilyn?

MARILYN is stunned to hear RITA speak. She freezes.

RITA is surprised herself.

Pause.

RITA takes MARILYN by the hand and leads her to the steps. The girls sit. RITA hands MARILYN the box and nods.

MARILYN starts to slowly untie the string, glancing up at RITA for approval. She lifts the lid of the box and examines the contents. She looks up at RITA.

RITA takes a rubber baby doll out of the box. She cradles it in her arms.

Long pause.

This was my practice baby. Mummy bought her for me last year when we were getting ready for our new *bébé.*

Pause. MARILYN is very still as she watches RITA.

The baby was… I didn't want a new baby. I said, "Mummy, can you send it back if we don't like it and get a refund, like at Eatons?" Mummy said *non, non* and showed me how to hold a baby. I didn't think it was funny. I liked it being just me and Mummy and Daddy. All the neighbours came over and just talked baby baby baby. And the house was filled with things for baby baby baby. I did *not* want it. But then one morning I woke up and Mummy was gone. Auntie was making porridge in the kitchen. She said Mummy had gone to the hospital in the middle of the night and I had a little baby brother.

Pause.

Mathieu. When Mummy brought him home from the hospital, he was all pink and wiggly. He cried like a kitten, and slurped on his fingers. I loved him right away, and wanted to just hug him hug him hug him. Mummy said *va laver* your *mains* first. Mummy said be careful with your *p'tit frère.* She was… she looked tired.

I held him with both hands like you're supposed to hold a baby.
I kissed him kissed him kissed him. *(gently hands doll to MARILYN)*
Mummy was crying. I said what's wrong? And Daddy said, it's okay
muffin, and he put Mummy to bed... I tickled my baby's toes every
day before I went to school, and at three o'clock I'd come home
and hold him till bedtime. Mummy would lie on the couch and
sleep sleep sleep. She would get up before Daddy came home to
put some TV dinners in the oven and get dressed. I wasn't allowed
to by myself, but—I—Mathieu... When Christmas holidays came?
I spent all my time with Mathieu except for one day. I was throwing
snowballs with my friend Susan across the street. When I was
coming home to change, I could hear Mathieu crying. I put him—
I ran inside and scooped him up out of his cradle, but he kept
screaming. His little face was all scrunched up and red like a tomato
from all the howling. I thought he was going to explode. Mummy
was lying on the couch with her hands over her ears. She was crying
too. Mummy said, "Muffin, *s'il te plaît* get Mummy *un* aspirin
from the cabinet please?" I got her the bottle. She fell asleep. *Merci.*
Mathieu was still crying. He was hungry hungry hungry. I'd never
warmed up Mathieu's milk before, but Mummy wasn't feeling well,
and *mon bébé* was starving. I put Mathieu on his baby blanket on
the floor near my feet so that he'd be close. I got him to suck on his
soother. His face started to turn pink again. It's okay, Mathieu, it's
okay. Shhh *bébé.* I put the pot on the stove and turned it on high.
I poured in the whole milk and waited... Mathieu smelled the
milk and cooed like a pigeon... I heard Mummy snore in the living
room... The burner turned red... Mathieu blew a spit bubble...
The milk is almost ready, Mathieu. Don't worry, your tummy will
be full soon... The formula was boiling... I clicked off the stove
and slid the pot off the burner... I picked it up with the handle,
but it was too heavy. I put my other hand under the pot to hold it
gooder and then I—ow!

> *Sound of pot crashing to the floor.*
>
> *MARILYN stares at RITA in shock.*
>
> *Long pause.*

(quietly) They wouldn't even let me go to the funeral.

> *Pause.*

I wish I was dead too.

MARILYN   *(gently)* No.

> *RITA starts to cry.*

MARILYN puts down the doll and goes to RITA. She wants to hug her, but finds that she is not able.

Pause.

RITA picks up the baby doll and holds it out to MARILYN.

MARILYN shakes her head no.

RITA   Please.

MARILYN takes the doll.

RITA kisses MARILYN on the cheek and exits.

Pause.

MARILYN looks at the doll, contemplating what to do. MARILYN pulls off her bride's veil and wraps the baby in it. Then she clasps the bundle to her chest, walking slowly up the steps and into the Marysh house. Inside, MARILYN crawls up onto the kitchen table, the baby in her arms. She kisses the doll gently. MARILYN falls asleep.

Scene Seven

RITA is inside the Lavoie house watching I Love Lucy. *After some time has elapsed, RITA begins to speak over the dialogue in the show.*

RITA   Hello.

Dialogue from television continues.

Bonjour in there, Lucille. Oh, what kind of pickle are you in today? Want to be in Ricky's act? *Que c'est dommage,* he won't let you. Sorry, Lucille.

Audience laughter from television set. RITA leans forward, trying to see inside the screen.

How many *personnes* are in there with you, Lucille? They must be happy happy happy, they're always laughing... How did they get in? *(She picks up her 3-D glasses and examines them. Then, she begins to inspect the television set.)* Is there a little magic door somewhere that I don't know about—Lucille? Or is everyone just born in there? Are they all black and white and three inches tall like you?

Dialogue continues. RITA waits for a reply. She turns away from the television.

You know, I used to want to live in televisionland with you... be your new *meilleure amie*. It would be fun fun fun 'cause I'd get to see you every day, not just once a week for half an hour. It's not enough, Lucille. *(annoyed, taps on screen) Bonjour*! Lucille, are you listening to me...? But now, Marilyn. The girl who lives next door? She and me are like you and Ethel...! Hey maybe you could come stay *here* sometime? I think Marilyn would like you; she wants to be an actress too. And I could keep you in my pocket... But, *je pense que* Ethel would miss you. Hello? *(tapping on screen)* Lucille?

Noise from television continues. RITA watches for a moment before she turns off the television. Then, she unplugs it before exiting.

Scene Eight

RITA is waiting for MARILYN. She sits on the chaise longue looking at the pictures in one of the movie magazines. Suddenly MARILYN bursts out of the Marysh house with the baby doll in her arms. MARILYN is a mess. The pillow under her dress has been bumped sideways. She hobbles down the stairs in one high heel, clutching the other, broken, in her hand.

RITA   What happened?

MARILYN   Oh, Rita. It was awful... I was on my way upstairs when I realized that I didn't have the baby. I took her into the pantry with me when I went to get some cookies and *forgot* about her. What kind of mother forgets about her child? And in the *pantry*! So I started back down the stairs to get her when I tripped on Evelyn's dress and con-se-quent-aly broke the heel off one of my favourite shoes. But... it's okay. She's fine.

                RITA takes the baby from MARILYN, cradling her with tenderness.

                Pause.

                (quietly) Can you teach me?

RITA   Teach you?

MARILYN   How to be a mother... Evelyn needs me.

RITA   …Okay.

> MARILYN *smiles gratefully at RITA.*

(*professional*) Well, first you gotta know how to hold a *bébé*. (*She arranges MARILYN's arms and places the doll inside.*) Both hands. *Tout le temps.* And never never never let go of the head.

> MARILYN *nods vigorously.*

Oh, she's crying! Is it a hungry cry or a wet cry?

MARILYN   (*confused*) What? Who's crying? I don't hear anything.

RITA   The *bébé*… Oh, you have to use your imagination.

MARILYN   I don't have one of those.

RITA   Of course you do. Everyone does—you just have to play pretend.

MARILYN   (*building anxiety*) But I never *play*. Everything I do is very, very real. I don't know how. I can't, I can't, I can't…

RITA   Marilyn. *Arrête*… okay.

> MARILYN *stops. She is frustrated with herself for not being able to express her sympathy to RITA. The girls exchange looks. Pause.*

(*putting hands over MARILYN's eyes*) What do you see?

MARILYN   Nothing. Your hands are over my eyes.

RITA   (*persisting*) Marilyn. What do you *see*?

MARILYN   Black… all right, all right. Um… black with little bits of red and yellow… and blue?

> RITA *takes her hands away from MARILYN's eyes. MARILYN keeps her eyes shut.*

RITA   And, what else?

> *Pause.*

MARILYN   Shapes that sort of look like… clouds… big creamy clouds that look good enough to eat like… like pie. Pie in the sky! (*opens her eyes*)

RITA   Mmm…

MARILYN   Cherry! Warm cherry pie that's crispy and soft in all the right places. And without a crust 'cause I don't like that part, and we can both eat it together with two big spoons—just eat and eat until we're all pie up to here! (*gestures at throat*)

RITA   (*delighted*) Marilyn!

RITA and MARILYN laugh.

MARILYN   *(serious)* It's a wet cry.

RITA   We need a diaper! *(She takes down a dish cloth from the laundry line and lays it on the ground.)* Maintenant, carefully place *le bébé* on top and we change the diaper *comme ça!*

>   *RITA shows MARILYN how to diaper. Then, MARILYN successfully diapers the doll.*

Perfect!

MARILYN   *(sing-song)* Perfect! Perfect! Perfect!

>   *Pause.*

>   *RITA looks away. MARILYN notices.*

Rita?

RITA   *Oui?*

MARILYN   I wanted to…

MARGUERITE   *(from interior)* Rita! *Mon p'tit chou!*

MARILYN   *(quietly)* Never mind.

RITA   I'd better go… Grannie and me are going shopping. I need some new knee socks. Bye-bye Marilyn. *(exits)*

>   *MARILYN sits down on the porch, cradling the doll. She picks up the jar of wilting dandelions, examining it. She glances down at the doll in her arms and notices the old shoebox lying on the porch. Suddenly, MARILYN gets an idea. She jumps up, grabbing the box, and runs into the house.*

Scene Nine

>   *RITA is sitting in her living room reading. MARILYN exits her house pushing a baby carriage and carrying the baby doll in one arm. She is wearing the pillow under a big black dress, obviously belonging to EVELYN. She picks up the wilting dandelions from their place on the porch. MARILYN is wearing a black hat with mesh that covers her face. She stops in front of the Lavoie residence and knocks on the door. RITA answers.*

MARILYN   Can you come out? Did you have supper yet?

RITA nods.

MARILYN pulls the shoebox from the carriage and holds it out to RITA, motioning for her to open it.

RITA slowly lifts the lid and pulls out a paper heart.

It's a heart... or at least it's supposed to be. I'm not very good with scissors.

Pause.

It's for Matthew. See? I wrote his name on top. We're going to bury the box in the garden and send it up to heaven.

Pause.

RITA   Like a funeral?

MARILYN   Yeah. A proper funeral.

RITA places the card back in the box.

You're the mourner, so you can wear my hat. *(places the hat on RITA)* I have to confess, I've never been to a funeral before. Evelyn's been... but I've seen them in the movies! Let's see... next, the widow is supposed to cry into her handkerchief. I guess you're the widow.

RITA   I don't have a hanky.

MARILYN   Oh, well... *(She pulls a handkerchief out of the bosom of her dress and hands it to RITA.)* Here.

RITA clutches the hanky.

Okay. This is the part where there's a big long sermon, and dreamy close-ups of all the sad relations and the broken-hearted lover, and lots of sad music plays. And we walk to the burial grounds. *(hums a few bars of funeral march music)*

RITA and MARILYN walk over to the flowerbeds in the Lavoie yard.

Now you take the flowers *(hands RITA the dandelions)* and put them in the coffin. Now you say, "In memory um."

RITA   In memory um.

Pause.

MARILYN   *(thinking)* In this movie, *The Egyptian,* people were buried in tombs with lots of nice things. Do you have anything you want to put in the box?

RITA	*(reaches inside her stocking and pulls out a creased and worn photograph)* It's Mathieu and me when he was a just-born *bébé*. I don't want him to forget.

Pause.

They all said it would be easier if I came here for the summer. That I would forget forget forget. *Mais*, he was *mon bébé* and I won't. I love you, Mathieu. *(places the photograph in the box)* What next?

MARILYN	Now we close the casket and sing a hymn.
RITA	Which hymn?
MARILYN	I don't know any off by heart. Um… what about "God Save the Queen"? It's kind of like a hymn.

RITA nods and they begin to sing. MARILYN and RITA dig a hole in the flower bed as they sing the lyrics. They place the box in the mound. RITA pulls a flower out of the perfect flower box arrangement and kneels down to place it on top.

Pause.

RITA	Marilyn? I…
MARILYN	*(whispers)* I'm sorry, Rita.

MARILYN rushes into RITA, tightly embracing her.

Scene Ten

Giggles start slowly, gradually building into laughter, peeling through the Marysh and Lavoie homes.

RITA	Ready?
MARILYN	Ready…! Wait! *(laughing, then regaining control of herself)* Okay, yes, ready.

Throwing open her screen door, RITA is wearing lipstick like MARILYN.

RITA	*(speaks with dramatic passion)* Parlez-moi d'amour!

MARILYN appears in her front-room window wearing simple play clothes like RITA. However, she still holds true to her lipstick. She throws up her arms and strikes a pose before sauntering over to her door. She opens the door and stands in the doorway like RITA.

MARILYN   *(with zeal)* Speak to me of love. Par-lez mwa damer!

RITA   *L'amour toujours. Toujours l'amour!*

MARILYN   Love *everlasting*! Lamer toogers!

RITA   *Votre beau discours...*

MARILYN   Tender words of love...!

RITA   Whisper those words to me...

MARILYN   *(struggling to do her best French accent)* Rep-eh-tez cez mos supremes...

RITA   *Je vous aime!*

MARILYN   Dear... I *adore* you!

MARILYN and RITA bow deeply to their audience and blow kisses to each other.

RITA   Marilyn—darling!

MARILYN   Rita—darling!

MARILYN and RITA sweep toward each other, meeting on the lawn. They air kiss each other with loud "mwa, mwa" sounds. The girls lock eyes and start to laugh hysterically.

Shall we dance, princess? *(turns on radio)*

Elvis Presley music begins to play. MARILYN and RITA begin to dance.

Oooh, this is my newest favourite song! *(swooning)* I think that if Evelyn has a girl we should name her Roxanne... Wow! Yes! And if she has a boy... we should name him Elvis! This *(indicating music)* is the wildest stuff I've ever heard! Sensational! The way he moves his hips. Oh, I hope it's a boy! I'd be the only kid on the block who could say she was related to Elvis! And did you see him on television last night, Rita?

RITA   No... a child could go blind from watching too much television. Besides, I was helping Grannie.

MARILYN   Too bad. He was spectacular!

A mischievous look crosses MARILYN's face. She tags RITA's arm and runs away.

Tag! You're it!

	RITA and MARILYN chase each other around the yard.
RITA	Gotcha! *(starts tickling MARILYN)*
MARILYN	*(laughing)* No! No!
RITA	*(Suddenly noticing, she points at MARILYN's flat stomach.)* Hey, what happened?
MARILYN	Huh?
RITA	Tallulah. Where is she?
MARILYN	Oh.
EVELYN	*(from interior)* Girls, Fred will be out in ten minutes! Get ready, please.
MARILYN	Okay! *(to RITA)* She can't come… Evelyn says that pregnant ladies, little kids, and cats can't go on rides at the Ex. Little babies like Tallulah get scared on roller coasters and Ferris wheels. They get all gooey and sticky from the candy apples. And they get sick from all the cotton candy, corn dogs, red hots, and waffle ice-cream sandwiches. Evelyn isn't coming because of it all. Ain't it a drag? I'm so glad we're ten so that we can enjoy ourselves. Poor Evelyn's stuck at home all alone. I told her she can listen to my Paul Anka records if she gets lonely. And besides, I think one baby in the house is going to be enough for this family. I'm going to be a big sister. I have to start helping Evelyn get ready for *her* baby.
	RITA smiles at MARILYN.
EVELYN	*(from interior)* Five minutes, baby!
	MARILYN and RITA scramble into their footwear.
MARILYN	Oh, you're going to *l'amour* the Exhibition, Rita. I wait all summer for this! Here. It's smudging. *(She takes her lipstick out of her pocket and re-applies it to RITA's lips.)* There. You know, we're like blood brothers, except *lipstick sisters!*
RITA	Forever…! Oh! I have something for you! Stay here.
	RITA rushes into the house, grabs a wrapped package and then runs back out with the gift behind her back.
	Close your eyes! Hold out your hands.
	MARILYN does as she is told. RITA places the package in her hands.
MARILYN	What is it?
RITA	Open it and see.

MARILYN	*(opens the gift)* A giant chocolate-chip cookie—my favourite! *(takes a bite)* Oh, this is sensational, Rita!
RITA	It's *homemade*. Grannie helped me… It's a going-away present.
MARILYN	Oh, Rita. I don't have anything for you. Wait…! *(rummages in pocket, pulling out a lipstick)* Here. It's called Canadian Sunset. It looks much better on you than it does on me anyways.
RITA	Are you sure?
MARILYN	Of course, I've got tons of lipsticks! *(kisses RITA on the cheek, leaving behind a lipstick mark)*
RITA	Hey! *(does the same to MARILYN)*
	MARILYN and RITA laugh at their new looks.
MARILYN	*(pause)* Are you really going back to Winnipeg?
RITA	Next week—day before school starts. *Mais,* I'll be back for Thanksgiving, *et Noël,* and…
MARILYN	And Evelyn promised that Fred would drive us all down to visit you during spring holidays. And we'll write each other every single day.
RITA	*Oui.*
	MARILYN and RITA turn to look out at the audience. They speak with intensity, almost overlapping each other's dialogue.
	Dear Marilyn…
MARILYN	Dear Rita…
RITA	I miss you…
MARILYN	Today, at school during recess, there was a hula-hooping competition and I won champion! All the girls want me to teach them…
RITA	Today, *maman* and *moi* went to the park and played on the swings. It was *fantastique!* I was flying flying flying!
MARILYN	I miss you…
RITA	*Embrasse* Elvis for me!
MARILYN	I'll write you again tomorrow…
RITA	Till tomorrow…
MARILYN	Love, your dearest friend in the whole wide world, Marilyn Marysh Esquire.
RITA	Love, xoxoxoxoxox forever, Rita Marie Dennis.

Pause.

MARILYN and RITA turn to face each other.

EVELYN *(calling from interior)* Gi-irls!

MARILYN and RITA clasp hands. They twirl.

MARILYN *(with a regal air)* Are you ready, Madame Rita?

RITA *Oui,* Madame Marilyn. *Allons-y!*

MARILYN and RITA begin to strut across the lawn, swinging their hips back and forth and batting their eyelashes. The friends begin to giggle. They stop the charade, throwing their arms around each other. They exit with their arms entwined, laughing.

The end.

Pie in the Sky creative team: (back row standing, left to right) Stephanie Atkins, Madeleine Cohen, Morgan MacDougall-Milne, and Katie Zulak; (front row seated, left to right) Livia Berius, Katelin Cook, and Morgan Norwich.
Photo by Victoria Dawe.

we all fall down

by Brenna McAllister

Mouth (Devon Howes) and his squeegee friends tell their stories of the street.

Photo by Brenna McAllister.

We All Fall Down was first produced by the students of Governor Simcoe Secondary School, St. Catharines, at the Niagara District Festival of the Sears Ontario Drama Festival at Brock University, St. Catharines, in March 2006, with subsequent performances at the Southern Regional Festival in Chatham in April 2006 and the Provincial Showcase in Toronto in May 2006.

Dodge	Patrick Murphy
Olivia	Sadie Isaak
Sammy	Jesse Cotton
Mouth	Devon Howes
Lydia	Mary Gray
Sid	John Henderson
Businesswoman	Lisa Van Oorshot
Street Kids	Valerie Beckett, Zach Cox, Ernie Gleeson, Gina Greco, Elissa Hibbs, Megan Lewis, Hillary Myers, Ryan Post, Fasiel Qazi, Alicia Tymoszewicz

Directed by Brenna McAllister
Stage Management by Justina Pabritsaite
Assistant Stage Management by Brittani Mulder
Costumes by Gina Greco and Ms. Habib
Lighting Designer/Operation by Kyle Greer
Set Construction by Dan McAllister
Hair, Tattoos, and Makeup by Mike McGreen, Nicka Noble, and Valerie Rodgers
Technical Crew: Matt Adams, Rebecca Clark, Jarret Flood, Mike McGeen, Ted Miller, Jake Plannic

Brenna McAllister

Brenna McAllister earned an Honours BA in Theatre and a BEd from Brock University. She is a drama teacher at St. Catharines Collegiate. Other works include *Fractured Mind*, *Toy Soldiers*, *Pianoman*, and *Project Dee*. *We All Fall Down* was performed in 2006 at the SummerWorks Theatre Festival. An extended version of this play was performed by St. Catharines Collegiate students in 2009.

characters

DODGE
OLIVIA
SAMMY
MOUTH
LYDIA
SID
ADDICT
BUSINESSWOMAN
STREET KIDS

The main stage area is filled with two sets of scaffolds. Each set has two levels of scaffolding with two platforms each, at various levels. An additional scaffold platform is positioned between the two sections of scaffolding on the top bar of each. The swing is attached to the arm holds on the underside of this platform with chains. SAMMY is silhouetted sitting on the swing. The STREET KIDS are present, lounging on the scaffolding. The STREET KID chorus can be expanded to fit production needs and their character types can be altered to fit the talents within the cast. There is a junkyard stage left, with a brick wall and tires. There are two upright platforms that have multiple layers of old, weathered posters on them. These platforms fold down to reveal two beds and a trunk, which creates The Palace. Everyone on stage is frozen except for SAMMY, who slowly swings back and forth. Singing is heard off/on stage. In the original production, LYDIA sang the song but the chorus may be used instead.

LYDIA   *(singing offstage)* Ring around the rosy.
Pockets full of posey.
Hush now,
Hush now.

The STREET KIDS remain frozen as they deliver their lines. SAMMY continues to swing.

TOUGH GIRL   What if I told you the whole story?

HOT RAVER   From the beginning.

TOUGH GIRL & ADDICT
Would it make a difference?

DJ SLIM   What if I helped you see the truth?

SKATER & DRUMMER
Would you see it?

ACROBAT   What if I was your

ACROBAT & SKATER
Son?

ARTIST   Your

ARTIST & HOT RAVER
Daughter?

ARTIST, DRUMMER, & BREAKER
Would you still walk by?

BREAKER   What will it take to make you care?

ALL	This is *my* story.
	This… is my life.

SAMMY jumps off the swing. The STREET KIDS sharply turn and stare at him. Transition music begins to play. It should be slow at first and then kicks in as the street comes to life. Everyone on stage moves in slow motion as they begin their day. When the song picks up they move quickly. MOUTH enters stage right on rollerblades and DODGE enters stage left, making a drug deal with the HOT RAVER. Everyone on stage is talking and trying to get money. Some speak directly to the audience. SID remains hidden in the background, watching the STREET KIDS and keeping a close eye on DODGE. OLIVIA enters from stage right and slowly makes her way to the milk crate centre stage. The ADDICT has approached DODGE as the music fades out.

DODGE	*(holding the money up)* What's this?
ADDICT	It's what I paid last time.
DODGE	*(turning away)* It's not your lucky day, kid… It's forty now. Inflation.
ADDICT	Come on. I need a hit.
DODGE	*(turning back)* Tell you what, I'll keep this as a down payment. You bring me the rest, you get the goods.
ADDICT	Forget it. Just give me my money back. *(pause, grabs DODGE's wrist)* It's all I've got.
DODGE	In the future, don't waste my time. *(pulling arm away)*

Everyone stares at DODGE. He flashes the gun hidden in the waistband of his pants.

Do we have a problem here?

STREET KIDS go back to work.

ADDICT	No.

ADDICT walks away, bumping into SAMMY who has entered stage right.

SAMMY	Watch it!
ADDICT	Screw you!
DODGE	What did you say?
ADDICT	Nothing.
DODGE	I think you owe my friend here an apology.

ADDICT   *(under his breath)* Sorry.

DODGE   I couldn't hear you.

ADDICT   I'm sorry.

DODGE   Get lost.

> *The ADDICT crosses stage right and sits on the stack of tires. The other STREET KIDS snicker and go back to their own activities. Attention shifts to DODGE and SAMMY.*

SAMMY   That was great! Did you see the look on his face?

DODGE   You're late. *(pause)* You were at that swing again. *(pulling SAMMY stage left)* Dammit Sammy! Sid's gonna freak. *(glancing over at SID)* I can't keep covering for you. He expects his payments on time.

SAMMY   I can do better. I promise. Just give me another chance.

DODGE   Fine. *(pause)* You can start with her. *(He nods toward OLIVIA. The STREET KIDS laugh.)*

> *DODGE pushes SAMMY toward OLIVIA. SAMMY awkwardly closes the distance. DODGE watches.*

SAMMY   Hey… what's your name? *(pause)* Don't feel like talking much, eh? *(walks toward DODGE and whispers)* She doesn't feel like talking… *(DODGE sends him back.)* My name's Sam. You're not from around here, are you? I can tell. You don't have that look in your eyes… *(becoming more uncomfortable)* Are you crying?

OLIVIA   *(wiping away tears defensively)* No.

SAMMY   There's nothing wrong with it.

OLIVIA   Well, I'm not.

SAMMY   I was just saying that it's okay. *(Pause. DODGE hands SAMMY a cigarette and a lighter.)* Do you want one? A cigarette?

> *SAMMY awkwardly lights the cigarette and coughs excessively. The STREET KIDS laugh. SAMMY puts the cigarette out. A STREET KID kicks a milk crate to SAMMY and he grabs it and sits beside OLIVIA.*

So, where ya from? I'm from St. Catharines. Been out here for about two months now. It's not great but it's not bad either. Just better I guess. I know where all the good pizza joints are.

> *SAMMY tries to reach around OLIVIA and get her bag. DODGE has signalled to MOUTH for backup. OLIVIA misinterprets SAMMY's action as a bad attempt to hit on her. He quickly pulls his arm back and tries to recover.*

	So… do you like trucks?
MOUTH	*(awkwardly blades over to join them)* Tiny!
SAMMY	The name's Sam.
MOUTH	Whatever, little man. What's happenin'? Who's your lady friend?
SAMMY	She won't…
OLIVIA	*(flirting)* It's Olivia.

> *SAMMY is exasperated.*

MOUTH	Well, well, well. Put her there. *(shakes hands with OLIVIA)* The name's Mouth. I see you've already met Tiny. *(ruffling SAMMY's hair)*
SAMMY	*(pushing MOUTH away)* It's Sam!
MOUTH	Oh… I see… *(makes out with his squeegee)*
SAMMY	What's with the blades?
MOUTH	It's a gimmick, man. Everybody's got one nowadays! The way I see it, these blades will be good for business. *(using squeegee to pull OLIVIA away from her bag)* Check it out. I'm under the Spadina overpass and… you know what I'm talking about, *(giving the signal to SAMMY to take her wallet)* the Gardiner… Q.E.W… Big Lou's there… Anyways, you hang till the people stop for the red. But there's another squeegee dude on the opposite corner and…

> *OLIVIA begins to turn back to her bag and MOUTH pulls her back using his squeegee. SAMMY puts her wallet in his jacket pocket and places the bag in it's original place. SID exits when he sees SAMMY has taken the wallet.*

	BAM! I roll over before dude on corner B has even stepped off the curb. There's only one problem.
SAMMY	*(joining them)* What's that?
MOUTH.	Some jerk punked my shoes… So dude, you got any stuff on ya?
SAMMY	*(patting his pocket)* Yeah. Over here. *(walking over to DODGE)*
MOUTH	Check ya later, Liv! *(awkwardly wheels over to DODGE)*
OLIVIA	It's Olivia! *(walks back and sits on crate)*
SAMMY	*(handing wallet to DODGE)* I did good, didn't I, Dodge?

> *DODGE pulls the cash out of the wallet, and hands some to MOUTH and SAMMY. He pockets the rest.*

DODGE	Yeah, you did good, kid. Listen, hang with Mouth for a bit.

SAMMY	But I haven't made enough today. Sid's going to be pissed.
DODGE	I'll handle Sid. Mouth will let you use his squeegee.
MOUTH	*(hugging squeegee protectively)* No, I will not!

DODGE signals OLIVIA.

Fine. But just this once.

> *He hits SAMMY in the chest with his squeegee as he hands it to him. SAMMY takes off with the squeegee, twirling it in the air and catching it.*

Be careful with her. *(awkwardly blading offstage after SAMMY)* Charlene!

> *DODGE watches SAMMY and MOUTH exit and his gaze shifts to OLIVIA, who has realized that her wallet is gone. DODGE throws the empty wallet in the trash bin as he approaches OLIVIA.*

OLIVIA	No! Dammit. Where is it? *(dumps bag out on stage)*
DODGE	*(kneeling beside OLIVIA)* Let me help you.

> *While helping OLIVIA collect her things, DODGE picks up a bracelet and hides it behind his back.*

OLIVIA	Unless you've got my wallet, there's nothing you can do for me. I had everything in there. Three hundred bucks.
DODGE	The name's Dodge. *(handing bracelet out to her)*
OLIVIA	Olivia.
DODGE	*(helping her up)* How about something to eat? A place to crash for the night?
OLIVIA	*(pulling hand back)* I'm not going to sleep with you.
DODGE	That's not what I had in mind. I remember what it was like when I first got here. Someone helped me out. *(STREET KIDS react to DODGE's offer to the newbie.)*
OLIVIA	Why should I trust you? *(pause)* Look, I don't want to owe anyone anything. I'm finally on my own and that's the way I want to keep it.
DODGE	*(defensive)* Give it a few days. No one wants to be out here alone.

> *DODGE begins to exit stage right and the STREET KIDS are satisfied that OLIVIA is alone again. DODGE stops himself and turns back.*

Look, if you change your mind, *(writing address on lip of cigarette package, rips it off and hands it to her)* You can find me here.

Transition music begins to fade in as OLIVIA takes the address. The transition music should be slow to help show the despair and hopelessness of nightlife on the streets. DODGE exits stage right. The ADDICT and ACROBAT begin to approach OLIVIA with ill intent. OLIVIA turns and bumps into the TOUGH GIRL, who blows smoke in her face. All other STREET KIDS taunt her.

OLIVIA   Dodge… *(a moment of indecision)* Wait up!

OLIVIA exits stage right after DODGE. The STREET KIDS prepare for their night on the streets. The platforms stage left are lowered, revealing two beds, and creating The Palace. SAMMY and MOUTH enter and sit on the beds stage left. They are playing cards. LYDIA enters and stands at the crate centre stage. Everyone on stage freezes as the music fades out and the lights on the street dim. LYDIA is clearly lit. LYDIA appears frazzled and has a black eye and bruises on her neck. She speaks directly to the audience, as if they are an interrogating police officer.

LYDIA   I wanted to file a report… *(clarifies)* A missing person report. My daughter. Her name is Olivia MacIntosh… *(sarcastically, with attitude)* Yeah… like the apple. I'm sorry. I don't know how to do this. She has long blond hair, blue eyes… She's about five feet, six inches… um… a hundred thirty pounds? We had a fight… she's been a pain in the ass lately. Olivia likes to test us. She's not too fond of my new husband. He's very… strict. *(adjusting sweater to cover bruises)* These bruises… *(sitting on crate, challenging)* I fell. *(changing the subject)* Olivia's run away before but she's never been gone this long. I told you already. I wasn't paying attention and I fell. *(standing and pointing at the audience)* No, I haven't been drinking! Who the hell do you think you are? Look, I just want to find my daughter. *(begins to pace slowly)* I don't remember what she was wearing… She had on black leggings… and boots… a green shirt, I think. *(looking at audience)* Yes, I have a picture. *(gets picture out of purse and stares at it)* Please, Olivia needs to come home… *(looking back at audience)* Before things get any worse.

LYDIA exits and her light dims to match the lighting level of the street. The STREET KIDS shift uncomfortably and freeze again. Lights brighten on The Palace. MOUTH is trying to teach SAMMY how to play poker. They have a milk crate between the two beds and are using it as a table. It is clear that SAMMY is high and his concentration is lacking. He begins to lay down his cards.

MOUTH	*(stopping him)* Noooooo! You need to decide if you're gonna raise.
SAMMY	I know. Just give me a sec... I have to figure out what these are first...

MOUTH and SAMMY laugh. Pause.

What would you do if you had a pair of tens?

MOUTH	Dammit Sammy! That's not how you play the game.
SAMMY	I didn't say I had a pair of tens, I was just asking what you would do, *(speeding up and hitting his cards)* if you had a pair of tens.
MOUTH	I heard you the first time. You can't go and tell me what you have in your hand. It's poker... that's the point.
SAMMY	*(trying to recover)* Well, maybe I was bluffing.
MOUTH	*(throwing cards down)* Five bucks says you have a pair of tens in your hand.
SAMMY	You don't have five bucks.
MOUTH	*(getting up)* Show me your cards.
SAMMY	*(jumping back away from MOUTH)* No, I was bluffing.

MOUTH chases SAMMY around the room and tackles him to the ground, trying to get his cards from him.

MOUTH	Show me your cards, Sammy!
SAMMY	No. I was bluffing!
MOUTH	Show me them!
SAMMY	I was bluffing!

SID enters.

SID	*(hitting his cane on the bed)* That's enough!

SAMMY and MOUTH freeze on the floor for a moment, then quickly scramble to get up. MOUTH stands like he is at attention and SAMMY sits on the far stage left bed, trying to be invisible.

(takes top hat off and places it on trunk) All right boys, what do you have for Sid tonight?

MOUTH digs through his pockets and pulls out various amounts of change and bills. Items fall on the floor and he picks them up and hands them to SID. SID stares at his hand. MOUTH takes a mint back and stands at attention again, bracing himself for a fist.

Just enough to cover rent and meals...

MOUTH   I know... but I was hoping I could borrow a little extra.

SID   Borrow a little extra? After everything I've already given you? You ungrateful boy.

MOUTH   I know... but I need to buy some shoes.

SID   Well, I guess you'll just have to work extra hard tomorrow then, won't you? *(slapping MOUTH on the cheek twice)* Tiny. *(putting end of cane under SAMMY's chin)* What do you got for me?

> *SAMMY quickly pulls out a wad of bills and hands them to SID. He does not want SID to realize he is high. SID eventually shifts his gaze to the cash, lowers his cane, and takes the bills from SAMMY. He begins to count them when DODGE enters.*

DODGE   Sorry I'm late, Sid. I was...

SID   *(grabbing DODGE by the throat)* Where the hell have you been? Do you know what time it is?

DODGE   *(fighting for air)* Let me explain.

SID   *(pushing DODGE on the bed)* You know the rules. *(raising his cane, holding it horizontally with both hands)* And you know what happens when they are broken.

DODGE   *(coughing)* I found someone... a girl.

SID   *(pressing cane down across DODGE's throat)* I don't like girls in here. Raises suspicion.

DODGE   *(trying to breath)* Could be good for business.

> *SID lets DODGE go, and DODGE collapses trying to catch his breath. SID straightens his suit.*

SID   How much did you get today?

> *DODGE hands over his cash. SID counts it.*

Good work, son. *(hands some back to DODGE)* Let me have a look at her.

DODGE   *(signals OLIVIA to enter)* This is Olivia.

SID   *(looking her up and down)* Are you hungry, my dear?

OLIVIA   *(clutching bag and looking around)* No. I'm fine thank you.

SID   Yes, you are.

> *OLIVIA turns to look at SID.*

Welcome to the family! You can stay as long as you'd like. We take care of each other here. Mouth… *(hands MOUTH some bills)* Get yourself some new shoes. Good night boys. *(picks up hat and twirls it on his head)* Sweet dreams. *(exits stage left)*

MOUTH   *(under his breath)* Prick.

SAMMY   *(jumping on bed)* You should have seen me tonight, Dodge. I was on fire! Mouth and I squeegeed for a bit but then we got bored so he took me to meet some of his friends.

MOUTH   *(trying to shut SAMMY up)* Slow down, little buddy.

SAMMY   We went to 7-Eleven. The clerk was so clueless. We stole so many snacks. I got some Juicy Fruit. Want a piece? *(SAMMY snaps a piece out of the pack, and it hits DODGE and falls to the ground.)* I'm gonna have a piece. *(SAMMY sits on the bed bedside OLIVIA.)* Hi, Olivia. You're so pretty. Has anyone ever told you that your eyes are the colour of the ocean…

DODGE   Dammit Mouth! What did you take, Sammy? *(SAMMY doesn't answer, and DODGE grabs him and pushes him stage right.)* What did I tell you? I don't want you getting mixed up with this shit.

MOUTH   It's good shit, man.

DODGE   Stay out of this.

SAMMY   Mouth does it and look at him

> *MOUTH has made a sock puppet and is sharing his cigarette with it. He talks to it and does a puppet voice. When he realizes that they are looking at him, he stops and pulls it off his hand.*

DODGE   You're better than this, Sammy. You have to think. Promise me that you'll never…

SAMMY   I promise.

MOUTH   *(doing scout's honour gesture)* I promise too. I will not do any more of that shit… tonight. *(collapses on bed laughing)*

SID   *(offstage)* Knock it off!

> *There is an awkward pause as they try to figure out who will sleep where.*

DODGE   Sammy, sleep with Mouth tonight.

> *MOUTH strikes a suggestive pose.*

SAMMY   No way, man!

DODGE   Sammy. *(indicating OLIVIA)*

SAMMY   Fine. *(glares at OLIVIA)* But just for tonight.

               SAMMY climbs into bed with MOUTH.

DODGE   You can sleep here tonight. You'll be safe.

DRUMMER   Please.

TOUGH GIRL   Help me.

ADDICT   Please.

OLIVIA   Thanks, Dodge.

               OLIVIA lies on the second bed and DODGE takes his place on the trunk. As the kids in The Palace fall asleep, the STREET KIDS come to life. MOUTH hooks his leg over SAMMY.

BREAKER & SKATER
               Please.

DJ SLIM   Help me.

BAG LADY   Help! Help!

SAMMY   *(getting up)* That's it! I'm sleeping on the floor. *(lies on floor)*

               Cross-fade to the streets. It contrasts the life and "security" of The Palace. The STREET KIDS slowly move throughout the scaffolds.

ACROBAT   I've only been here

BREAKER & SKATER
               A day.

DRUMMER   A week.

TOUGH GIRL   A month.

HOT RAVER   A year.

BAG LADY   A lifetime.

ADDICT   Did you hear me?

TOUGH GIRL   Listen!

DJ SLIM   I'm hungry.

HOT RAVER   Tired.

ACROBAT   Weak.

ARTIST   Cold.

BAG LADY   Sick.

BREAKER   Afraid.

DRUMMER   Alone.

SKATER & TOUGH GIRL
                 Tired.

BAG LADY & DJ SLIM
                 Sick.

ARTIST & HOT RAVER
                 Cold.

TOUGH GIRL & ADDICT
                 Sick and tired.

HOT RAVER   I need money.

BAG LADY   A dollar.

DJ SLIM   Loose change.

DRUMMER & ARTIST
                 Compassion.

BREAKER & SKATER
                 Please.

BREAKER, SKATER, ACROBAT, & DRUMMER
                 Please.

ALL STREET KIDS
                 Please.

> *The STREET KIDS wait for a beat and then the lights begin to fade on the streets. The STREET KIDS begin to try and make money by selling their talents, talking directly to the audience. In the transition, the kids in The Palace fold the beds up. The STREET KIDS quiet down when The Palace kids re-enter the street. DODGE and the others make their way stage right and hang by the flat. DODGE and OLIVIA are sitting, and MOUTH and SAMMY are standing. MOUTH has no shoes on and is carrying his rollerblades.*

DODGE   There's a lot of money to be had on the street.

SAMMY   Are you sure she's ready for this?

DODGE   You need to be patient. Observe everyone and everything around you. Only strike when you know no one is watching.

SAMMY   If she screws up, we'll all get caught.

MOUTH   Come on, little buddy, you can help me with my new gimmick... tada! *(producing a harmonica)*

SAMMY	What do I get to do?
MOUTH	*(torn between his harmonica and his squeegee)* You can… hold my squeegee. Let's go.
SAMMY	*(to OLIVIA)* Don't screw up.

> MOUTH pulls SAMMY away stage left in a playful headlock. They are met at centre stage by DJ SLIM, who hands them a flyer.

DJ SLIM	Mouth… Rave… Friday… Be there.
MOUTH	Check ya later, raver dude.

> MOUTH stuffs the flyer in SAMMY's face, and SAMMY pulls it away as they move to the crates stage left. A BUSINESSWOMAN enters stage right and is talking on her cellphone.

DODGE	Just stick to the plan. When I give you the signal, *(runs his hand through his hair)* you move in. Ready?

> OLIVIA nods and DODGE gets up and approaches the BUSINESSWOMAN.

BUSINESSWOMAN
Yeah Jim. I'll be there in ten minutes. What do you mean there's been a delay?

DODGE	Excuse me, ma'am…

BUSINESSWOMAN
(to DODGE) Hold on a second. *(to phone)* That's not good enough, Jim. The Mercer file needs to be on my desk by two. *(folds phone)* What do you want, kid?

DODGE	I want a job.

> DODGE runs his hand through his hair but OLIVIA is unable to move.

BUSINESSWOMAN
(laughing) A job? You've got to be kidding me. *(begins to walk away stage left but DODGE circles around and stops her)*

DODGE	I bet you could use a creative individual like myself.

BUSINESSWOMAN
If you'll excuse me… *(puts phone in purse)*

DODGE	Ma'am, please. I don't like to beg but I really need some cash.

BUSINESSWOMAN
For drugs? You'll get nothing from me.

> DODGE gives the signal again but OLIVIA doesn't move.

DODGE   Sammy!

> *SAMMY drops the squeegee and joins DODGE.*

MOUTH   Hey!

DODGE   This is my kid brother *(SAMMY pulls back from DODGE.)* and
               I promised that I'd look after him once we got here... Our father
               died. He hasn't eaten anything in...

> *OLIVIA has worked up the courage and runs into the back of the*
> *BUSINESSWOMAN, who spills her coffee on her suit and drops*
> *her purse. In the confusion, DODGE picks up her purse, takes her*
> *wallet, and hands it to SAMMY.*

BUSINESSWOMAN
               Dammit!

OLIVIA   Oh my god! I am so sorry.

BUSINESSWOMAN
               My suit is ruined!

OLIVIA   Let me help you with that.

BUSINESSWOMAN
               Just get out of my way.

> *She turns to exit and DODGE hands her back her purse.*

               You street punks are all the same.

> *BUSINESSWOMAN exits.*

DODGE   *(calling after her)* What about the job? Come on, lady... for
               my brother!

SAMMY   Why did you say that, Dodge?

DODGE   I needed your help.

SAMMY   *(pulling wallet back)* We split it three ways.

DODGE   Let it slide just this once, Sammy.

SAMMY   You're breaking your own rules, Dodge.

DODGE   There'll be more.

SAMMY   What ever you say... *(hitting DODGE on chest with wallet as he*
               hands it over) Bro.

> *SAMMY joins MOUTH stage left and DODGE moves toward*
> *OLIVIA.*

DODGE   Do the honours.

OLIVIA	There's over a hundred dollars in here!
MOUTH	Any cards?
DODGE	No cards, Mouth. Too easy to trace and Sid won't bail you out. What is it, Liv?
OLIVIA	There's a picture… She has kids. This isn't right, Dodge.
DODGE	Look around you, Liv. What do you see?
OLIVIA	It doesn't make it right.
DODGE	This is your life now. Your values and morals mean nothing out here. *(takes wallet back)* I've learned the world owes me nothing. So I take. Payback's a bitch, Liv.
OLIVIA	Why are you talking like this? This can't be who you are.
DODGE	You know nothing about my life!
SAMMY	Dodge killed a man once.
MOUTH	Robbed a gas station before coming out here.
OLIVIA	I don't believe that.
SAMMY	Believe it. No one messes with him, right Dodge?
DODGE	*(pause)* Look, this money is a drop in the hat for that lady. It means nothing to her. But to us, it means we get to eat tonight and it buys us another night at The Palace. *(taking money out of wallet)* If you're too good for this, too good for us, *(throwing money at OLIVIA's feet)* then maybe you should go back to mommy and daddy.
	DODGE exits stage right. SAMMY runs after him. Transition music begins to play as OLIVIA slowly sinks to the ground. The STREET KIDS climb out of the set. OLIVIA sinks to her knees and picks up the money, staring at it. The STREET KIDS move in and surround OLIVIA, taunting her. The transition music fades out.
TOUGH GIRL	Lose your dignity.
ADDICT	Sell your soul.
SKATER	Fight the fear.
DRUMMER	Don't close your eyes.
ACROBAT	Never turn your back.
DJ SLIM	Trust no one.
BAG LADY	Don't let your guard down.

ARTIST	Ignore the hunger.
ACROBAT	Disguise your broken pride,
BREAKER	Your shattered hope.
HOT RAVER	Push through the humiliation.
DRUMMER	They won't recognize you from your poster.
TOUGH GIRL	They don't even see you.

ALL STREET KIDS
(raising hands, begging to audience) Can you spare some change?

The STREET KIDS freeze as MOUTH crosses to OLIVIA and crouches beside her.

MOUTH   Liv, it's getting late… (offering her his hand) Are you coming home?

OLIVIA   Yeah. (putting money in her pocket, accepting her new life and MOUTH's hand) I'm coming home.

MOUTH and OLIVIA get up and exit stage right. Once they are off the stage the chorus drop their hands.

ALL STREET KIDS
That's what I thought.

The STREET KIDS climb back into the set and back to their places for the night. DODGE and SAMMY enter upstage right and make their way to the swing. SAMMY sits on the swing and DODGE leans on the stage right side of the scaffold.

DODGE   Sorry about earlier. I didn't mean to play the brother card.

SAMMY   I know.

DODGE   (pause) You don't talk about him much anymore.

SAMMY   I thought that when I got out here it would all just disappear. But it's harder now.

DODGE   What do you mean?

SAMMY   At home I had pictures… memories.

DODGE   And now?

SAMMY   I can't remember what he was like before he got sick. When I think of him now, all I see is him hooked up to all of those machines, rotting away in that hospital.

DODGE   What was he like?

SAMMY   You.

DODGE	Really?
SAMMY	I used to believe him too. But you both lied.
DODGE	Sammy...
SAMMY	It's true. Half the things you say are lies, aren't they? *(DODGE remains silent.)* And I believed all of it, Dodge. I thought you cared.
DODGE	I do care, Sammy. I get it.
SAMMY	*(standing)* You don't get anything!
DODGE	I get that you don't belong here, kid. You should be at home with your parents. You should be going to school.
SAMMY	I'll never go back there. Everyone around me was lying. Just like you. I'll see you at The Palace.

SAMMY exits upstage left as OLIVIA and MOUTH enter upstage right.

DODGE	*(calling after SAMMY)* Sammy... Sammy come on.
MOUTH	Check it out, Dodge.

MOUTH plays an indistinguishable tune on the harmonica. DODGE walks away and sits on a milk crate. He pulls out a cigarette and begins to smoke.

Harsh man. Harsh. Check ya later, Liv.

MOUTH exits upstage left, trying to play his harmonica. There is an awkward moment between OLIVIA and DODGE.

OLIVIA	*(breaking the tension)* What is this place?
DODGE	It's the secret swing. Some artist put it in a couple of years ago. *(pause)* Try it.

OLIVIA sits on the swing, and DODGE gets up and crosses behind her.

Close your eyes.

OLIVIA	*(looking back at him)* Why?
DODGE	*(leaning in)* Just do it.

OLIVIA closes her eyes and DODGE gives her a push. OLIVIA continues to swing and DODGE makes his way to the crate, where he sits and continues to smoke. As DODGE speaks OLIVIA is carried away to another place and her happiness is reflected on her face.

I use to come here to forget. I'd sit on that swing, and the lights and noise of the city would just fade away. I'd be somewhere else... No past... no future... just happy. *(pause)* But I can't even dream here anymore. At some time you have to open your eyes again and you're just in a dirty alley.

> *OLIVIA opens her eyes, realizes where she is, and stops swinging. Her dream has evaporated.*

OLIVIA   *(pause)* Can I ask you something?

DODGE   Depends on what you're asking.

OLIVIA   Did you really rob a gas station?

DODGE   *(pause)* No.

OLIVIA   *(hesitant)* Did you... kill someone?

DODGE   No.

OLIVIA   Why lie about it?

DODGE   *(getting up, tossing cigarette away)* Too many questions.

OLIVIA   *(standing)* You can still dream, Dodge.

DODGE   What's the point? I've spent my entire life dreaming of places to run to that would be better than where I was at. Where did it get me? *(motions to his surroundings)* I'm done with dreaming.

OLIVIA   Do you miss your old life?

DODGE   No use looking back.

OLIVIA   *(pause, makes her way back to the swing and sits)* I miss my mom. I never thought I would but I do. She use to sing to me when I was sick or afraid. When my dad left, my *real* dad, she just stopped.

DODGE   Sorry about your dad.

OLIVIA   Me too. *(standing)* I spent so much time hating her after he took off that I forgot that she was human. She was just sad too.

DODGE   Do you want to go back?

OLIVIA   It doesn't matter what I want now. She's not the same and I guess I'm not either. Things can never go back to the way they were. *(pause)* But I still miss her.

DODGE   *(changing the subject)* Sorry about earlier.

OLIVIA   *(pulling money out of her pocket)* I understand how things work. I don't like it... *(holding money out to DODGE)* but I understand it.

DODGE   *(folding money back in her hand)* Keep it.

> *OLIVIA leans in for a kiss and they almost do but DODGE pulls back.*

It's getting late. We should get going. Sid will be waiting for us.

> *Transition music begins to play. DODGE and OLIVIA exit upstage left. The STREET KIDS remove their winter clothing to show the passing of time. LYDIA enters and stands centre stage.*

LYDIA   I have been in and out of this station almost every day for the last four months and you are no closer to finding my daughter. No. Don't tell me to calm down! You have no clue where she is. Would you care more if she had been kidnapped? *(pause)* I'm sorry. *(sitting down)* I didn't mean that. *(trying to collect herself)* Do you think that I don't see the way you look at me, officer? You think this is my fault. My daughter is out there somewhere, hungry, with god knows who, and you think I'm the one to blame. Well you know what... You're right. I'm her mother. I'm suppose to be the one protecting her. She saw it happening every day and she tried so hard to get me to leave him. But I just couldn't. *(defending)* He wasn't always like that. I used to believe that he didn't know what he was doing because he was drunk. *(protecting)* He never hit Olivia... *(coming clean)* until that night. I knew she wasn't going to come back this time and I just let her go. *(pleading)* Everything has changed since Olivia left... I've changed. *(standing)* You have to believe me. I finally have the strength to leave him. I know that Olivia is seventeen and I know that she ran away from me but she's still my little girl. Can you understand that? Please, just help me bring Olivia home.

> *LYDIA picks up her purse and exits stage right. The streets come alive. DJ SLIM is beat-boxing and the others gather around him. The BREAKER begins to break dance. DODGE, OLIVIA, MOUTH, and SAMMY are hanging in front of The Palace, preparing for the rave. SID enters and pulls DODGE aside to provide him with E to sell at the rave. DODGE removes some pills. He takes one and rejoins the group. The STREET KIDS filter off the stage, dancing and cheering.*

DODGE   I have a surprise. *(producing the pills)* A new branch of Sid's business.

OLIVIA   What is that?

MOUTH   E... Ecstasy?!

DODGE   My treat.

> *DODGE hands one to OLIVIA and MOUTH. MOUTH promptly swallows it.*

OLIVIA	Haven't kids died from taking E?
DODGE	I took one earlier and I'm fine. *(laughing)* You've been high before, right?
OLIVIA	I smoked pot once.
SAMMY	Big deal.
MOUTH	It's better than pot.
DODGE	It speeds everything up.
MOUTH	A real rush! Your vision may start to blur and you could feel cold or faint. You may grind your teeth or bite through your tongue... It'll be fun!

> *DODGE has pulled OLIVIA aside.*

| DODGE | *(to OLIVIA)* Do you trust me? |

> *OLIVIA pauses and then takes the pill. DODGE holds her hands and stares at her. MOUTH gets excited at their shared E experience.*

SAMMY	Where's mine?
DODGE	I told you already. I don't want you getting mixed up with this shit.
SAMMY	You're such a hypocrite!
DODGE	That's a pretty big word for such a tiny individual.

> *They all share a laugh.*

SAMMY	Don't call me that, and stop treating me like a little kid!
DODGE	You are just a kid.
SAMMY	She's changing you, Dodge, and you don't even see it. You're becoming mean... just like Sid.

> *In a quick move DODGE grabs SAMMY by the collar.*

| DODGE | Don't you say that. *(shaking him)* Don't you ever say that! |
| MOUTH | Why so serious? Leave the little dude alone. |

> *DODGE, realizing what he is doing, lets SAMMY go and backs away.*

| SAMMY | Stop saying that! |
| DODGE | I'm tired of being your babysitter. You want to try it... go ahead. *(hands pill to SAMMY)* Mouth, he's your problem tonight. Let's go, Liv. *(pulls OLIVIA offstage)* |

MOUTH	He'll cool off.
SAMMY	Get off me.
MOUTH	No going back.
SAMMY	I know.

MOUTH pulls the pill away from SAMMY. SAMMY grabs it, swallows it, and begins to walk away. MOUTH catches up to him and drapes his arm around him.

MOUTH	It's going to be a good night! You'll see, Sammy. Remember to drink lots of water and kiss lots of ladies.

SAMMY stops. MOUTH takes a few steps then stops and turns to look at SAMMY.

You have kissed a girl before, right?

SAMMY	Well... technically... my mom...
MOUTH	Shut up! You've got a lot to learn, my man. *(leading SAMMY offstage)* It's definitely going to be a good night. I'll teach you everything I know. And believe me, I know a lot about the ladies! Stick with me, kid, and you'll never go horny again!

As they exit the stage, lights begin to dim and the stage is filled with coloured lights, and sound. DJ SLIM enters.

DJ SLIM	All right party people. This is DJ Slim spinning for ya till five a.m. Everybody get up and dance. I wanna hear you scream.

Everyone screams offstage and then they begin to enter. DJ SLIM makes his way to stand on top of the tires stage right. As everyone enters, they are dancing and swinging Glow Sticks. As the rave continues, there is a slow-motion bit and the lights go to black. When the music kicks in again, everyone dances at normal speed. OLIVIA collapses. DODGE helps her offstage. As the rave dies down, The Palace is lowered and everyone makes their way back into the scaffold. They throw their Glow Sticks in the garbage bin on stage and fall asleep. MOUTH and the HOT RAVER are frozen in a flirtatious pose at the swing. DODGE and OLIVIA enter The Palace, and DODGE helps her onto the bed.

OLIVIA	I feel like my heart's going to explode. I can't breathe.
DODGE	*(grabbing water from the trunk and handing it to her)* Drink this.
OLIVIA	I just want to go to sleep.
DODGE	You can't... Not yet.
OLIVIA	Why not?

DODGE	You might not wake up.
OLIVIA	*(annoyed)* Oh god.

OLIVIA sits up and takes a drink of the water.

DODGE	You're going to be fine.
OLIVIA	Talk to me, Dodge. How'd you end up here? The truth.
DODGE	The truth is a tricky thing, Liv. I've invented so many stories it's hard to distinguish the truth from the lies.
OLIVIA	I know there are some things you can never forget. I want to know you.
DODGE	No, you don't.
OLIVIA	Please, Dodge. It will help me focus. How'd you end up here?
DODGE	Where do I begin? *(getting increasingly angry as he continues)* How about the foster mom who spent every cent of her welfare cheque on booze or maybe the one who used to lock me up in the closet every night. Or how about the one who fed me nothing but Alphagetti for a month. Pick one, Liv, I've got thirteen more to tell you about. Is that what you want to hear?
OLIVIA	I'm sorry. I didn't know. *(pause)* Well, what about your real parents?
DODGE	Father, never knew him. Neither did my mother, if you want to get technical. My mother... eighteen-year-old with a coke habit and not a whole lot of patience for kids if I can remember correctly. She use to drop me off with a neighbour... One day, she never bothered to pick me up.
OLIVIA	That's awful.
DODGE	*(begins to change)* Compared to my childhood, juvie was a breeze. Hot meal everyday, warm bed. Guess that's why I kept going back.
OLIVIA	Can you be serious for once? I know what it's like.
DODGE	Give me a break. Do you know what it's like to be unwanted, Liv?
OLIVIA	Of course I...
DODGE	No. I mean really unwanted. It eats away at you until all that's left is an empty shell. You don't even recognize yourself anymore... At least here, I get respect. People listen to me. Especially Sammy. I'm all he's got... me and Sid.

OLIVIA is creeped out at the mention of SID and she moves to the other bed to be closer to DODGE.

OLIVIA	Let's just leave, Dodge. You and me… We'll catch a bus and fade away into the sunset. We'll just keep going till the money runs out. We could go to BC or Montreal.
DODGE	I don't speak French, do you?
OLIVIA	There are shelters, *good* people who could help us.
DODGE	*(thinks about it and almost believes it is possible)* I have a life here. People who need me.
OLIVIA	*(taking his hands)* I need you. I don't even know you're real name but you know what I think?
DODGE	What?
OLIVIA	*(playing with his hands)* I think… *(moving in for a kiss)* I think… I think I'm going to be sick.

> *DODGE helps ease OLIVIA into bed, where she quickly passes out. DODGE moves her hair out of her face. SAMMY enters unnoticed.*

DODGE	The name… *(kisses her forehead)* is Gavin.

> *SAMMY enters and DODGE stands up. SAMMY moves to the other bed and lies on his back.*

	Where's Mouth?
SAMMY	Don't know.
DODGE	Are you feeling okay?
SAMMY	Fine.
DODGE	You're sure you're okay?
SAMMY	Yeah. *(turns his back to DODGE)* Night, Dodge.
DODGE	*(to himself)* Night, kid. *(climbs into bed with OLIVIA)*

> *Attention shifts to MOUTH and the HOT RAVER, who unfreeze.*

MOUTH	So… need a place to crash? You could always come back to my pad.
HOT RAVER	Got any money?
MOUTH	Are you serious? *(searches his pockets, comes up empty handed and tries a new tactic)* You know, there's a lot of love to go around.
HOT RAVER	I don't think so. You're good from far… but far from good!

> *HOT RAVER climbs into the scaffold and the other STREET KIDS snicker. MOUTH is clearly deflated by the rejection.*

MOUTH	Harsh, man! Harsh. *(to TOUGH GIRL)* I guess some things never change. *(sits on the swing as she hands him a cigarette and lights it)* Some people look at me with disgust. They see that I haven't showered and assume I own one pair of clothes. They make eye contact with me and I can feel their annoyance. They drive by and I don't give them another thought. *(pause)* They aren't as bad as the ones who don't look at me at all. They're the ones with the power to shame. *(getting up and walking slowly to centre stage)* Oh, they know I'm there. *(grabbing his shirt)* I make their skin crawl. But they keep their cold stare on the pavement ahead, listening to the tunes in the shelter of their fancy cars. They're the ones who haunt me because they're the ones who make me feel like I'm nothing. I'm worthless. Not worth their spare change, not worth their kindness or compassion. Not even worth a glance in the rear-view mirror. *(pause)* But what am I suppose to do? I can't give up. I sure as hell can't go home. *(pause, points to audience)* Can I squeegee your car? *(pause, shakes head and tosses his cigarette aside as he exits stage right)*

The lights come up on The Palace as SAMMY wakes up. He roots through DODGE's jacket. He finds the gun and a bag of pills. He takes some pills then holds the gun up and aims it. OLIVIA groans and stirs. SAMMY quickly puts everything back. DODGE wakes up, rubs his eyes, and looks around.

DODGE	Where's Mouth? I didn't hear him come in last night.
SAMMY	He didn't.
DODGE	Does Sid know?
SAMMY	Sid knows everything. *(lights a cigarette now with ease)*
OLIVIA	*(sitting up)* I think I'm going to be sick again.
SAMMY	Lightweight.
OLIVIA	If I lie down, my head spins and I think I'm going to puke, but when I sit up I get this sharp pain behind my eyes.
SAMMY	*(yelling)* Does princess have a headache? *(blowing smoke in her face)* Poor baby.

DODGE smacks SAMMY as OLIVIA coughs. She covers her mouth, stands up, and runs off stage left past SID, who has entered.

SID	*(yelling after OLIVIA)* Where do you think you're going? *(to DODGE)* Where's Mouth? He owes me my commission.
DODGE	He got up early.

SAMMY	He's lying.
DODGE	Sammy!
SAMMY	Mouth didn't come home last night.
SID	He'll get what's coming to him. *(sensing tension between DODGE and SAMMY)* Sam, you've been pulling in a lot of cash lately. I think it's time you started to take on more responsibility with our little operation.
SAMMY	Dodge doesn't think I can handle it.
SID	Dodge isn't in charge. I am. What do you say?
SAMMY	*(staring at DODGE, challenging)* I'm in. *(starts to walk away)*
	SID *goes about organizing money and drugs to give to SAMMY to sell.*
DODGE	*(stopping him)* What are you doing?
SAMMY	Just looking out for number one, right Dodge? *(walking past him)* That's what you always say.
DODGE	*(going after him)* We look out for each other.
SAMMY	I'm tired of you telling me what to do.
DODGE	I only do that so you won't make the same mistakes as me.
SID	*(enticing)* There's a lot of money to be had on the streets, my boy.
DODGE	You don't belong on the streets, Sammy.
SID	There's power in this business. People need you to feed their habit and because of that, they give you respect.
DODGE	*(places a hand on SAMMY's chest to stop him)* Don't listen to him.
	SAMMY *knocks DODGE's hand down and sits on the other bed across from SID.*
SID	*(holding out a bag of pills that SAMMY grabs)* You'll have more money than you know what to do with. *(handing him cash)* I can give you everything you've ever wanted.
DODGE	*(back to them)* It's not worth selling your soul.
SID	I'm the devil then, am I? *(getting up to face DODGE who has turned around)* A devil that's provided you with food, shelter, and an income for three years. *(walking away)* You wouldn't have lasted a week out there with out me.
DODGE	Shut up!

SID	(*moving toward DODGE and grabbing him*) I'll teach you respect. (*raising his cane*) Seems you've forgotten how things work around here.
DODGE	What are you going to do? Hit me again? I'm not afraid of you!

SID lets DODGE go and SID backs away.

	Do whatever you want to me, just leave him out of this.
SAMMY	What do you care? You're leaving anyways.
SID	Leave? Where would you go? What could you possibly do? You would be nothing without me. You want to leave, go ahead, but the kid stays. He's a partner now, right Sam?

SID offers his hand. There is a pause and then SAMMY shakes hands with him.

	Get to work. (*twirls his hat on and exits*)
DODGE	Sammy, I don't know what you've heard but you've got to believe me…
SAMMY	Got more lies, Dodge? 'Cause that's what you do, right? Invent things so people believe you're something you're not. Well I'm done listening. (*walking away*)
DODGE	Don't you see what's really happening here? This is exactly what Sid wants. He wants you to deal so he doesn't have to do the dirty work. What happens when you get caught, Sammy? Do you think Sid will be there to help you? Whatever is going on in your head, don't do this because you're mad at me. Trust me, it's not worth it.
SAMMY	(*opening bag of pills to take one*) Stop telling me what to do. I can think for myself. (*DODGE grabs the bag from him.*) You're not my brother!
DODGE	You're right. I'm not because he's dead, Sammy! (*softening*) He's dead but I'm standing right here. Your brother didn't choose to leave you. He got sick and he died.
SAMMY	Shut up!
DODGE	It sucks and I'm sorry it happened.
SAMMY	(*pause*) He said he was going to be fine. That he wasn't going anywhere.
DODGE	I know what you're going through.
SAMMY	You know nothing about it!

DODGE	Do you want to end up like him? Is that what you want? How much have you been taking, Sammy?
SAMMY	*(trying to grab pills)* It's none of your business.
DODGE	These pills will not make the pain go away. They'll screw up your brain till you can't think anymore.
OLIVIA	What's going on?

> *OLIVIA enters. DODGE looks at her and SAMMY grabs the pills back.*

SAMMY	This is your fault. Everything was fine before you got here. I hate you. I hate both of you!

> *SAMMY quickly exits stage left.*

DODGE	There's no point talking to him now. He needs to come down before he'll hear me. *(goes to trunk and pulls out pill container)* But I need to keep an eye on him. Here take these.
OLIVIA	No more drugs.
DODGE	Tylenol. Stay here today. You'll be no good on the streets like this.
OLIVIA	Don't get angry with him... Just talk to him, Dodge.
DODGE	I'll be back soon.

> *DODGE exits. OLIVIA takes her Tylenol and lies back in bed. Transition music begins to play and the streets come to life. LYDIA tries to hand out flyers with her daughter's picture on them, but people ignore her and go about their business. SAMMY doesn't notice DODGE has followed him.*

LYDIA	Please, could you just take a second to... just look at the picture... It will only take... Have you seen... Please... here take one... Could you just... I need your help... Would you just STOP!

> *Everyone stops and stares at her. The transition music cuts off. LYDIA speaks directly to the audience.*

Look at her picture. Take a good look. Have you seen my daughter? Her name is Olivia MacIntosh. She's been missing for six months now. She has blond hair and blue eyes. She has small hands, just like mine. *(Everyone begins to move again.)* Please don't walk away from me.

> *DODGE has picked up a poster from the ground and is staring at it. In the next scene SAMMY realizes that DODGE is following him and he exits stage right. The ADDICT and the ACROBAT*

follow him. DODGE is unable to follow because LYDIA has him trapped.

(to DODGE) Have you seen my daughter? Do you know her? Please, if you know where she is…

DODGE   I don't know your daughter.

LYDIA   *(grabbing DODGE's arm)* Her name is…

DODGE   Let go of my arm. I don't know your kid, lady.

LYDIA   Please…

DODGE   I'm sorry.

He pockets the poster and exits upstage left.

LYDIA   *(looking around lost)* I can't do this.

LYDIA exits upstage right as SID enters The Palace carrying a dress and makeup bag. He smells the dress, then notices OLIVIA and places the dress and makeup bag on the bed.

SID   What are you still doing here?

OLIVIA   I wasn't feeling well.

SID   *(sitting on the bed with her)* There, there, my dear. Rest up. You'll need your strength for tonight.

OLIVIA   *(shifting away from him)* What are you talking about?

SID   *(moving closer again)* I have a friend. Said he'd pay good money for a night with a pretty little thing like yourself. *(pulling cane back)* I got you a nice dress and some makeup *(running cane up her thigh)* so you'll look real good.

OLIVIA   *(standing up and crossing arms protectively)* I'm not a prostitute.

SID   *(puts cane down and walks up behind her)* Do you know what happens to pretty girls like you on the street? You should be thanking me for picking a businessman for your first trick. He'll be gentle. *(running hand around her stomach)* Real attentive.

OLIVIA   *(turning to face him)* You're a pig!

SID   Oh really… *(slaps OLIVIA across the face and she falls to the ground)* The free ride stops here, honey. You've been sponging off me for six months now and it's time you start earning your keep. *(crouching down behind her, running a finger up her leg)* You owe Sid this favour… and you'll do it.

SID gets up and begins to walk toward the bed. OLIVIA slowly gets up on her knees.

OLIVIA I can't... I won't.

SID *(grabs her by the wrists, pulling her up)* No one gives a damn about you. Do you think mommy and daddy are out looking for you? I see it every day. They're not because you're nothing. *(throwing her back to ground)* Now put on this dress *(throws the dress at her)* and paint your face. *(throws makeup bag)* Look real nice for my friend. *(crouching beside her, grabs OLIVIA's face)* Do not test my patience, little girl. I won't ask so nicely next time. *(pushes her face away)*

> SID begins to exit stage left and runs into DODGE as he enters. OLIVIA is left crumpled and crying on the floor. She slowly sits up and hugs her legs.

DODGE What's going on? *(OLIVIA continues to rock back and forth. DODGE kneels beside her.)* What happened? *(He reaches out to comfort her.)*

OLIVIA *(pushing him away)* Don't touch me! *(realizes it's DODGE then goes back to rocking)*

DODGE Okay... okay.

OLIVIA I'm so ashamed. He wanted me to... to... oh god! I was actually thinking about doing it... selling myself. It wasn't suppose to be like this. It wasn't suppose to be so hard. *(DODGE moves to her but she gets up.)* I have to get out of here. I can't stay.

> OLIVIA goes to the trunk and begins to frantically pack her things on the bed. She sees that DODGE has pulled out the gun.

What are you doing with that?

> DODGE goes to exit stage left.

Where are you going?

DODGE He's not getting away with this!

OLIVIA Screw Sid! This isn't about him anymore! *(DODGE backs away from her. She makes her way to him.)* Let's just leave. There's a big world out there, Dodge. I haven't been here long enough to forget that. There's a place for us.

> OLIVIA manages to take the gun away from DODGE and she cautiously places it on the bed. DODGE has pulled out the poster and is staring at it.

DODGE There's a place for you. *(hands flyer to OLIVIA)*

OLIVIA Where did you get this? Did you tell her I was here? *(sitting on bed)* She can't see me like this.

DODGE She loves you. Maybe you should go home.

OLIVIA   I can't go back. Not while he's there. You don't now what it was like in that house. *(pause)* You don't know!

DODGE   No one's looking for me! No one gave a damn about me until I came here.

OLIVIA   I would rather die than settle for this. You control your life, Dodge. You make the choices.

DODGE   I can't just leave.

OLIVIA   Yes, you can.

DODGE   No, I can't.

OLIVIA   Why not?!

DODGE   Because I'm scared! *(sits on bed)*

OLIVIA   *(pause)* Of what?

DODGE   That Sid's right. That I am nothing. That maybe this is all I deserve.

OLIVIA   *(approaches DODGE)* Dodge…

DODGE   *(shifting away)* Don't.

OLIVIA   You deserve more than this.

DODGE   Stop it.

OLIVIA   More than anyone I know.

DODGE   *(getting up)* Quit screwing with me.

OLIVIA   *(turning him around)* You deserve more. *(holds his face in her hands)* Listen to me, you deserve so much more than this, Dodge. *(hugs him and eventually he returns the hug)* You deserve so much more. *(The embrace moves into a kiss and they eventually pull apart holding hands.)*

DODGE   I won't leave Sammy.

OLIVIA   Then we'll take him with us.

              OLIVIA grabs her remaining things. DODGE picks up the dress and makeup bag and angrily tosses them in the trunk. He goes to the bed and picks up his jacket. He picks up the gun.

              Are you ready?

              DODGE thinks about it and then places the gun back on the bed.

DODGE   Yeah. *(grabbing her hand)* Let's get out of here.

              DODGE and OLIVIA exit stage left. The STREET KIDS come to life as MOUTH enters with posters and markers.

MOUTH	*(handing out supplies to the STREET KIDS)* All right boys and girls, we need posters.
	Lots of posters.
BREAKER	What should they say?
MOUTH	*(He is holding up a sign with "STUPID" written in big letters down the left-hand side. After each big letter is a corresponding word.)* Squeegees of Toronto Unite Producing Independent Dollars.
	MOUTH celebrates his genius and in his head he can hear the crowds cheering.
TOUGH GIRL	Mouth… Mouth… Mouth! How do you spell squeegee?
DRUMMER	Is it squeegee or squeeg-eee? *(clear emphasis on the extra E)*
	MOUTH thinks about this and writes it in the air.
SKATER	One E or two E's, Mouth?
MOUTH	One… no… maybe two… could be three…
ARTIST	Mouth?
MOUTH	It doesn't matter how you spell it! It's about the idea!
	DJ SLIM drops down from the scaffold.
	Wow! You're just in time. I'm starting a union and these are my people. I have a dream that one day every squeegee kid will belong to my union. Everyone who joins will receive better wages… skilled representation…
ALL STREET KIDS	Yeah right.
MOUTH	And buttons!
ALL STREET KIDS	Buttons! *(cheers)*
MOUTH	Or a membership pin! I don't know, I have so many ideas!
	The STREET KIDS eagerly make their signs.
DJ SLIM	Your union… It's STUPID.
MOUTH	Thinking too small, eh? I thought about that too. How about Southern Ontario Squeegees of Toronto Unite Producing Independent Dollars! *(MOUTH does a celebratory dance and sings his next line.)* That's the new one… it's so much better… I just made it up in my head!
DJ SLIM	Mouth… Mouth… *(slapping him)* Focus man!

MOUTH	Ouch! What! I am focused!
DJ SLIM	Look. *(showing him the sign)* Now you're SO STUPID!
MOUTH	Why do you have to be like that?
DJ SLIM	Read the sign!
MOUTH	I read it when I wrote it, man.
DJ SLIM	Why don't you look closer?

> *DJ SLIM holds the clock around his neck and holds his fingers up counting to three.*

MOUTH	The shading's perfect... I could have probably used more colours but I didn't want to cloud the... Oh snap! *(pulling DJ SLIM aside)*
DJ SLIM	It took you long enough.
MOUTH	How is anyone going to take me seriously?! Hi, I'm Mouth and I'm with STUPID!
DJ SLIM	You can still change it.
MOUTH	No. They've already made the signs. *(stopping in his tracks)* Do you think they noticed? *(All STREET KIDS are angrily staring at MOUTH. MOUTH slowly turns to face them.)* I think they noticed. *(clearing his throat)* Will you look at that! She made a sign with a butterfly... and a squeegee for a body...

> *MOUTH takes off running and exits stage right. All the STREET KIDS take their signs and throw them in the trash and go back to their places in the scaffold. ADDICT and ACROBAT have entered and sit at the swing waiting for SAMMY. SAMMY enters The Palace.*

SAMMY	Dodge, I need your... *(realizing he's not there)* help.

> *He quickly moves to the trunk and searches it, realizing that DODGE and OLIVIA's stuff is gone. He sits on the trunk. After a moment he notices the gun. He slowly picks it up and spins it around in his hand. As he exits stage left, transition music plays. The STREET KIDS talk amongst themselves. SAMMY re-enters upstage left and meets the ADDICT and ACROBAT at the swing. The transition music fades out.*

ACROBAT	Well, well, well. What do we have here?
ADDICT	It's my old pal, Sammy.
ACROBAT	Where's Dodge?

SAMMY	I make the deals now. *(All the STREET KIDS laugh.)* How much do you want?
ADDICT	Half gram. *(hands SAMMY money)*
SAMMY	*(walking forward)* It's forty-five now. Inflation.
ADDICT	It was forty last time.
SAMMY	Take it or leave it.
ADDICT	Just give it to me.
SAMMY	Forty-five or I'm outta here.
ADDICT	Please.
SAMMY	*(laughs and throws the money at him)* You're worthless. *(begins to walk away)*
	ACROBAT laughs.
ADDICT	Where do you think you're going?
ACROBAT	Relax, Ray.
ADDICT	No. He's gonna pay for all the times Dodge screwed me over. Hand over your stash.
SAMMY	No.
ACROBAT	We'll just buy it from someone else.
ADDICT	Your cash too.
SAMMY	Screw you!
	SAMMY turns to leave but the ADDICT pushes him to the ground.
ACROBAT	Dammit, Ray!
ADDICT	Pick him up... do it!
	The ACROBAT reluctantly picks SAMMY up and holds his arms behind his back.
	You tell Dodge the next time he messes with me he's dead.
SAMMY	Tell him yourself!
	SAMMY spits in the ADDICT's face. The ADDICT punches SAMMY in the stomach and begins to go through his coat pockets. He takes the drugs and the money, and then finds the gun. He pulls it out and is pointing it at SAMMY.

ACROBAT	*(letting SAMMY go and slowly backing away)* What are you doing with that?
	SAMMY lunges for the gun.
SAMMY	Give it to me! It's mine!
ADDICT	Let go!
	They continue to struggle over the gun until it goes off and everyone hits the ground. SAMMY and the ADDICT are in shock, and then SAMMY eventually falls to the ground clutching his stomach.
ACROBAT	What did you do...
ADDICT	*(dropping the gun and slowly backing away)* I didn't... oh god.
ACROBAT	What did you do?!
SAMMY	Help me... please.
ADDICT	I'm sorry, kid.
	Everyone has cleared the streets. DODGE and OLIVIA enter upstage left, holding hands. They make their way to the swing.
DODGE	Sammy?
OLIVIA	He's over here.
	They see SAMMY on the ground and figure he is drunk or high again. SAMMY has his back to the audience.
DODGE	I'm gonna kill him.
OLIVIA	I'll get him. Come on, Sammy. Get up. *(turning him over, sees blood for the first time and begins to go into shock)* He's hurt, Dodge.
DODGE	*(moving downstage to SAMMY)* What did you take this time...
	DODGE slowly backs away and brings his hands to his head. OLIVIA begins to panic. While OLIVIA is kneeling with SAMMY, she applies fake blood to his T-shirt and her hands. While SAMMY is on the ground, he puts blood capsules in his mouth.
OLIVIA	You're going to be okay. Do you hear me? *(looking at her hands which are now covered in blood)* There's so much blood. Dodge. Stay with me, Sammy.
	DODGE drops his jacket.
	Dodge! Help me get him up!

> *DODGE and OLIVIA try to pick SAMMY up and move him but they collapse to the floor. Blood comes out of SAMMY's mouth. OLIVIA starts to lose it as DODGE tries to comfort SAMMY.*

SAMMY *(whispering and gasping)* I don't want to die, Dodge.

DODGE You're not going to die.

OLIVIA I can't get it to stop!

DODGE Sammy… Sammy! Look at me! .

OLIVIA Sammy, don't close your eyes.

DODGE You're going to be fine. I promise… we'll get you back to The Palace. Sid will know what to do.

OLIVIA Dodge…

DODGE Did you hear me, Sammy…

OLIVIA Dodge, he's gone.

DODGE Sammy… *(shakes him frantically)* Sammy!

> *DODGE gets up and walks away, leaning on the construction pylon stage right, like he is going to be sick. As OLIVIA is talking, he slowly turns back to them and notices his gun for the first time. He falls to his knees.*

OLIVIA *(whispering and crying over SAMMY)* Sammy, you have to get up. We're leaving… You're coming with us… You have get up, Sammy…

DODGE *(picking up the gun)* Get out of here.

OLIVIA Dodge…

DODGE *(standing)* Get out of here! Go!

OLIVIA *(moving toward DODGE)* You can't stay here! Not now!

DODGE *(grabbing her by the shoulders)* Don't you get it? This is my life!

OLIVIA Dodge… please!

DODGE *(pushes her to the ground)* Get out of here! *(pointing gun at her)* Go!

> *OLIVIA picks herself up and runs off stage left. DODGE drops the gun and moves to SAMMY. He slowly sinks to the floor and cradles SAMMY's head, rocking him. LYDIA begins to sing offstage. The lights slowly begin to fade.*

LYDIA *(singing)* Ring around the rosy.

DODGE Why didn't you listen to me? You stupid kid!

LYDIA   *(singing)* Pockets full of posey.

DODGE   I tried to tell you...

LYDIA   *(singing)* Ashes...

DODGE   I tried... *(breaking down and slumping over SAMMY)*

LYDIA   Ashes...

OLIVIA   *(offstage)* Mom... it's Olivia. Can you come and get me? *(pause)* I wanna come home.

LYDIA   *(singing)* We all fall down.

               Fade to black.

Dodge (Patrick Murphy) is the neighbourhood dealer in this insightful portrait of addiction and street kids.

Photo by Brenna McAllister.

WHITECHAPEL

Book and Lyrics by Maya Bielinski
Music by Donald Rankin and Charles Hoppner

Emily Delpero as Lady Castlethorpe.
Photo by Michelle Valberg.

Whitechapel was first produced by the students from Bell High School, Nepean, at the 2008 Ottawa-Carleton District Festival of the Sears Ontario Drama Festival at Woodroffe High School in Ottawa in March 2008.

Mary Kelly	Maya Bielinski
Inspector Abberline	Don Rankin
Charlotte	Ellen McAteer
Reporter	Scott McLarens
Jonas	Dylan On
Lady Castlethorpe	Emily Delpero
Chief Inspector Warren	Josh Murray
Lord Raff	Hamza Ul-Haq
John	Dan North
Tony Blunt	Martin Shaw
Lord Denning	Trevor Stalkie
Mother Pearl	Lisa Aalders
Woman/Thug	Megan Honey
Woman/Lunatic	Laurie Cooper
Salvationist/Salty Man	Billy Jeans
Goon	Martin Martinov
Salty Man/Soloist	Julian Zanetti
Citizens of London	Julia Blakey, Carter Barnaby, Marco Ferraris, David Haberl, Cameron Harvey, Evan Kinsman, Tiffany Lam, Jocelyn Ma, Lewis Whitely

Director/Staff Advisor: Perry Van Allen
Dramaturgy by Scott McLarens
Stage Management by David Carson
Assistant Stage Management by Martin Martinov
Set Design by Ronald Young
Costumes by Alice Jones and Perry Van Allen
Technical Advisor: Thom Sparks
Lighting Design by David Carson
Sound/Projections by Martin Martinov
Additional Music by Julian Zanetti, Ellen McAteer, Maya Bielinski
Orchestration by Peter Grant Mackechnie
Apprentice Den Mother: Karen Headley

NOTES

Whitechapel would not have been possible without the support of James Risk, Sharon Davidson, the original cast, the families of those involved in the show, the administration of Bell High School, and of course the inspirational and visionary Perry Van Allen. Thank you for your time, your talents, and your generosity. Many thanks also go to Gabriel Walton for his indispensable input, and Ashley Williamson for her insightful comments.

This play contains the following pieces of music:

"Dies Irae," Music by W.A. Mozart. Orchestration by Don Rankin.

To access music samples from *Whitechapel*, visit:
http://whitechapelthemusical.wordpress.com
or email: whitechapelmusical@gmail.com.

This play quotes from material that appeared in newspapers and in anonymous letters to the police at the time of the murders. More information can be found here:

W. Evans Hurndall, "Black Winter in East London." *Morning Advertiser* (London), 14 November, 1888. http://www.casebook.org/press_reports/morning_advertiser/18881114.html

"What we think." *The Star* (London), 5 October 1888.

http://www.casebook.org/press_reports/star/s881005.html

maya bielinski

Maya Bielinski is studying English Literature and Art History at Queen's University in Kingston, Ontario. She is following her passion for theatre through performance and writing, currently developing a full-length musical tentatively titled *Belle Gunness* (which she is co-writing with Peter Grant Mackechnie, the orchestrator of *Whitechapel*).

characters

MARY
ABBERLINE
CHARLOTTE
REPORTER
JONAS
LADY CASTLETHORPE
WARREN
LORD RAFF
JOHN
TONY BLUNT
LORD DENNING
PEARL
WOMAN
THUG
LUNATIC
SALVATIONIST
SALTY MAN
GOON
CITIZENS OF LONDON

Downstage right, almost on the apron of the stage, is the REPORTER's desk with a typewriter, a chair, and a coat and hat stand. The main area of the stage is set with a gated fence stage left, and a raised platform with staircase attached upstage right (variously the Ten Bells Pub, the police station, etc.). Behind the platform is the façade of a Victorian building upon which headlines are projected.

Prologue

Rolling fog. A haunting melody is played on a solo violin as three figures emerge, their voices interlacing: CHARLOTTE, MARY KELLY, and ABBERLINE.

Song: "Prologue"

CHARLOTTE *(singing)* Abberline…? Where are you…?

ABBERLINE *(singing)* Charlotte… I've lost you…

MARY *(singing)* Can anyone help me…? I'm too young to die…

The caw of a crow. The REPORTER is revealed to be sitting at his desk, ready to type.

REPORTER It begins.

The Streets of the East End

London, 1890. ABBERLINE, NEWSPAPER BOYS, a crowd.

NEWSPAPER BOYS
    Murder, murder! Blood flows through Whitechapel! Jack rips London!

There is a general bustle as passersby pick up the paper and read the headlines. ABBERLINE, haggard and empty, makes his way through the crowd to grab a newspaper.

Headline: "Return of the Ripper?"

ABBERLINE Give it here, boy.

ABBERLINE takes a paper and studies the headline as attention focuses on him for a moment.

(quietly, to himself)

Song: "DARK OBSESSION"

This dark obsession reigns again?
A flash of metal, streams of red...
This is the work of long ago;
Another soul now ripped and dead.

I trailed behind your path of deeds.
You scarred my life and stole my time.
I saw the women, dead and cold:
The crimson markers of your crime.

You used to hold me by the throat.
I was a victim; you made sure
To rip my very life in two—
I lost my life when I lost her!

He reads the article quickly.

(to himself) Ahh, nothing but a copycat. He finished his work years ago.

ABBERLINE tries to disappear into the crowd.

SALTY MAN   Nothing but a copycat? Says who?

REPORTER   Inspector Abberline, what luck to see you! Tell us about the case, Inspector. Do you have leads? This new murder—will it finally point the investigation in the right direction?

ABBERLINE   Leave me be. I'm not in charge of that case anymore.

REPORTER   But surely you have some insight about this new development. You said that this was only a copycat—how are you so sure?

ABBERLINE   Leave me in peace!

REPORTER   Peace, Inspector? You ask for peace? The whole of London asks for peace! We demand it! But we won't have it until this murderer, this Ripper is found and brought to justice!

SALTY MAN   That's right, you never caught him! You never caught the murderer, and now he's back to take more lives.

Similar attacks from the rest of the crowd.

REPORTER   But why ask you, the burnt out detective of years ago? You couldn't catch him then, you won't be able to catch him now. You're right to have given up, inspector.

ABBERLINE   I gave up when I had nothing else to give.

REPORTER   We all know the story of your failure, Abberline—your defeat. We
            all know how you turned your back on London when you turned
            your back on the case!

            *The booming bells of Whitechapel are heard. We go back in
            time to…*

Day of Wrath

*Two years previous, late summer 1888. A severe Latin hymn is
heard while a funeral takes place—that of Annie Chapman, the
second victim of Jack the Ripper.*

REPORTER   Late summer, 1888. Watched by an agitated crowd, a battered coffin
            was carried from twenty-nine Hanbury Street in Whitechapel.
            It was obvious from the speed of the police carriage that the
            unfortunate girl was beyond medical help.

            Song: "Dies Irae"

CHORUS   *Dies irae! Dies illa*
            Solvet saeclum in favilla,
            Teste david cum sybilla!

            Quantus tremor est futurus,
            Quando judex est venturus,
            Cuncta stricte discussurus!

            Day of wrath! O day of mourning!
            See fulfilled the prophets' warning:
            Heaven and earth in ashes burning!

            *As the coffin is getting transported through the streets, the funeral
            setting turns from mournful to sour—into the setting of the
            streets of London. Mourners go back to their daily work.*

The Character of London

The booming bells of the Whitechapel church are heard.

REPORTER   Annie Chapman was the poor girl's name; fallen woman and victim
            of the second atrocity in the East End. A universal fear among
            women strikes at the downtrodden poor; this man, this monster,
            Jack the Ripper!

Song: "Character of London"

CHORUS Like a call to funeral, the bells of London ring.
Nightmares come when mallets drum
On iron bells that sing!

Our work is done down by the docks when heavy bells are heard,
We travel to the rookery like blackened swarms of birds.

The chapel's bell toll may be heard across the district wide—
People stop and close up shop when iron bells collide.

Cover comes with darkness and the heavy London mist,
The pitch and noise bewitches boys
Who wander the abyss.

The bells of London call the moon to climb the nighttime skies.
She's frightened, though: the clouds below
Conceal her as she flies.

Darkness comes! Save yourselves! Take cover, lock the door!
Go away or take the risk that Jack will strike once more.

LORD RAFF *(to an UNFORTUNATE WOMAN, singing)* I'm looking for a bit
of fun to put my mind at ease.

So here's a coin—now hurry up and try your best to please...

JONAS *(singing)* Please help me, sir, I haven't got a penny to m' name;
I'd like a bed to rest me head and dinner all the same.

LORD RAFF *(singing)* You're red eyed—

JONAS *(singing)* Hungry!

LORD RAFF *(singing)* ...Savage! And I never help a rat.
You scurry like you're vermin, and there's nothing good in that.

IMMIGRANTS *(singing)* In Poland, Russia, Latvia, we dreamed of living here,
But now we're having second thoughts standing on this pier.

My life back home was dangerous; I lived in constant fear—
But standing here alone I see it's not too different here.

JOHN *(with a police whistle, singing)* Move along, now move along,
you're crowding up the street.
I won't have dirty lice like you begging on my beat.

PEARL *(to a MOTHER huddling outside the Ten Bells, singing)*
You're gonna have to pay for something if you want to stay,
So come inside and buy some beer or piss off—go away!

MOTHER *(singing)* The baby's crying, all I need is shelter from the rain.
Just let me huddle on your stoop—to you it's all the same!

PEARL   *(singing)* I can't afford no charity, I'm barely scraping by,
             My customers ain't thirsty when they hear your baby cry.

CHORUS   *(singing)* Only here in London will you hear the bells resound—
             Their chilling ring and mournful song means refuge can't be found!

             The daughters of the nighttime emerge when shadows grow.
             They call them the Unfortunates, a name by which they go.

UNFORTUNATES
             (singing) They call us the Unfortunates, a name by which we go…

             Headline: "Social Reform Unlikely for Unfortunates"

REPORTER   The women of the notorious East End of London, whose whole
             lives are struggles against extreme poverty, are considered unworthy
             of the attention of our social reformers. And yet the condition of
             these unfortunate women requires immediate attention…

             The UNFORTUNATES are trying to sell their wares by the gate.
             JONAS is in the shadows.

UNFORTUNATE ONE
             Of course there aren't any prostitutes in all of London… No, just
             a whole lot of unfortunate women.

MARY   The unlucky sods which fate has tossed into this filth.

UNFORTUNATE TWO
             We either find our way out, or die. It's all a game of luck.

UNFORTUNATE ONE
             Lady Luck ain't exactly a workin' girl, is she? So much for looking
             out for your own.

MARY   Since when does anybody look out for anybody?

             Song: "Tough Life"

             (singing) It's a tough life, pet, when you're workin' in the street
             Lookin' for a farthin' to buy some food to eat.

UNFORTUNATE ONE
             (singing) There's nothing left to do, ducky, nothing left to say…

UNFORTUNATES
             (singing) Work your bit and live, or you'll starve and waste away.

             We are the unlucky girls, desperate right from birth.
             The dice are thrown, our fates are known to everyone on earth

             We blunder in the darkness, not knowing up from down,
             Offering our bodies to anyone around.

> *Enter the SALTY MEN and Tony BLUNT. BLUNT goes for MARY.*

SALTY MEN   *(singing)* Come on, ladies, hows about a friendly little kiss?

UNFORTUNATES
             (singing) Lust is love and all you get is "love" in the abyss.

SALTY MEN   *(singing)* Hows about some company—I'll give you what you need,
             And I shall get what I want now when one of you concedes…

UNFORTUNATES
             (singing) Living in the darkness, no love and no romance.
             A business deal with nighttime—each night we take the chance…
             It's heads or tails with Lucifer, and either way we lose…
             It's better left to fate, I find; I'd hate to have to choose.

> *The UNFORTUNATES go off with their respective customers, leaving MARY alone for a moment.*

MARY   *(singing)* It's better left to fate, I find; I'd hate to have to choose.

BLUNT   Mary Kelly. I'm waiting.

> *MARY follows TONY BLUNT into the darkness.*

JONAS   Don't go, Mary!

In the Police Station

> *In the police headquarters. WARREN is putting on his cloak and hat, ready to go home, when he sees ABBERLINE at his desk. He pulls out a folded newspaper before he approaches ABBERLINE.*

WARREN   Abberline, I've been meaning to talk to you. I'm sure by now you've had a chance to glance at the morning papers?

ABBERLINE   I have, sir.

WARREN   Did you catch this rather precious nugget? "There have been no startling developments in the East End murder case."

> *Headline: "No Developments in East End Murder Case"*

ABBERLINE   I did read that, sir.

WARREN   It goes on… "The police…"

> *The REPORTER writes the article.*

REPORTER	The police seem to be absolutely at sea. Sir Charles Warren, chief of police, will say nothing; perhaps because he has nothing to say. He displays an irritability that is in itself strong evidence that he and his team are completely baffled.
WARREN	Would you say that this is an accurate article, Inspector? Are we lost at sea? I, for one, know that I am indeed displaying a certain irritability…
ABBERLINE	We're working on a new lead, sir, that may prove to be quite promising—
WARREN	It's not fast enough, Abberline. We must take action.
ABBERLINE	Arresting someone now only to let him go would surely have the press on our heels in—
WARREN	I want an arrest, Inspector! Pull in an immigrant, a butcher—any dirty scoundrel from that rotting East End. See to it that Jack—any Jack, Abberline—is in one of these cells before the week is out.
ABBERLINE	Sir—
WARREN	They're all guilty of these crimes, the whole of Whitechapel. You know it as well as I. The entire district is filled with ruthless criminals, wicked men, murderers, and rough women. They've bred this Jack the Ripper. Modern England indeed.
	Abberline, I'm coming to the end of my patience with this case. Do that—or do something. You've got to make some headway in this case. My neck is on the line… as is yours.

WARREN leaves the station. ABBERLINE stays for a few moments in his chair, then picks up the paper to look at the headlines again.

ABBERLINE	"No startling developments…"

Outside, JONAS is seen pilfering an apple from a vending cart.

JOHN	*(singing)* Watch it boy, I see you!
JONAS	*(singing, hiding the apple behind his back)* Who, me, sir?
JOHN	*(singing)* Yes boy, you!
	You'll pay for that, you will, and you'll smile when you do…

JONAS grins and places the apple back in the cart. The policeman's back is turned, and the apple is once again in JONAS's hands.

JOHN goes into the station and notices ABBERLINE alone in WARREN's office.

Sir, I'm sorry to interrupt. We've just got news from the docks of a man called Klosowski who may have been…

Headline: "New Suspect in Leather Apron Investigation"

ABBERLINE   It's no use, John.

JOHN   I'm sorry, sir?

ABBERLINE   I said it's no use. I've been on this case for weeks with nothing to show for it—nothing but dozens of articles telling the world that London has fools in Scotland Yard.

JOHN   This, sir?

He picks up the paper.

Excuse my boldness, sir… but these are tabloids! Since when do you listen to tabloids?

ABBERLINE   But it's all true, John. We *haven't* had any new developments for weeks. No one's been caught; the killer is still at large.

JOHN   So he is. But London couldn't ask for a better inspector. Frederick, I'm telling you that you haven't been bested. We're on to him! We've got leads. He's bound to blunder sometime, and when he does… you'll be there to bring him to justice.

ABBERLINE   I suppose you're right. I can't stop now.

JOHN   You speak true, sir. Now. About that Klosowski chap… We've gotten a tip to meet at the docks tonight. I think this may prove to be quite the lead. Here.

JOHN hands ABBERLINE a lead report.

ABBERLINE   Thank you. Now go. I want no disturbances. We'll go to the docks this evening, and we'll see where this takes me.

CHARLOTTE is coming up to the station and sees WARREN on his way out.

WARREN   Charlotte, how do you do?

CHARLOTTE   How do you do, Sir Charles? Is Inspector Abberline still in the station?

WARREN   He is. I'm sure he'd welcome a visit from such a lovely face.

CHARLOTTE   Thank you.

WARREN   Will I be seeing you tonight at the Vigilante Committee's gala? The members are so very excited to meet you and Inspector Abberline.

CHARLOTTE   Of course we'll be in attendance. I wouldn't miss it.

WARREN	Good evening, my dear.

CHARLOTTE goes into the station to look for ABBERLINE. She is intercepted by JOHN instead.

CHARLOTTE	John! How are you?
JOHN	I'm well, thank you, Charlotte. If you're here to speak with the inspector, I'm afraid he's quite busy with the case… Could I pass on a message?
CHARLOTTE	May I not speak with him for just a moment? I won't be long.
JOHN	Well… he's quite busy… and he asked not to be disturbed… but how could I say no?
CHARLOTTE	Thank you.
JOHN	Good evening.

CHARLOTTE goes into the office. ABBERLINE hears her footsteps, but is reading a file.

ABBERLINE	John, if this information is correct, we may be able…
CHARLOTTE	Good evening, Inspector.

ABBERLINE turns to see her.

ABBERLINE	Charlotte! What a surprise! How did you get here?

They embrace.

CHARLOTTE	Oh Frederick. I had to see you. I have such wonderful news.
ABBERLINE	You do.

Pause.

CHARLOTTE	Yes! Are you not going to ask me what news I have?
ABBERLINE	*(not unkindly)* What is it?
CHARLOTTE	Father says that we have his blessing as soon as you're done the case. He's to announce our engagement tonight at the gala!
ABBERLINE	Oh Charlotte.

Headline: "Society Pages: Engagement!"

That's wonderful.

CHARLOTTE	I can't tell you how happy this makes me, Frederick. Finally we'll have a place of our own and a life of our own… You'll not have to spend long hours in this awful station, I'll not have to spend long hours wishing for you to be beside me. We'll find a place… not too

far from here, but far enough… and it will be you and me and our future.

ABBERLINE   Of course.

CHARLOTTE   I'll leave you be. I know you must be very busy. Sir Charles says that the Vigilante Committee is quite anxious to meet you. Don't be late this time.

ABBERLINE   I won't be late.

Exit CHARLOTTE.

I love you.

On the Streets

The many characters of London go back to their daily business and attention focuses on JONAS with his stolen apple. He goes into an alleyway to enjoy it when he is accosted unawares by a GOON.

JONAS   Hey! Let go of me! What do you think…

GOON   Shut your mouth. You're Jonas, ain't you?

JONAS   Who're you?

GOON   A debt collector, mate. And a bully. Tony Blunt says you're past due on your payments…

The GOON winds up to strike JONAS when Tony BLUNT appears from the shadows. BLUNT makes a motion and the GOON stops in mid-blow. Instead, he holds JONAS so that he can't run.

BLUNT   *(to the GOON)* The modern world, mate, runs on transactions— am I right? The provision of services, the promise of a payment…

GOON   You're right, boss.

BLUNT   *(to JONAS)* You're still alive and kicking…

JONAS struggles in the GOON's arms.

So I expect to be paid. Unless, of course, you want to entrust Lady Fortune to protect you.

The GOON brandishes a knife. The glint catches the eye of MARY, who is on the other side of the stage.

From what I heard, you and her ain't on the best of terms.

The GOON laughs and brings the knife closer to JONAS's throat. There's a small struggle from JONAS. MARY interrupts the scene.

MARY   Hey! Leave him be!

BLUNT spins on his heels.

BLUNT   Mary Kelly. What a pleasant surprise. Why don't you come join us? I believe we have a bit of business to clear up ourselves, don't we?

MARY   There's a policeman just down this stretch, boys. Leave him be or I'll holler.

BLUNT   With a mouth like that, you should be glad that we're in a good mood today. You're lucky we don't want any trouble, Mary. No, we're just having a bit of a follow-up appointment with Jonas here. Aren't we, Jonesy?

JONAS   I'll get you the money by Friday. Really I will.

BLUNT   Friday's too late, I think. Accidents do happen.

The knife again.

MARY   How much is it, Tony?

BLUNT   A mere sixpence.

MARY   *(shocked)* Sixpence?

BLUNT   Just enough to save your friend from a few accidents. Plus I want the four pence that you owe me.

MARY   Here. Leave him alone, Blunt.

BLUNT   What do you have with all that? No matter... I appreciate doing business with you, Mary Kelly, but if I were you, I'd watch how bold I was from now on.

He grabs her jaw.

You don't want to be making any enemies.

He kisses her. After a nod from BLUNT, the GOON drops JONAS. BLUNT and the GOON leave. JONAS dusts himself off. He looks at MARY.

JONAS   I'll pay you back.

MARY   Forget it.

JONAS   I *will* get the money, and it'll go straight from my pockets to yours, I promise you.

MARY	The only thing I want you to promise is that you'll keep out of these messes! I'm broke as it is without having to bail you out of trouble every two weeks.
JONAS	It won't happen again, honest.
	Mary, can I ask you something?
MARY	Anything.
JONAS	However did you end up here?
MARY	My father died when I was about your age, Jonesy. My mum, soon after.

Song: "A Violet From Mother's Grave/Stick With Me"

(singing) Scenes of my childhood arise before my gaze
Bringing recollections of bygone happy days.
When down in the meadow in childhood I would roam,
No one's left to cheer me now within that good old home.

(speaking) I had nothing left back in Ireland... so I came here.
They said I'd find a new life.

(singing) My childhood days are over, memories remain—

JONAS	*(singing)* My childhood's forever gone, and will not come again.
MARY	*(singing)* But things start looking up, you know, they really do, When you stick with someone,
JONAS	*(singing)* And someone's there for you.
MARY	I'll stick with you, lad.
JONAS	You'll stick with me.

A SALTY MAN appears. He taps MARY on the shoulder and grabs her by the waist.

SALTY MAN	You open for business, pet?

MARY pushes him away.

MARY	No, I ain't "open for business." Leave us be!
SALTY MAN	I was trying to help you out, is all! In a few hours, when it's dark, you'll wish you had a few pennies to buy yourself a doss.
MARY	In a few hours, mate, I'll have forgotten about you and your charity.
SALTY MAN	You'll regret it, pet, you will. Have you not heard? Have you not heard it in the news? There's danger in the streets of London!

Headline: "East End Paralysed in Fear"

This is Jack

In the next song, men in top hats and cloaks tango with the UNFORTUNATES.

Song: "This is Jack"

SALTY MAN   *(singing)* He comes in the dusk as the sun falls down
When the shadows grow long and thin;
As darkness coaxes gargoyle frowns,
The Unfortunates hear from him.

He'll call on you like a gentleman bold
With his top hat and black cape
But his eyes will make your blood run cold
And the hair stand on your nape.

He lures you down, or so I'm told,
To some dark alleyway.
He'll promise you sweet grapes and gold
And a new life far away.

And however empty is his heart,
His promises are true:
The grapes he gives are poisoned, tart!
And the gold ain't meant for you!

He'll place the gold coins on your eyes
When Jack is done his work.
His red hot knife don't cauterize.
The press will go berserk!

So now you're bleeding on the street,
Your life will ooze away
And one policeman on his beat
Will blow his whistle and say…

CHORUS   *(singing)* This is Jack! (Is it Jack?)
His deadly knife will strike again.
This is Jack (Is it Jack?)
But no one dares say how or when.

This is Jack! (Is it jack?)
His deadly knife will strike again.
This is Jack (Is it Jack?)
But no one dares say how or when.

As the women leave the stage, the men gather on the platform upstage and remove their top hats and cloaks. Welcome to the fundraising party.

The Vigilante Committee

At the gala. CHARLOTTE, RAFF, and LORD DENNING are gathered, as well as other guests, in LADY CASTLETHORPE's ballroom.

REPORTER   Now there is only one thing to be done at this moment…
The people of the East End must become their own police.
They must form themselves at once into Vigilance Committees…
These again should at once devote themselves to volunteer
patrol work at night, as well as to general detective service. The
unfortunate women who are the objects of the man-monster's
malignity should be shadowed, and funds should be raised to help
these innocent victims…

Headline: "Concerned Citizens Form Vigilante Committee to Stop Killer"

LORD RAFF   Charlotte, where is Inspector Abberline, the man of the hour?

CHARLOTTE   He'll be arriving momentarily, I'm sure, Lord Raff.

LORD RAFF   Of course. How very fashionable of him to be late for a party in his honour.

LORD DENNING

Perhaps we should write a letter to the police headquarters and
advise them to give Abberline leads one day in advance—that way
he may unintentionally be on time to catch the killer!

He laughs.

Raff. What a pleasant surprise to see you here. Charlotte, this has
been quite a successful evening! The Vigilante Committee has
certainly done its job to organize such a wonderful gala.

The orchestra begins a waltz as LADY CASTLETHORPE appears at the top of the staircase.

Song: "The Vigilante Committee"

LADY CASTLETHORPE

(singing) Welcome! Eat! Move your feet!
Gents, take your ladies in hand.

What a treat: you all look sweet,
but I look simply… grand!

LORD RAFF   Charlotte, may I have this dance?

GUESTS   *(singing)* The Vigilante Committee, aren't we witty?
Raising funds to help catch Jack!
We're all looking pretty, a toast to the city!
We plan to keep the case on track.

The wine is flowing, the funds are growing,
We're socially aware—how fine!
The ladies are glowing, our wealth is showing,
This soiree's divine.

LORD RAFF   *(to himself, singing)* Abberline is tardy to his own damn party.

End music.

CHARLOTTE   Thank you for the dance, Lord Raff.

LORD DENNING
This fundraiser is certainly a step in the right direction. I'm
convinced that since Abberline has taken the case, the East End
situation has cleaned up considerably!

CHARLOTTE   Thank you, Lord Denning. We're all very proud of Frederick.

LADY CASTLETHORPE
Lord Denning, the inspector has only been on the case for a few
months. Surely a considerable change can't be noticeable in such
a short time.

LORD DENNING
Au contraire, Lady Castlethorpe! Why, even last night on my way
back from the courthouse, I saw *not one* whore trying to sell her
wares. An unbelievable change! My carriage ride takes me right
along Bishopsgate. And Bishopsgate has never been so sterilized
as I witnessed it to be last night… It's remarkable!

LORD RAFF   Perhaps your praise falls to the force opposite Inspector Abberline,
Denning. After all, it's not the inspector who is, as you put it,
"sterilizing" our streets.

There is a silence. LORD DENNING laughs.

CHARLOTTE   If you'll excuse me.

LORD RAFF   Of course, my dear.

(to DENNING) All the same, I agree with you. The East End is
literally cowering in fear from this caped character—and it's better
for it, I think!

LADY CASTLETHORPE
Surely you don't mean that.

LORD RAFF   Indeed I do. The East End has plagued London—and, consequently, all of England—for years. You cannot deny it.

LADY CASTLETHORPE
In my humble opinion, murder and fear are not the best ways to keep people off the streets and out of the gutters, Lord Raff. Social programs, education, organization: *these* are the tools of a modern era.

LORD RAFF   I mean no disrespect, of course. But while we have been wasting our time using these conventional methods of betterment, some independent genius has taken the matter in hand! Jack the Ripper, the Whitechapel Murderer, the Leather Apron: he's a social revolutionary, I'm sure!

Another silence. CHARLOTTE has obviously been uncomfortable for the length of the party.

LORD DENNING
(He finds CHARLOTTE again.) Now where is our little celebrity, Inspector Abberline? Charlotte, have you any knowledge as to his whereabouts? Why, the evening is almost over, and still we've no word from him!

CHARLOTTE   I apologize, Lord Denning. I can't imagine how he could miss such an event... I'm sure he's held up by something very important at the station. The evening has been wonderful, Lady Castlethorpe— but I must say good night. It's getting late.

LORD RAFF   What a pity! I beseech you to stay, Miss Charlotte.

CHARLOTTE   I couldn't.

LORD RAFF   At least accept my invitation to dinner tomorrow night. The inspector, of course, is also quite welcome, should he decide to show up.

CHARLOTTE blushes.

Wonderful. Allow me to escort you to your carriage, if you absolutely must go.

CHARLOTTE   That's quite all right, I've arranged to have it at the front gate. Thank you again for a wonderful evening.

Abberline and Charlotte

CHARLOTTE *steps outside and the rest of the party fades away.*
There is no carriage; no one is there to meet her. She is alone.

Song: "We Still Have Time"

CHARLOTTE *(singing)* We still have time.
Mistakes that we've made till now can be undone.
We still can dream.
With time, the night will give way to the sun.

But yet you're never here,
And it's never now,
And it's always later, Abberline…

We still have time,
And time can help us mend this lonely dream.

And though I'm scared
That somehow we'll be lost and far apart,

We still have time
And time can help us find a brand new start.

I still have love
It's given me the strength to carry on.
We still have love
To help us through the night toward the dawn.

CHARLOTTE *hears slow footsteps, sees the shadow of a man*
in a top hat. Only when she hears his voice does she realize
it is ABBERLINE.

ABBERLINE Charlotte.

Pause. She collects herself.

CHARLOTTE *(cold)* Inspector.

ABBERLINE I'm afraid… I'm late.

CHARLOTTE I noticed, Mr. Abberline.

ABBERLINE I got caught up with a lead, Charlotte, I'm sorry. We got a tip and
it was urgent that I…

CHARLOTTE It's always urgent, Frederick. It's either something at the station,
or a new lead, or the paperwork… Last week you missed Lady
Tattington's welcoming party. The week before that, it was the
earl's dinner.

ABBERLINE   I understand that you're angry with me, Charlotte…

CHARLOTTE   *(warmer)* Oh, Frederick. I'm not angry with you. Father can
              announce the engagement another time. I'm worried about you,
              that's all. You don't need to tell me that you wanted to be here…
              and you also don't need to tell me how important your work is
              to you. It's important to me, too, Frederick. But you must find
              a balance. You are isolating yourself… and it's unhealthy. I'm not
              questioning your intentions—I can see in your eyes that your heart
              is in the right place. But remember what is important to you. You
              must remember what is important to you.

ABBERLINE   Just give me time.

CHARLOTTE   I will, Frederick. I am. But I only hope that you'll find a balance.
              And before it's too late.

              Pause.

              Oh, Frederick.

              She fixes his coat collar.

              Well, you've got another chance. Lord Raff has invited us to dinner
              tomorrow night. Don't be late.

Abberline's Obsession

Headline: "Police Still Fumbling for Clues"

*Back at the station. JOHN is just locking the door as he sees
movement in the shadows.*

JOHN   Who's there? Show yourself!

              JOHN drops the keys and tries to shine his lantern into the night.

ABBERLINE   Good evening, Constable.

JOHN   Oh, Inspector, it's you. You gave me quite a fright. I'm not usually
              one to be shaken by harmless shadows, but I've been in the morgue
              since you left… Well, you know it's not exactly precious paradise in
              there. God rest their souls.

ABBERLINE   Go on home then, John. It's been a long day. Rest up so that we can
              try the docks again tomorrow.

JOHN   And what of you, Inspector? Did you forget about the gala?
              Charlotte is expecting you!

ABBERLINE	It's fine, John, fine. But I left a notebook in the station that I must retrieve.

JOHN physically blocks ABBERLINE from entering the station.

JOHN	Now, Inspector. It's already locked up. I'm sure you can do without your casebook for one night. Charlotte is waiting for you! You are hours late!
ABBERLINE	Excuse me, Constable. I've already seen Charlotte. Now please step aside.
JOHN	You've seen Charlotte? The gala can't have ended this early…
ABBERLINE	Step aside, John.
JOHN	What happened? What did you do?
ABBERLINE	Step aside!
JOHN	Is that a command, sir?

Pause.

As your friend, I must advise you to re-evaluate. Turn your back on this place—at least for a time. Go back to Charlotte. She loves you, Frederick.

ABBERLINE	I don't think there's anything in the morgue that can possibly do me harm, John.
JOHN	That's not what I'm worried about! You're possessed by the case. It's taking control of your life.
ABBERLINE	Nonsense. I can go home as soon as I have that casebook. Step aside.
JOHN	This is an obsession, Abberline. You spend more time with the deceased than you do with the living. You must get perspective.
ABBERLINE	I don't need you to turn on me as well, John. Please, help me… and step aside.
JOHN	You're not hearing me. This murderer and the mystery behind him is tearing your life apart.
ABBERLINE	Step aside, Constable. That's an order.

ABBERLINE receives the keys from JOHN and steps inside the station.

Double Event!

*The next morning. In the following, people dictate letters
in individual spotlights. They overlap and build against
a background of tense, almost atonal music.*

Song: "Double Event"

REPORTER   Mr. Lusk:

I send you half the kidney I took from one woman—preserved
it for you. T'other piece I fried and ate. It was very nice. I may
send you the bloody knife that took it out if you only wait
a while longer...

Catch me when you can, Mr. Lusk!

WRITER ONE   October 2, 1888

Dear Mr. Editor,

I am not satisfied with the level of policing in the East End
of London. It is my belief that if we had modern lighting and
sufficient police officers, this heinous Ripper character would not
have had opportunity to begin his work in the first place.

LADY CASTLETHORPE
To the Editor of the *Daily News*:

The moral of the whole business is plain enough. It is poverty
which lies at the root of what we perhaps rightly call the social evil,
and it is by aiming at the abolition of poverty that we shall cure a
variety of woes which we usually set down to an entirely different
set of causes.

The Whitechapel murders are indeed a tardy visitation on us for
our neglect of obvious social duties, for our hopeless individualism.
In a city where very few of us know the names of our next-door
neighbours, we cannot be surprised that a crafty scoundrel like the
Whitechapel murderer should be able to hide his misdeeds. But
there is a far more rooted unfriendliness in our so-called Christian
society than that which concerns the isolation of neighbour from
neighbour. There is the alienation of the rich from the poor; there
is that especially unneighbourly form of dealing which consists in
one class abstracting the fruits of the labour of another...

WRITER TWO   Dear Mister:

My mother says that liver is good for me, but I read in your paper that Mr. Jack eats liver. I tell my mother that I don't want to be like Mr. Jack, but she says that it's different with me...

WRITER THREE October 5, 1888.

To whom it may concern:

The streets of Whitechapel have become a very breeding ground for...

REPORTER Say Boss—

You seem rare frightened, guess I'd like to give you fits, but can't stop time enough to let your box of toys play copper games with me, but hope to see you when I don't hurry much.

WRITER FOUR An open letter to Jack the Ripper:

You are among us. You live in the gutters and cracks of our very society, shrouded by the fear you have created among the honest people of England. You have cracked the very foundation of our nation, which now crumbles...

MISSIONARY Sir,

Black winter has already settled down on East London. Many people are foodless and fireless. My blood curdles as I find decent respectable folks going without food for two days together! When funds run out, I am powerless. If friends of the suffering care to send help, I will see that it is used to the best advantage...

WRITER FIVE October 7, 1888.

Dear Sir,

As chairman for the Society of Westmont Furriers, I must complain on behalf of my colleagues about the complete lack of...

WRITER SIX ...The simple truth is that as long as this murderer, whether he be maniac or not, continues as he does, choosing victims who make themselves accessories to his escape, and leaving behind no clues for the police, the crimes will continue...

REPORTER I write you a letter in black ink, as I have no more of the red stuff. I think you are all asleep in Scotland Yard with your bloodhounds, as I will show you tomorrow night. I am going to do a double event, but not in Whitechapel. Got rather too warm there. Had to shift. No more till you hear me again.

Signed Jack the Ripper

NEWSPAPER BOYS
Jack Strikes Again! Double Murder! Double Event in Whitechapel! Catherine Eddowes and Elizabeth Stride—found brutally murdered in Whitechapel this morning...

WRITER SEVEN To the Editor:

As a poor woman living on an honest few pennies a day, the trade of the Unfortunate becomes more and more appealing...

CHARLOTTE Dearest Frederick,

Allow me to start this letter of uncertainty and confusion with something that stands true and strong in my heart even during these times of doubt and despair: I love you...

WRITER EIGHT Kind Sirs:

In this time of fear and propaganda, neighbour turns against neighbour, suspicions fly, and no one feels safe. What have we come to as a nation if we cannot...

SALVATIONIST Half beast, half man—the devil himself—has come on this day of retribution. Sinners beware! He chokes the doubters, rips the blasphemers, murders the unbelievers. Take heed! You have a choice before you, you damned creatures of God: to find food and earthly pleasures to satisfy your lustful and selfish desires, to find death and face judgement and surely be damned to eternal hellfire, or to find salvation! Find salvation and be saved, ye wretched and heathen sinners...

WRITER NINE October 8, 1888.

To the Editor of the *Star*:

I am a butcher; fallen under suspicion by my patrons, neighbours, and friends...

WRITER TEN Dear Sir,

I am suspicious of a character who lives two doors down from me. He is a widower, keeps odd hours, and is often seen wandering along Bishopsgate. Last night, I heard a dreadful scream of "Murder!" which was quickly silenced. It is my belief that this man may indeed be the murderer of Whitechapel...

REPORTER I'm not a butcher, I'm not a Yid, nor yet a foreign skipper... But I'm your own light-hearted friend.

Yours Truly, Jack the Ripper!

End music. Blackout.

SOCIALITE   *(offstage)* Inspector Abberline, the main detective searching out
             the notorious Whitechapel murderer, was seen today in the Ten
             Bells Pub. It is rumoured that his fiancée, Miss Charlotte Barnett,
             was seen with Lord Raff, Chief of Surgery at the London Hospital,
             walking at eight-thirty Thursday evening along Spitalfields, near
             Christ Church.

The Ten Bells Pub

*ABBERLINE, MARY, and practically the rest of the East End find
refuge in old matron PEARL's rowdy Ten Bells Pub.*

Headline: "Tensions High in East End"

REPORTER   The public are looking for a monster, and in the legend of Jack
             the Ripper, the Whitechapel part of them seem to be inventing
             a monster to look for. This kind of invention ought to be
             discouraged in every possible way, or there may soon be murders
             from panic to add to murders from lust of blood. It seems that
             suspicions are giving rise to action: tensions ride high in this
             district, and it seems that just one spark might set the whole
             East End on fire.

             Song: "The Ten Bells"

TAVERN MAN ONE
             (singing) Double murder! Double murder! Have you heard
             the news?

             They say it was a butcher!

TAVERN MAN TWO
             (singing) I heard it was the Jews!

TAVERN MAN ONE
             (singing) A royalist conspiracy: maybe its the queen!

TAVERN MAN TWO
             (singing) I hear the first one lost her kidney: that's some fine cuisine!

             Enter JOHN.

JOHN   *(to ABBERLINE, singing)* I heard some talk before I came that
             Tony Blunt's in town.
             You know he's got a lust for blood and tie-ins with the Crown.
             He could have killed 'em both, you know—he's got the sickly mind

TAVERN MAN ONE
(singing) Or maybe Sweeney Todd's around and needs some meat to grind!

CHORUS
(singing) Meet me at the Ten Bells, I'll see you there tonight.
Have some pints and ladies and maybe feel all right.
Forget our lives, cheat our wives, and drink a lot of gin.
Maybe then we can forget this awful lot we're in!

UNFORTUNATES
(singing) The night is just beginning when gaslights all get lit,
We all go to the Ten Bells and rouge our cheeks a bit!
There's nothing like the nighttime to chase away our woes—
And nowhere like the Ten Bells, so this is how it goes...

CHORUS
(singing) Meet me at the Ten Bells, I'll see you there tonight.
Have some pints and ladies and maybe feel all right.
Forget our lives, cheat our wives, and drink a lot of gin.
Maybe then we can forget this awful lot we're in!

TAVERN MAN ONE
(singing) Did you hear about that woman found dead on Mitre Lane?
Her throat was slit and dress was ripped, though otherwise quite plain.
Catherine Eddowes, she was called, though many knew her well
As Polly-Sue the Prostitute, and Nicely Naughty Nell.

The REPORTER notices ABBERLINE at the bar.

REPORTER
(to ABBERLINE, singing) I wrote it in the news today, if you'll excuse me, sir...

CHORUS
(singing) That you ain't got a clue 'bout who yer lookin' fer!

MARY
(singing) Correct me if I'm wrong, sir, but now, upon my life:
Isn't it your job to save us from Jack's knife?

CHORUS
(singing) Meet me at the Ten Bells, I'll see you there tonight.
Have some pints and ladies and maybe feel all right.
Forget our lives, cheat our wives, and drink a lot of gin.
Maybe then we can forget this awful lot we're in!

PEARL
(singing) Maybe all you need, Inspector, is a pint of beer—

MARY
(singing) Relax a bit, unwind! We'll whisper in your ear.
We're good at what we do, Inspector, that we know for sure—

UNFORTUNATES
(singing) So call us up, Inspector; hey, what are ladies fer?

The CHORUS finishes the song with a rowdy verse of laughing.

PEARL   All right, all right. That's enough. If you've got a room, you can stay. The rest of ya is more trouble than you're worth. I'm closing up.

TAVERN MAN ONE
               Aw, Pearl, you don't mean it. We's just havin' a little fun with the inspector!

PEARL   I do mean it. I want no more hassle for Inspector Abberline. Go on: we're closing early. Go on, now!

               There is bustle as the customers leave PEARL and ABBERLINE alone in the public house.

Just Like Jack

ABBERLINE   You shouldn't have kicked them out. Tonight was a busy night for the Ten Bells: you just lost a lot of business.

PEARL   Oh, they'll be back. Most of 'em don't pay their tabs anyhow. Now I don't mean to be presuming, sir… but will you be needing board?

ABBERLINE   No, miss. I best be home soon.

               PEARL goes behind the bar. ABBERLINE is alone downstage.

               Song: "Just Like Jack"

               (*singing*) My two natures battle—they tear me apart.
               One is more human, having soul and a heart.
               The other is ruthless, corrupt, uncontrolled.
               My throat's in his hands in a very firm hold.

               This fiend, Jack the Ripper, is doing dark deeds,
               Shredding apart what society needs.
               Love disappears, trust is gone, hope is lost.
               We lash out in fear and revolt—at what cost?

               Somehow I've got to repair what has shattered,
               Forget my obsession, return to what mattered,
               Put this away, place it back on the shelf.
               Before I save others, I must save myself.

               Thank you, Pearl. Now lock the door behind me, if you're not inviting any customers in. I wouldn't dare be alone and vulnerable tonight, if I were you.

               ABBERLINE leaves the Ten Bells. PEARL locks the door behind him.

Outside the Ten Bells

Outside the Ten Bells Pub. Quick footsteps. MARY and JONAS appear. MARY knocks on the door to the pub.

MARY Closed! At this hour?

JONAS Closed the door for fear of Saucy Jack! Closed the door and barred him from entering—and us out, too! But she's still in there, I see a light. She'll take us, won't she, Mary?

MARY Of course she will, don't be a twit.

JONAS What if she doesn't take us, Mary? It's getting late. Do we go back to the lodging house?

MARY Those lodging houses ain't fit for rats, Jonesy. No fear, now, Mother Pearl'll take us both. She may be hard, but she has a heart. She'll give us a room.

MARY knocks again, louder, more urgently.

I know she's in there. I can hear her bones creaking.

JONAS And hows about a breakfast? Bread and honey…

MARY That's an honest enough meal, boy. If we can get our foot in the door, Mother Pearl will get you your honey. And hot, strong tea.

JONAS You think so?

MARY I know so, chum. As soon as that old goat opens up this door!

MARY knocks at the door, louder and louder. PEARL opens the door.

PEARL Who's that? Oh, Mary, it's you. Now stop this racket. It's not everybody that works the night and sleeps the day. It's a wonder you haven't alarmed me guests. Sleep is all the liberty they get, methinks, from the trouble of the streets.

MARY We've a mind to sleep the night, too, if there's a place for us, Mother.

PEARL A place? Closing the door I thought I'd be safe from beggars like you. There's no more room here, be off!

MARY Not even for a shilling?

PEARL A shilling?

She warms a little.

	Ahh, well now, Mary, it ain't safe to be out on a night like this. You've heard the news, you must've. The streets ain't safe; you best stay the night here…
JONAS	A shilling! Where are we going to find a shilling?
MARY	Hush, Jonas!
PEARL	No shilling? No board!

PEARL almost shuts the door.

MARY	Oh, come now, Mother. No room for an underfed boy and a stick of a girl like meself? Jonas can fit in the cracks between the boards in the floor! And me, I'll squeeze between the barrels in the storeroom.
PEARL	Oh, aye, 'tween the barrels. Be gone, you two. If you ain't got the coin, I said there's no room.
MARY	Mother, you know I'm good for it. I've got… sixpence—that's half. Let us stay. You said yourself it wasn't safe these nights.
PEARL	That's enough for one of yous. I like you both—Mary, Jonas… But an old slag has to look out for herself, you know. As soon as I let you both in, half the East End'll be knocking off my door. And then I will have to fit you in between the floorboards!
MARY	Here.

MARY gives PEARL the money and pushes JONAS forward.

JONAS	Mary, where are you going to stay? You can't be alone on the streets.
MARY	Don't you worry about me. I'm tougher than I look… And if I'm lucky, I may be back here before the night is through.
JONAS	You can't go. Mary, you stay here, and I'll look for some money. I once found a penny in a gutter; it can happen again.
MARY	I've found my share of pennies in the gutter, myself. Don't you fret. I'll meet you at the Old Aldgate Pump in the morning.

Abberline's Choice

CHARLOTTE is at an engagement party. Spotlight. She is in her own thoughts, with her mind on her relationship with ABBERLINE.

Song: "We Still Have Time (Reprise)"

CHARLOTTE   *(singing)* We still have time.   ·
            Mistakes that we've made till now can be undone.
            We still can dream...

            And though I'm scared
            That somehow we'll be lost and far apart...

LORD RAFF   *(offstage)* Darling.

CHARLOTTE   Frederick, you've made your choice. You chose your work.
            I'm sorry.

> *She backs out of the light to blend into the party. Swell of music.
> ABBERLINE is truly alone.*

Abberline's Failure

> *ABBERLINE is on patrol. MARY is also on the streets, looking
> for business. Both are alone, both are victims of fortune and fate.*
>
> *Song: "Midnight Creeps Closer"*

ABBERLINE   *(singing)* Where have I gotten? What have I done?   ·
            My old life is over, a new one's begun.
            A cold, dark obsession has made itself known—
            Corrupted, I'm driven... and very alone.

MARY   *(singing)* Alone in the streets on an eve such as this,
            I'm wary and frightened: something's amiss...
            The fog seems much thicker, the stars are less bright,
            The moon—she looks lonely, like me, in the night.

            (speaking) Come now, Mary—chin up and fight.
            One bit of misery pays rent for a night!
            What kind of a girl do you think you've become?
            Be awake with the moon, but alive with the sun...

BOTH   *(singing)* Is there still time? Can I turn back?

ABBERLINE   *(singing)* Midnight creeps closer, secret and black.

MARY   *(singing)* Who's in the shadows? Are you a friend?

BOTH   *(singing)* Will this dark night soon come to an end?

> *The REPORTER dons a top hat and cloak and approaches
> MARY.*

MARY   Hello, sir. I've been waiting for you. Seems like a lonely night tonight. How about some company?

No response from the REPORTER. He gives her his hand. Mary takes it, and he leads her offstage.

Headline: "Another Prostitute Found Murdered in Whitechapel"

The caw of a crow and the bells of Whitechapel are heard once more.

Blackout.

Don Rankin as Inspector Frederick Abberline and Maya Bielinski as Mary Kelly.
Photo by Charles Hoppner.

wayne Fairhead

Wayne Fairhead is the Executive Director of the Sears Ontario Drama Festival. He has worked as a teacher (at all levels of education), director, adjudicator, writer, editor, advisor, and arts advocate. After leaving OISE/University of Toronto he became Consulting Director of Educational Services at the Lorraine Kimsa Theatre for Young People in Toronto from 2006 to 2007.

Jane Gardner

Jane Gardner is the general manager of Carousel Players, a theatre for young audiences touring company located in St. Catharines, Ontario. She previously managed the Blyth Festival and the Great Canadian Theatre Company, and is a former executive director of Theatre Ontario.